UNCOVERED

Best Wishes

[signature]

THE AUTOBIOGRAPHY OF
PAT CASH

First published in Great Britain in 2002 by
Greenwater Publishing
A division of Crystalsight Limited

A CIP catalogue record for this book is
available from the British Library

ISBN 1-903267-08-0

Printed and bound in Great Britain by
The Bath Press Limited

Greenwater Publishing
Suite D, Pinbrook Court, Pinhoe, Exeter EX4 8JN

Photographic Acknowledgments
For permission to use copyright photographs the
author and publisher wish to thank
Popperfoto, Tommy Hindley/Professional Sport,
Andrew Carne-Ross, Nick Ayliffe
Cover/Front Flap: Nick Ayliffe
Back Cover: Tommy Hindley/Andrew Carne-Ross

Acknowledgements

It's a common joke about finishing one's autobiography, or not finishing it as it may be. If you couple that with the fact my memory isn't the greatest, I have found that it has been difficult to complete. Although the concept has been in my mind for years I am glad I waited until now.

I have done my best to recollect correctly. The recent years are easy to remember but in some early ones I may have made some little screw ups so forgive me if you notice one. Sorry to the people I have forgotten or not mentioned you are no less special to me but I have been limited in some ways. My thanks must go to Barry Flatman who painstakingly pieced it all together and put up with all the last minute additions. Without him this would not have been possible.

Of course I know some of my family and friends will be shocked by some of the things written. They know how I demand privacy in my own life and admire it in those of other people. I have done my best to respect privacy of others and have withheld incidences and names when I felt it was appropriate.

Partial reason for this book is to dispel the myth of sports people being super human. I am like all the others, very human indeed as you will see.

Pat Cash
2002

Contents

Chapter One

UPWARDLY MOBILE CHAMPION

Everyone is supposed to have his or her one defining moment. For some people this comes when they are in total isolation, for others it is in the privacy of their own home, and for the lucky ones it is in the presence of just a few close loved ones. Me? I just happened to have the company of 12,433 spectators crammed around one of the most hallowed lawns ever mown. And for good measure, you can add to that figure millions of television viewers all around the world.

Strangely I was totally oblivious to them all for a few moments: I had something else on my mind, something I had been thinking about and planning for months. Elation does strange things to you, but in my case it turned out that winning the one all-important prize I had always set my heart on wasn't paramount in my thoughts. Maybe people actually on the court were talking to me, but I didn't take in a word they were saying. Looking into the crowd I could see thousands of waving arms and pumping fists, but I was cut off from them, somehow isolated - but now I was desperate for that feeling to come to an end.

I had always played my tennis as if I were locked in a cage, a segregated animal at a zoo, with people looking in but not able to get too close. Lay me down on the psychiatrist's couch and you'll find it was a defence mechanism; certainly to me there was no grander enclosure than Wimbledon's Centre Court. For a long time I had pictured myself triumphantly breaking through the bars: I had always wanted to get through that invisible barrier, and planned to do it in my finest hour. Now was the time - but for a second or two I felt something holding me back, something making me wonder whether it was the right thing to do.

Champions of the past had celebrated their wins in time-honoured fashion. Most used to jump the net and run up to commiserate with the person they had just beaten; this was the style of the great Australians such as Laver, Emerson, Hoad and Fraser. But I wasn't prepared to do that with Ivan Lendl; I didn't like the guy at all and I wasn't about to sympathise with him. The fact that he had again been denied the elusive title he so craved wouldn't make me any more popular! I remember Jimmy Connors rushing over to kiss his wife - or was it girlfriend - in the front row, but I had always planned to take things considerably further.

Don't get me wrong: I'm a great lover of Wimbledon's traditions and everything they stand for, but I wanted to go where no champion had ever gone before. Suddenly I made up my mind, and nothing or nobody was going to stop me. I had looked up to the players box, and so many of the people who meant so much to me were there: my coach Ian Barclay, my girlfriend Anne-Britt, my dad, my sister Renee, my uncle Brian, and the woman who had helped me become one of the fittest players ever to walk on a tennis court, Ann Quinn. I had to be up there with them, and I was going to show my gratitude by climbing up to them.

Why did I do it? Growing up I'd always seen myself as just a normal Aussie kid who liked rock and roll music, football and girls, but I suppose I was just a little bit left of centre. I was kind of crazy, and always tried to be a bit different. My family upbringing had never involved a lot of hugging, but I had it in my head that if I ever won Wimbledon I would show the world how much I actually felt for those people. I wanted to be with them for these most memorable minutes of my life, and the most public way of showing my thanks was to do it in this greatest arena in tennis. So off I went.

I don't know if anyone tried to stop me: if they did, too bad. Up I climbed, through that invisible cage and over the little green wall that surrounds the court, tripping over the first seat and then barging my way between the mass of fans who in those days stood on the old terraces (nowadays fully seated). The film *Crocodile Dundee* had done the rounds of the world's movie theatres a couple of months previously, and there's a scene near the end where Paul Hogan walks over the top of the crowd, using peoples heads like stepping stones. We are both Australians, but I can honestly say it never entered my head at the time to do this as a copycat thing: I had more important matters to worry about.

Contrary to what I have always said in the years since, I had always planned the climb though not too well, perhaps because I figured too much thinking about it might jinx my prospects. But getting higher, I now suddenly realised there was a ten-foot climb to the box. Nevertheless, even though I wasn't quite sure how to get up there, I wasn't about to stop: millions were watching, and an admission of failure would have been too embarrassing. I can remember standing on the shoulder of somebody dressed as a priest - quite appropriate for a kid brought up as a God-fearing Catholic, you might say! As it turned out he was only wearing fancy dress, a strange choice of attire on an afternoon when temperatures were sweltering. But he served the purpose and, as many of us are aware, the good Lord works in mysterious ways.

Next problem was climbing onto the commentary box roof. I really wasn't too sure whether it would take my weight, although victory celebrations in more recent times have proved I had no need to be concerned: a couple of years ago Richard Williams used it as his own personal dance stage to celebrate his daughter Venus' victory over Lindsay Davenport. Then, of course, there was Goran Ivanisevic, in the greatest demonstration of unbridled joy and sheer relief that our sport had ever seen. Back then, however, I was breaking new ground, and in the whole of Wimbledons 101-year history, no champion had even contemplated what I was doing. So the thought of crashing through the roof onto the head of broadcasting legend Dan Maskell or Tony Trabert would certainly have spoiled a good show.

In the end I risked it. And each time I looked up, I kept seeing more people who meant so much to me: Jeff Bond, the psychologist who made the whole process of going out and winning a Wimbledon final so clear and straightforward in my mind; Gerry Moran, the surgeon who had carried out a couple of operations on me; then I spotted a childhood mate of mine from Melbourne called Richard Caston, as well as my best English friend Geoff Lamb, a huge guy who was strong as an ox and used to tell everyone he was my bodyguard. He wasn't, but it was good for the image. Behind the box was Paul McNamee, Australian tennis player, great mate, Davis Cup colleague, doubles partner and probably the most helpful figure amongst my peers (and consequently god-father to my son Daniel).

I heard my Dad shouting to me, and this was also kind of appropriate, because the sound of his voice reverberates throughout my career - sometimes for the right reasons, and sometimes, in my opinion, for the wrong ones. He's never been much of a style guru, my father, but I do remember that day he was bedecked in a huge white cap he used to wear to the footy back home. Things had obviously got a bit rough up there, and it had been knocked to an even more comical angle as the celebrations took hold.

Finally I made it, I reached the summit. I gave Dad that hug I'd always wanted to give him and wished we'd done many times previously. Next I went for my second father, my coach Barkers: I wouldn't have won that day but for him indeed, I probably wouldn't even have been playing the tournament. Without doubt he was the most important contributor to my career.

Royalty was near at hand, too: Princess Diana was seated only a few feet away, and I am hoping she didn't hear all of our expletives though if she did, she couldn't have minded that much, because some years later on we became friendly. So in the excitement of the moment I shouted at the top of my voice: 'We fucking did it, Barkers, we fucking did it! Actually I didn't really care who overheard. Winning that title was really like a team effort, and that was the way I wanted to treat everyone in that box. I was the car and they were the mechanics or rather, I was just the tool who drove it all. Nearby sister Renee was in hysterics, and Uncle Brian, one of Melbourne's most eminent criminal lawyers - now there is a character who merits a book all of his own - decided to steal my black-and-white chequered headband for a memento.

I didn't know the headband had gone, but if I had, I really couldn't have cared less. I was on a complete high, and I have no idea how long I stayed up there. It was probably quite a while, but it felt like a couple of minutes. Then I was suddenly struck with the thought that I had to get back down on court, as there was the small matter of the trophy to collect from the Duke and Duchess of Kent. Deciding it probably wasn't a good idea to go back down the way I came up, I nipped down the stairs by the players' box, through a couple of doors, back past the words of Rudyard Kipling (that frankly didn't mean a whole lot to me), and out onto the Centre Court where everybody was waiting.

Later, in the privacy of the locker room, a gentleman by the name of R. E. H. Hadingham, or simply Buzzer as he was known to all the top players, took me to one side. As chairman of the All England Club Lawn Tennis and Croquet Club it was his duty to inform me that my actions might have caused a problem or two, in that the British tabloid newspapers were to trying to put together a story that I had purposely kept British royalty waiting. Such behaviour was unprecedented in the history of the Championships. Normally the two finalists just shake hands at the net, then shake hands with the umpire, and go back to their courtside chairs to towel down and rest, whilst waiting for everything to be put in readiness for the presentation, when the royals would walk out on to the court, always involving a couple of ball kids in conversation.

Buzzer wasn't joking, either; but he was so good as to insist that if anything untoward were to happen because of the whole business, I would have his total support. Later he confessed to having copped a lot of flak, and I certainly appreciated his support and integrity, to my mind one of the most important of all qualities. In return I had to promise that if I retained the trophy in twelve months time, or indeed ever won it again, I would not repeat the climb. However, he needn't have worried, since I never got beyond the quarter-finals again. But it seems like I set something of a trend, as Martina Navratilova was scaling her way up the same ascent a year later (just to prove that women's tennis *does* follow in the

Upwardly mobile champion

wake of the men's game!).

More recently there have been Venus Williams and Goran, as already mentioned, while I think Steffi Graf climbed up there at least once. Pete Sampras made his way even further back in the grandstands a couple of years ago when he broke Emerson's record by winning his thirteenth Grand Slam title. His parents, rarely seen at any tennis match, chose not to sit in the box, but sought the anonymity of a seat amongst the public. Pete found them, though, and I know exactly how he felt: he wanted to give his old man a hug, and good on him.

As for keeping royalty waiting, I don't think anyone minded. The Duke and Duchess were full of congratulations, and naturally I've watched film footage of the whole thing. Princess Di seemed to enjoy the whole episode, while the lady next to her in the Royal Box even had her camera out, snapping away as I hauled myself up to the people who really mattered to me.

Much as I love Wimbledon and revere it as the greatest tournament in the world, there are times when I wonder if the Clubs powers-that-be really want the public, the great unwashed, to come through their gates at all - whether they wouldn't really be happier for their tournament to be played out in front of just the members and a few honoured guests. Do they only let the paying fans in because they have to? If it were left to the members, I think there's a good chance it would be a private tournament.

But I was brought up on the tradition of the place, as are most Aussies who love tennis. And even though we have our own Grand Slam tournament, which has made enormous progress since the days even when I was playing, tennis means Wimbledon. Nevertheless I always felt we were playing for the benefit of the members, and there has always been a certain arrogance about the

All England Club - although this has noticeably taken a change for the better in the last few years.

And I would like to think that I and my climb had something to do with that. Nothing makes me prouder than to see my name in gold embossed type up on that wooden board, in amongst the list of all the champions, and it's something that can never be taken away. But if I have to identify the most precious moment of the greatest day of my life, then it wasn't the match, or holding the trophy afterwards: it was breaking my way out of that lifelong cage, and going up to those I really cared about to share my moment of glory.

Having said all that about the members, I actually became one of them that day, as is customary for all champions (with the temporary exception of John McEnroe, whose membership was suspended for one year as punishment for being somewhat outspoken); though I don't think I have put on the famous purple and green tie since I was photographed wearing it at the Champions Dinner that evening. My dislike for ties probably dates back to those strict years at school, and being ordered to wear one. Nor do I set much store against sentimental keepsakes - in fact I lost track of the replica trophy given to me until I found it in the bottom of a cupboard, wrapped up in brown paper, where my wife Emily had put it just before we were about to have some building work done at home.

What I do hold very precious is the memory of my achievement, and the fact that I did what I did in victory. And it is all the more surprising, given that I am really an intensely shy person. My parents love to tell my children about my first day of school, when I ran away. Much to my dismay my mum dragged me back again, but I managed to jump out of a window a second time, and escape again.

Upwardly mobile champion

I take any form of criticism deeply to heart. Very early in my career I learned it was best not to read the newspapers or to watch the televised coverage of my matches because people were bound to write and say things that would hurt me. I dread being embarrassed in public, and react negatively to critique. Many is the time I have been sitting in my parents' house and *The Age* newspaper is on the table - my Dad won't read anything else - and I would *love* to glance at the sports pages to know about the cricket or the footy: but I won't, because my name might be mentioned somewhere, and the context might upset me.

One person who has always been there throughout my career is John McEnroe. He's been a rival, a colleague, a friend and, in my opinion, the most talented man ever to pick up a tennis racket. Yet I remember playing him in an exhibition tournament in Adelaide a few years ago at the back end of both our careers. The match really didn't mean too much at all, but I beat Mac and, true to type, he was truly livid in defeat.

Next morning at breakfast in the hotel I decided I wouldn't speak unless he spoke to me. As usual he walked in with that big wall of natural defence around him, because he never knows whether anyone is going to jump up and accuse him of anything. These days you see him wandering around Wimbledon or Flushing Meadows in between his commentary slots, wearing a baseball cap and wrap-around sunglasses in the forlorn hope that nobody will recognise him. In effect he is really giving off the vibe: 'Don't even try talking to me!' which is understandable, if you think about it. If people have been calling you an arsehole your whole life, there may come a time when you start believing it, and you would certainly then have a problem trusting anyone.

I looked across the breakfast room at Mac. He's reading the

newspaper report of how he lost to me the night before, and he is getting more and more annoyed; it's almost like he is back out there on court. He is scratching at what's left of his hair, and shaking his head, and finally he throws the newspaper down on the floor and looks seriously pissed off. The article apparently referred to him as a has-been and yet he is one of the greatest players that has ever been. He has more money than he knows what to do with, a lovely wife and great kids; every television company that screens tennis wants him to commentate for them - but still he can get incredibly upset because of something written. I could have told him he needn't, and shouldn't, have read a word. I learned the lesson a long time ago, but you don't say that sort of thing to a furious Johnny Mac. Maybe when he's a little bit more laid back and mellow - but not when the most infamous temper in tennis is coming to the boil.

When it comes to tantrums, my temper has caused me more than a few problems over the years. It has also been the root cause of plenty of criticism aimed in my direction, and consequently has caused a great deal of heartache. The repeated barbs of one critic have consistently hurt more than most, and unfortunately for me, that person used to be one of my real heroes. A little earlier I mentioned a list of great Aussies who had won Wimbledon before me and there's no doubting the acheivements of John Newcombe decree he should be included in that list. Absolutely right but I cannot bring myself to do it after all the stick I have taken from him over the years. One of my most vivid childhood memories is sneaking through a back entrance into Kooyong as a nine year-old and hanging from the scoreboard to watch Newcombe beat Jimmy Connors in the 1975 Australian Open final. He won in four sets that day, and it was the last of his seven Grand Slam titles. Reading some of the history books, it says his game relied on a heavy

Upwardly mobile champion

service, forceful volleying, and solid, powerful ground strokes, with his best performances coming on grass. Which Australian player who came along a few years later does that remind you of?

However, Newcombe never once had a good word to say about me. He relentlessly slated me in his weekly newspaper column in Sydney, ghost written by a certain John Thirsk. Every time I lost a match, there was Newcombe laying into me; and every time I won, he would say it's about time. He was forever criticising my behaviour on court, insisting that my actions - the odd disagreement with an official and bouncing of a racket - was letting down the great heritage of Australian tennis. He never once cared to praise me for winning the country two Davis Cups, or following him as the first Aussie to win Wimbledon for sixteen years.

Newcombe undoubtedly contributed to my dislike of reading the newspapers, to the point where I wanted to confront him and discuss the whole vendetta openly. My dad warned me against this, however, largely because of Newcombes popularity in the eyes of the media. He was then, and still is, remarkably high profile. A lot of people take notice of what he says. He was a one-man publicity machine and he's still at it to this day. Even though he's retired as Davis Cup captain, he's still milking his popularity by appearing in every commercial break during the Australian Open, waving magazines, eating sausages and trying to convince people that they should move into brand new housing estates in the middle of nowhere. Come off it Newk, everyone knows you live in the United States for a large proportion of the year. I am learning to come to terms with this sort of vilification now, but it used to be very hard for me though I wasn't the only one to be the butt of Newcombes pen in the 1980s. McEnroe, Gerulaitis and Connors, to name just three good players, suffered his criticism, and there were others. Its not as if I was the first player to query a decision or toss a racket, either: Mac, Jimmy and Ilie Nastase had been doing it before I came along!

There were times when I got mad at myself on a tennis court, and this was primarily because I was a perfectionist: I just wanted to hit a winner off every point - and as Ian Barclay pointed out and Ian knew my character considerably better than many - if you took away my inner fire, then you would take away much of my natural game. It would have been great if somebody of Newcombes experience and standing, who had been through it all before and knew all the pressures, could have talked to me and given me his advice.

Sadly he did completely the opposite, apparently at every opportunity; it was almost as if he was in some way jealous of my success, perhaps fearing that it would compromise his reputation, even threaten his earnings - he was always worried about money! Two instances I remember in particular: one was the year before I won the Wimbledon title, when Newcombe attended a prestigious dinner in London, at which he insisted that my emotional and erratic behaviour on court was because I had been taking drugs. I was incensed, and my father, as a practising lawyer, realised I had good reason to sue for slander. In the end we decided that, with my career still on the up, the last thing I wanted was a big litigation case against somebody who was globally famous at the time.

Newcombe clearly had a problem with me, even though I had hardly met the guy - I was just a teenager, and he had been my hero. It would have been a great boost for me to know that the last great Aussie player was on my side, and surely that would have been good for the country's tennis as well. Whereas instead he constantly waged this campaign against me.

Upwardly mobile champion

The other instance was considerably more public. Just before Australia played Sweden in the 1983 Davis Cup final, he previewed the match in his newspaper column. Now you would think that Newcombe, as a fair dinkum Australian and national hero, would have wanted his country to win although everyone got an inkling of what was going on several weeks earlier. His subservient ghost writer Thirsk was seen and heard cheering on Sweden's Joakim Nystrom as he beat me in the semi-final of the New South Wales Open.

At the time, Mats Wilander and I were the nation's two number one players: I was eighteen years old, Mats just nine months older and the newly crowned Australian Open champion. Newcombe and Thirsk collaborated to write that comparing Mats' talent with mine was like comparing the Grand Canyon with a crack in the wall.

Isn't that just the sort of thing you want to hear before the biggest match of your life when you are representing your country? Looking back over my whole career, I can honestly say that no words have ever struck more painfully, and it was hurtful not only to myself, but to my father, my whole family, and my coach Ian Barclay. Basically the person who is being vilified in this way can react in two ways: as it turned out, I was probably more fired up to prove the man wrong, though it effectively caused me to view the press with dislike and suspicion for ever more. And it made me question exactly what I had done to be treated in this way.

And shall I tell you the reason for all this slander and ill-feeling? Four years previously Newcombe had wanted me to join his national junior squad, sponsored by McDonalds. However, at the time I was being coached by Ian Barclay, and was doing really well; I was happy where I was, and making good progress - but that was no good to Newcombe, who considered he should have the pick of any good youngster. He arranged for one of his colleagues, Allan Stone, to write a derogatory piece about Barclay's coaching ability, saying how I would be better advised teaming up with another good junior called Mark Kratzmann in the McDonalds squad. Nowadays I think 'Rolling' Stone is a really nice guy: he is one of my commentating colleagues on Channel 7 in Australia, and probably understands the situation a little better now.

At the time everyone around me decided I was better staying with somebody I knew and liked. Unfortunately Newcombe couldn't tolerate this sort of rejection, and from then on went out of his way to belittle me at every opportunity. Things never really changed in our relationship, but I stopped concerning myself with the problem a long time ago. I'm sure that over the years Newcombe has baulked numerous opportunities that would have been advantageous to me, but it is water under the bridge now.

Back then I had plenty of other matters that needed my attention. One of the strangest was a letter I received from an elderly lady claiming to be a Hungarian princess living in Los Angeles. She wrote telling me she was a big fan of mine, and how much she had enjoyed the way I played at the previous year's US Open. She told me she was old, and didn't have anyone to whom she could give her money, so because of the pleasure I had given her, she wanted to make me a gift of $1 million. You could say I was more than a little bit shocked. Imagine just how much money a million bucks would have been, back in 1985: it would have set me up for life. To put things into perspective, Lendl picked up less than a quarter of that amount for winning his first US Open title at Flushing Meadows that year, and I'd pocketed a £155,000 cheque as Wimbledon champion two years later.

Initially I thought the offer was genuine, although, of course, there was an element of suspicion. Naturally I talked to my dad about it, because he kept an eye on all my money matters (still does, as a matter of fact), and we decided to employ somebody from the International Management Group - who acted as my agents - to go and check the whole thing out. A girl actually walked up to the large house and knocked on the old lady's front door to ask a few questions.

Soon I got another letter from her, asking what was happening: here she was, offering me a million dollars, and all I did was get one of my agents to go round and find out if she was genuine. Meanwhile the Hungarian consulate insisted she couldn't possibly have been a princess, so I was beginning to think she must be just a lonely old woman who wanted a little excitement in her life. Then my younger brother Daniel recalled something he'd read in a newspaper about Jimmy Connors being made such an offer from a rich old lady. But for Daniel I wouldn't have known this, because by then, of course, I didn't read the newspapers.

I decided to telephone Connors and see what action he had taken. I always had an immense amount of respect for Jimmy, even though he wasn't exactly popular with most of the other guys. He confirmed that the very same old lady had offered him a million dollars, saying similar things about how she was a fan of his, and how she liked the way he always involved the crowd.

Jimmy said he had thought about the offer for a long time. Even though he had won considerably more than I had from his playing career, and could boast numerous endorsements, a million bucks was still a huge amount of money to turn down. But he realised that if he accepted, then he would have been committed to the woman, and might possibly have been obliged to do something back. So because he didn't know where it was going to lead, he turned it down; and I must admit I felt exactly the same way. So reluctantly I wrote her a letter back thanking her very much for her extremely generous offer, but regretfully declining. I never heard another word from her, and to this day don't know whether the offer was genuine, or a hoax. However, there have been many moments over the years when I have speculated on what I might have done with that million bucks.

It goes without saying that tennis is an extremely mercenary sport, and although money may not be quite everything, it accounts for a huge chunk of the game. Agents are everywhere, everybody has their price, and nobody does very much for nothing. Unlike some of the current players - Mark Philippoussis and Jan Michael Gambill spring to mind - I've never been one for flashy cars or expensive possessions; in fact I'm more than happy to go around with a plastic watch on my wrist, though I do allow myself a few luxuries for instance, I own more than one guitar. But I prefer to spend my money on my family, as they are *the* most important in my priorities.

My children mean more to me than anything else in the world: Daniel and Mia from my relationship with Anne-Britt, and the twin boys Shannon and Jett, who keep my wife Emily and I on our toes. Let me tell you here and now, the elation of becoming a father beats anything you can achieve on a tennis court: winning a Grand Slam title is wonderful, but being there when a baby is born is like witnessing a miracle. It's breathtaking, and there is no comparison. When I won Wimbledon I had already become a father, and maybe that's why the whole thing quickly became a little bit of a let-down. Sure, there was a great sense of achievement and pride as I sat there in the locker room with a big grin on my face; but deep down I couldn't honestly say I felt ecstatic as I had done when the kids were born.

Looking at the trophy, I can vividly remember feeling extremely exhausted and hugely relieved. For some reason beforehand, I thought that nothing else would matter once I got my hands on that prize: the heavens would open up, and I'd be happy forever. Of course that's not true, and I've come to realise that it's just a bit of tin with some gold plating around - and let me say here and now, being a Wimbledon champion isn't a passport for anything.

Perhaps it was because I thought I *would* win, and because everybody convinced me I was right in my optimism; so in effect all I did was fulfil the promise. Or perhaps it was just a feeling of natural progression, because so many Aussies before me had won it. It's a bit like building something: you work and work, seeing it come together all the time, and by the time it's finally completed, you just think: 'OK that's done, but it's no big surprise because it was always going to happen.'

I suppose this sort of thought started entering my head within a minute or two of walking off court, and one of the first things I said to my coach Barkers was: Let's go and win the US Open now!

I could have enjoyed the moment a bit more, without thinking about the next big one so quickly; but such is the nature of tennis, and many other big sports. It's always the expectation of the next one, rather than the savouring of the one before. Now I realise it's a character flaw, and a social problem of champions: too much goal searching and trying to keep up with the Jones's will ultimately send you crazy. Believe me, in my case, it did.

You can never live in the present because you're always looking for the next mountain to climb. How many people have said the important thing is to hang around for a while and smell the roses? Well, I'm another one to add to the list - but try and tell that to a twenty-two-year-old.

Give credit to Goran Ivanisevic last year. He was so different, because that one win meant so much to him, after the most amazing comeback I have ever witnessed - and that compliment is coming from somebody who attempted quite a few comebacks in his time. Goran had been written off by almost everyone, and as he celebrated that title he really couldn't have cared less if he never hit another tennis ball as long as he lived. That's a feeling many champions must really envy, because they are immediately trapped in the pursuit of the next big one.

Now I have retired, I can sit back and watch Wimbledon, thinking I have actually won this, and it's no mean feat. But it took a very long time to appreciate that the Wimbledon title isn't that easy to attain. Even though it was Pat Rafter, who is both an Aussie and a mate, who was beaten last year, I think seeing Goran finally win gave me more pleasure than any win since mine. However, it also made me distinctly remember all the moments when I wondered whether I could ever handle the pressure again.

Maybe it would have been different if I had been older, but for a twenty-two-year-old it took a huge toll in terms of stress, concentration, effort and nerves. When you are so young, you question your ability to go through it again. There were only two occasions during the whole of my career when I had those feelings: winning the Davis Cup as an eighteen-year-old, and Wimbledon.

In later years I have found that both victories, coupled with such a heavy weight of expectation, exacted deep psychological damage. Maybe that's why I never achieved anything of note ever again. So why did I continue to enter and persist with tennis through numerous agonies, arguments and heartaches? Well, it's a long story.

Chapter Two

SHOULD OUTLAWS DRINK WARM ORANGE JUICE?

Once I used to tell people that the reason I might have appeared to be tennis's Wild Colonial Boy was that I was descended from one of Australia's most notorious criminals. Martin Cash was a legendary Tasmanian bushranger, second only in notoriety to Ned Kelly himself. Having been sentenced to the infamous Port Arthur penal settlement for shooting his girlfriend's lover, Martin then became the only inmate ever to escape. After being recaptured, the laws of the land at the time decreed that he should be hanged; but, always popular amongst the ladies, the governor's wife Lady Franklin was persuaded to lead a petition for his pardon.

I loved the story, and used it to brighten up a few press conferences in my time. It seemed to give a historic sense of credence to my behaviour on court, and there were certainly times when I felt something of an outlaw myself. The trouble was that my father, another Patrick, knew his history and had traced back the Cash family tree, and unfortunately he refutes the likelihood of any family connection - which to my mind is a downright shame. To this day I'm not totally convinced, although my dad insists that my great-grandfather, yet another Patrick Cash, was an Irishman from the town of Inniscorthy in County Wexford.

Setting sail to become one of the forty-niners in the Californian gold rush in the middle of the nineteenth century, he arrived late and didn't get to the west coast of the United States until something like 1851. By that time nearly all the gold had been claimed, and he quickly realised that he would have to look elsewhere to make his fortune. After boarding a whaling boat, he journeyed across the Pacific and jumped ship in Adelaide, where he married a local girl of Irish descent called Mary O'Sullivan. I don't think he ever did get too rich, but so began this branch of the Cash family of Australia. Even so, who is to say that old Martin the bushranger, who apparently used to spread his favours amongst the ladies by all accounts, didn't figure somewhere in my ancestry.

This particular Pat Cash - the third, if I was to follow the example of a certain American golfer - came into the world on 27 May 1985 at the Boxhill Hospital in Melbourne's eastern suburbs. My parents had met when my father, one of a family of nine and owner of the law firm Patrick Cash and Associates in Footscray, was asked by my mother Dorothy to serve some divorce papers against her first husband. He wondered at the other guy's sanity in letting such a good-looking woman go, and set about courting her himself.

My mother comes from Chicago, and had immigrated to Australia with three children a couple of years earlier. So the new baby immediately had two stepbrothers and a stepsister. Within two years another girl, Renee, came along, and a year later my kid brother Daniel completed the family. To this day my mum is a pretty amazing woman. She makes furniture for the house, fixes more or less anything that breaks down, and keeps everyone in line. My teenage son Daniel has moved from Oslo to spend some time with

28

me at the tennis academy, I have set up with Gavin Hopper at Hope Island on Queensland's Gold Coast. When I'm in London or somewhere else around the world, Daniel's grandmother moves up to look after him and make sure he does his homework and gets to school in good time.

At the age of fifteen, Daniel decided to try and become a tennis player, just like his old man - although I hold my hands up and say I had nothing to do with the decision. Going back almost a quarter of a century, I came to the same decision a little earlier in life, although for a long time the sport I saw as my best opportunity wasn't tennis, but Australian Rules football. To my mind, footy remains the best sport in the world, and there's only one team for me: the mighty Hawks of Hawthorn. My dad used to play for them in the 1950s - one year he was even their top goal scorer.

I was playing footy every day, and could drop-kick goals by the age of six. By the time I passed my tenth birthday, all I wanted to be was a player in the Australian Football League, and I think I had a pretty good chance of succeeding - an early growth spurt seemed to make me bigger and stronger than all the other kids of my age, and I never missed a goal. One year I kicked more than a hundred, besides also winning the best and fairest player award. My team Kew Rovers got so good they had to move from the Hawthorn League into the much stronger Doncaster League. Did we find our level? Not a bit of it, because next year we went out there and won that as well. We firmly believed we were the best junior team ever, and a couple of the lads actually went on to wear that very special yellow and brown guernsey for Hawthorn in the AFL. Despite everything I've achieved in tennis, deep down I still really envy them.

Like any other Aussie kid, I also played cricket and got to be captain, although I didn't really know which fielding positions the other boys should have been filling. I really was one of those lucky kids. Without any proper training, I used to win the 100m, 200m, high jump and long jump at school sports day every year; in fact I used to win everything I tried! Tennis became part of the agenda after Mum and Dad started playing socially near where we lived in Balwyn; later on we moved to a place then called North Ringwood, but for some reason now renamed Park Orchards. I guess I was about nine years old, and the three of us kids went down there with my parents because at the end of their session, Dad used to let us hit the ball around a bit.

The first courts I really played on were at school, Our Lady of Good Counsel at Deepdene. They were very basic, with holes in the nets and cracks in the surface with weeds growing through. But amazingly, those courts spawned two players who went on to make the world's top ten and become Wimbledon champions: Peter McNamara and myself. Later on I found out that Ann Quinn, who played such an important role throughout my career, also began playing tennis there as well.

At weekends a guy used to come down and give me lessons, and I took to the game quickly - which frankly didn't come as a huge surprise. In fact at around this time there were only two things I didn't excel at: distance running and swimming; but with so many other options available, I just avoided the track and the pool. What with footy, tennis and the odd game of cricket, there were more than enough pursuits to fill my spare time.

However, it was tennis that rapidly took precedence. I had a couple of coaches, Bill Mattea and Will Coughlan, and was getting on fine. Then when I was something like eleven years old, my dad took me down to a Heatherdale Tennis Club in Melbourne's eastern suburbs for a meeting that was to prove one of the most important in my life.

Ian Barclay looked much the same then as he does now: slight build, moustache, and that hair which I consider must have turned grey when he was seven or eight years old. He had been a commercial artist who did a bit of tennis coaching in his spare time, and now he had a squad that included the Minter sisters, Anne and Liz, as well as a twelve-year-old left-hander called Mark Hartnett. Barkers' sporting background was in horseracing, and as a youngster he'd pushed his way through betting rings at the tracks to run the tote odds. He's played a fair bit of tennis, but he used to complain that his father was so engrossed with his horseracing that he had only seen his son play twice; on one occasion this was at St. Kilda when he beat Bob 'Nails' Carmichael, the former coach to Darren Cahill and Indian Grand Slam doubles champion Leander Paes; the other when Emerson thrashed him at Kooyong.

However, he'd faced all Australia's top players of the time, and picked up something from each match. Though he wasn't sufficiently talented to progress as a player, he was perceptive enough to become a very good coach, particularly of juniors. I'd heard about Barkers from a classmate of mine at the time called Warren Brennan, a good tennis player who used to face Mark (Hartnett) in a great many state finals. I thought I was doing all right with my game, but just needed to hit with better players, so Barkers' first opinions of me were interesting: he thought I had one great quality, and that was I wanted to be a champion as well as the world's best player. Thus my competitive spirit immediately impressed him, along with the fact that I seemed to have no fear; he also liked my athleticism and speed around the court. But he marked me down as a young man in a hurry who wanted everything to happen yesterday.

At the time I played all my tennis pretty much from the baseline, probably due to the fact I'd learned the game on quasi clay courts known as *en-tout-cas*, which best suited the often inclement local climate (you know what they say of Melbourne's weather: if you don't like it, hang around for a little while and it's bound to change). I don't think I had ventured near the net before I went to Barkers, and I probably wasn't big enough to serve and volley.

Physically I hadn't grown too much at all since that early growth spurt which helped me at footy, but before long my new mentor had to order me to hold back on the attacking. Neither Mark Hartnett nor I were particularly tall kids, so Barkers used to joke there was enough room to drive a truck down the sidelines past us, let alone a tennis ball. Not that I was allowed to call him Barkers in those days: it was strictly Mr Barclay, or Mr B. As coach he had to show great patience as I struggled to come to terms with the vagaries of shots which in later years would become my great weapons: the volleys, and most particularly the overhead smashes that in the early days really caused me a lot of problems. One time my mum came down to practice with me, and we ended up on a brand-new court that had just been laid. She was feeding lobs to me, and if I top-edged one into the mud surrounding the court, I must have top-edged two dozen. Mr B probably thought he had quite a job on his hands - but I was really determined, and often used to turn up at the courts when I should have been at school while he was coaching a group of ladies on a weekday afternoon.

You may have noticed that I have hardly mentioned school in my childhood recollections. The reason is quite simple: it didn't mean too much to me. My parents were middle class, my dad a successful lawyer who put a lot of importance on his kids having the best schooling possible. I was always going to have a strict Catholic education, we were that type of family and always used to go to Mass every Sunday morning. My early schools weren't too bad, but by the time I was making progress at tennis I was attending Whitefriars College where the teachers were Carmelite Fathers, and I disliked almost everything except the physical education lessons.

It's fair to say that I have never been much concerned about discipline, as a few supervisors and umpires around the international tennis circuit came to find out in later years. The only two teachers I ever got on with were sports masters: one was Garry Wilson, who used to captain Fitzroy Football Club; and the other was Ray Keane, the team's fitness adviser. Otherwise, apart from a nice Irish teacher whose name I forget, I'm afraid I don't have much to say about the rest of the teaching staff, although I used to do plenty of talking back to them in class. I was bright enough, but I just wasn't interested, and as I travelled more with my tennis, I got further behind in lessons.

At the end it was hard for the teachers not to pick on me, because it was public knowledge that I was earning more money than them. Even at that early stage of my career, racket manufacturers and clothing companies were willing to pay me endorsements because I had finished runner-up at Junior Wimbledon.

With my future becoming increasingly clear, my parents reluctantly agreed to take me out of school when I was fifteen years old. To me it was certainly a decision for the best, as I sat examinations in only two subjects in my final year. The day before I left, I threw a big garbage bag full of water through the window of the school's new pride and joy, the computer room. Long before making that last rebellious gesture, I decided I would never, ever go back, regardless of what I achieved in my career.

More than twenty years later I have stayed true to that decision, although with kids of my own, I now want the best possible education for them. Yet for a long time afterwards I had very bitter memories of Whitefriars, and hated all teachers. I considered they tried to subdue me through intimidation, and thought they treated their pupils with complete lack of concern and sympathy, behaving with the brusque authoritarianism characteristic of some policemen or sergeant majors in the army. This is a shame, because I know many people who have happy memories of their schooldays; but sadly I'm just not one of them.

Nevertheless, if school was not the most formative of experiences, my budding tennis career was faring much better. Barkers used to bundle all us pupils into his old Ford Fairlane sedan and head off to faraway tournaments in upstate Victoria and even further afield. Titles came along with increasing rapidity: both Mark Hartnett and I captured the national age-group singles title, and we were also developing into a formidable doubles combination.

By the time I was fourteen years old I could beat just about everybody, with the exception of Mark and a new guy a couple of years older from Canberra who had joined the squad. His name was Wally Masur, and he became a close mate of mine for the duration of my career; he currently fills the role of Australia's Davis Cup coach.

By this time Barkers realised we'd gone just about as far as we could go in Australia, and needed to travel overseas in search of better opposition. But for that we needed money, and there was none forthcoming from the national federation. Australia might have had the most magnificent tennis tradition in the world, and there was no shortage of old stagers who liked reminding people of

Should outlaws drink warm orange juice?

the fact; but in those days we didn't even have a junior tennis programme to create players for the future. So the coach got networking, and eventually in 1978 a private syndicate was formed which became known as MATCH: Make A Tennis Champion Here.

One person who immediately showed an interest in becoming involved was Michael Edgley, one of the country's new entrepreneurs and impresarios. Michael was responsible for bringing to Australia enterprises as diverse as the Moscow State Circus and Bob Marley and the Wailers, and his son Mark was one of Western Australia's top junior players. He promised two years of funding to Barkers little squad, so long as young Mark Edgley was included in the plan. No worries, everybody said: he's in.

There were several others who underwrote our enterprise, and at risk of this appearing to be a roll call, every one of them deserves a mention: Arthur Liddle who was Dunlop-Slazenger's manager in Victoria at the time; John Bee, a Commercial Bank of Australia executive; Peter Thorpe, Simpson's sports clothing managing director; Kevin Turtle, national promotions officer of Australian Airlines; my uncle Leo who was secretary-treasurer; my dad who set up the legal structure; and of course Barkers himself.

Over the next three years the syndicate spent the extremely modest amount of $Aus 6,000 flying the squad around to junior tournaments in Europe and the United States. For that money we ultimately achieved one Wimbledon title, one junior Wimbledon title, two US Open junior singles titles, as well as a doubles, a French Open junior singles title, two Davis Cups, two Avvenire Cups and a Galea Cup (both European junior team events), eleven tour titles and probably three times as many Australian event titles. Not a bad investment compared to the millions frittered away by Britain's Lawn Tennis Association every year with hardly anything to show for the money. One great sadness was that Arthur Liddle, who had supported us right from the outset, died of cancer the day after I won Wimbledon.

Our first trip to Italy was in 1979. I was still thirteen when we left, and one of my earliest memories was practising against this Swedish kid with hair everywhere and a more-than-impressive set of ears. I used to call him Koala Bear, while Barkers preferred Teddy Bear; the tennis world soon came to know him as Mats Wilander. And was he good?

I can remember playing two-on-ones with him for more than twenty minutes, and he never missed a single ball. For me the trip was a real eye opener as to how us Aussie kids were so far behind the Swedes and other Europeans. Initially the Swedes were so much better organised. Bjorn Borg had already won the French Open and Wimbledon three times in a row, and every one of their six teams had both a coach and a manager to conduct business details.

All their youngsters played just the same way as Borg, but more importantly, they were all so fit. I always used to run out of steam, and seemed to lose in the first round of everything. Then I looked at some of the trophies: of course there was Borg, but there was also Lendl, Navratilova and Mandlikova engraved on the silverware, and seeing those names made me realise the improvements I needed to make.

By the time I got home, playing footy had to be a thing of the past: it was tennis, tennis, and a bit more tennis, with fitness work thrown in for good measure. In Melbourne I was playing for Grace Park against some really experienced guys just off the professional circuit. I knew I needed to get much fitter, and I used to go for special training under John Fraser, brother of Neale, and Australia's Davis Cup doctor, at 7.30 in the morning before school.

Should outlaws drink warm orange juice?

Up until then my game had all been based on natural ability along with brute power, and I detested running anything further than a 200m sprint because my endurance levels were pretty pitiful. I always had speed, and nobody could beat me over 50m or 100m, but when it came to running laps, I was in trouble. Doc Fraser did his best to change things, but it was tough, and I used to trudge off to Whitefriars for another series of bouts with the despised teachers, totally exhausted before the day had even begun.

The following year I had my first real experience of playing on grass in the National Championships at Sydney's White City, losing in the quarterfinal to Simon Youl. My next European trip also went considerably better, and I won singles trophies in Bologna and Bari before returning to the scene of the previous year's education at the Avvenire Cup in Milan.

We weren't quite the novelty of a year before, and Mark Hartnett and I made a few people sit up and take notice. Mark won the singles, and we won the doubles, beating the French pair of Loic Courteau and Tarik Benhabiles (these days the latter has the highly enviable task of coaching the exciting young American Andy Roddick). Barkers saw something special in me during that match: much later I found out that as he walked away he told his wife Jackie that I would win Wimbledon one day.

After I left school I became a resident at the Australian Institute of Sport at Canberra. The place may be famous now, after all the success enjoyed on the cricket field and in the swimming pool, but in those days the tennis set-up was a big failure. The one thing the institute did do, however, was finally improve my fitness, because I was basically lazy when I went there. I still hated distance running, and although I could play tennis all day long, the very sight of a track made me feel weak at the knees.

It wasn't until I started hitting balls in practice with the Australian Davis Cup squad, which then included players such as Paul McNamee, Peter McNamara, John Alexander, Brad Drewitt, and that grumpy old bear of a man Mark Edmondson, that I came to appreciate how hard they worked.

The guy in charge of tennis at the AIS was Ray Ruffels, a former Davis Cup player who was regarded by many as both dedicated and a wily wielder of the racket. He was said to be the perfect man to take a team of youngsters around the world, and later on coached the record-breaking Woodies (Mark Woodforde and Todd Woodbridge) to some great trophies. But in all honesty, in my opinion you could write down Ruffel's technical knowledge of tennis on the back of a postage stamp.

In a couple of years I learned just two things from Ruff. During a junior tournament in Italy I stayed up late talking to this extremely attractive girl, and next day lost my match because I was tired. To compound my disappointment, Ruff fined me for my nocturnal behaviour - so that did instil a bit of professionalism. He also taught me never to let the opponent know that you were down - so whenever it looked as if defeat were on the cards, I was to make it look as if I was going to win. He said good players should always have that walk, with their head held high and an air of confidence.

Apart from the financial blow of that fine, my third European trip showed that great things were by now a distinct possibility. To start with, I finally managed to win the Avvenire Cup singles prize in Milan. First I had to beat two players who would certainly go on to make their mark on the game: Emilio Sanchez in the quarterfinals and Karel Novacek in the semis. My reward was a place in the final, and a first confrontation with another young Swede who would figure prominently in my career.

Should outlaws drink warm orange juice?

In those days Stefan Edberg played the traditional Borg way. Like all the others he rarely strayed from the baseline, hit with a double-fisted backhand, and seemed to regard the net as something carrying rabies. Although feeling extremely nervous, I beat him without too many problems, and my rapidly rising junior ranking escalated still further. However, my supposed knowledge of Stefan tested the strength of my friendship with Wally Masur a year or so later.

The two young Aussies arrived in Lisbon to try and qualify for a tour event. Wally was drawn against Edberg, and I told him there was nothing to worry about because he was a typical Swede who just stayed back on the baseline. But sitting courtside, I couldn't believe what I saw: there was this supreme young fair-haired athlete who served and volleyed everything with the crispest single-handed backhand I'd ever seen.

Two pretty swift sets later, a soundly beaten and decidedly pissed off Wally stumbled his way from the court to the locker room. On his way, he gave me the unfriendliest of looks and I thought I heard him utter, thanks for the tip, mate. I'd like to think they were the exact words he used, but I know for a fact they were interspersed with others considerably stronger.

Within a couple of weeks of winning the Avvenire Cup, I made it to the quarterfinals of the junior singles at the French Open, where I lost to Wilander. The next contest saw me treading British turf for the first time, though my game still hadn't properly developed into the all-out serve and volley style that became my trademark and was so suited to grass.

Back then I was a bit of everything, and I used to be called a hacker in some quarters; but Barkers had a plan, and insisted I serve-volley everything. I was still good enough to overcome the

American Todd Witsken, tragically no longer with us, and then beat Wally to win the Thames Ditton tournament that traditionally prepares youngsters for the big one the following week: Wimbledon.

I have to say, my initial recollections of Wimbledon itself are tinged with disappointment. Ruffels arranged practice facilities for us next door at Aorangi Park - a strange name for somewhere in Wimbledon, but apparently at the time the All England leased it to the New Zealand Sports and Social Club, and Aorangi, meaning Cloud in the Sky, is the Maori name for Mount Cook.

All of that was irrelevant to me at the time; I just remember the grass courts being pretty bare, the clubhouse little more than a garden shed, and that the drinks, on hand to cool you down, were all lukewarm. Needless to say, nowadays things have changed, and the practice facilities are some of the best in the world, as befitting such a great event. Back then, however, it didn't make a great impression on a sixteen-year-old from Down Under who was used to have his drinks ice cold.

Nevertheless, the disillusionment cant have been too bad because I made it through to the final of the junior boys singles - admittedly with a little good fortune along the way. In the semi-final I came up against an extremely talented and equally precocious young Frenchman called Henri Leconte; but luckily for me, Henri twisted an ankle and had to retire. This sent me through to the final against an American kid called Matt Anger, whom frankly I didn't take that seriously because Wally had beaten him easily the previous week at Thames Ditton.

The dangers of over-confidence were another tough lesson which had to be learnt on the now-demolished Number One court that day: with the noise almost deafening next door on Centre while

Should outlaws drink warm orange juice?

McEnroe and Borg played out that historic tie-break, I got deservedly beaten 7-6,7-5.

Apart from the gripping disappointment of defeat, one other thing sticks in my memory from that final: for the first time in my life I felt pressure as I made my way on to a tennis court, and I didn't like the feeling. The stupid part was, the thing that prompted the screwed-up sensation in my stomach was just a simple telegram from a relative back home in Melbourne wishing me good luck. Suddenly it didn't feel as if I was playing just for myself: it was as if I had the weight of other people's expectations resting upon my shoulders. It was a problem I struggled to come to terms with for the rest of my career, and there were times when I craved to play in complete silence - I used to get annoyed if somebody beside the court just yelled something as innocuous as 'Come on, Pat'.

The way I heard it, they weren't offering me support in my bid to win, but were saying I wasn't trying hard enough, or that they were disappointed with my game and should put in more effort. Looking back, I appreciate now that it was only encouragement, but far too often I just couldn't see it that way. I regularly told courtside spectators to shut up, to get out on court themselves if they thought they could do better, and not to be such smart arses. I also used to ask them if they thought I wasn't trying, and in retrospect it all looked very like a lack of gratitude. In later years my psychologist Jeff Bond really got to work on this problem, and hence the fact I played my matches in an imaginary cage where nobody could get to me.

After Wimbledon I went back home for a few weeks, where I attracted the attention of another prospective financial backer, a guy called Chris Gleeson, who was managing director of a company that sold medical equipment overseas. He was also another friend of Barkers. Bolstered with a little more finance, I headed across the Pacific to play the junior events at both the Canadian and US Opens.

At the time there was a tale going around saying that after arriving at John F. Kennedy Airport, this sixteen-year-old Aussie kid became somewhat flustered by all the hubbub and was befriended by a more mature American woman, who actually took him home for a couple of days. Evidently I proved untraceable as she allegedly fed me, washed my tennis shirts and taught me a few other things beside.

Sounds like a cracking story to me - a Mrs Robinson situation, and if somebody else were telling it, I'd sit back and enjoy the yarn. Unfortunately, and extremely sadly, I don't have any recollections of it at all - the woman, the meals, the clean tennis shirts or anything else so I must conclude that it never happened. I blame I. Barclays over-active imagination.

What certainly did happen was that I won the Canadian title and reached the semi-finals of the US Open; so by the time it got to the Australian Open, played in those days at the end of the year in December (rather than in its current place on the calendar as the circuit's first Grand Slam in January), I was in line to become the world's top-ranked junior.

Frankly I was under no misapprehension, thinking that Wilander was still far better than me. By then, however, Wilander had moved into the main draws at most tournaments, and within six months was the French Open champion. On the face of it, I had problems with another young Swede called Jorgen Windahl, who beat me in the final of the Australian juniors. But the truth of the matter was, that the problem was with myself.

I take nothing away from Windahl that day. He was a very flashy player, a bit like Leconte, and another to break the Swedish mould by attacking the net and playing with a one-fisted backhand. Frankly I didn't play that well - but the real problem was that I got upset because my dad was shouting encouragement from the courtside.

So here was that same problem rearing its head again. My dad just wanted me to do well: it was as simple as that. However, I thought he was telling me I wasn't trying hard enough, and was letting myself, the family, and the whole Australian nation down. I took it as a downright criticism - so what did I do? Grit my teeth and give it a little bit extra? No way, I shouted at my dad to shut up, and then plunged straight into the tank. For a while I just didn't give a shit about the match; it was almost as though I *wanted* to lose, to piss him off. Ultimately my losing focus meant I *did* end up beaten - but my dad wasn't angry with me (or to be more honest, he didn't let it show).

As always he was really sympathetic afterwards, and by the time I had cooled off in the locker room and let the disappointment sink in, I knew he was only offering me support. Nevertheless, some part of me regularly clicked into negative when I was out on the court, and it happened many times during my career.

In spite of that defeat, I still ended the year Junior World Champion, and consequently had to waltz with the world's top girl at the glittering awards dinner held in Paris the following June. Zina Garrison was my dancing partner, and if I have never apologised to her for my performance on the floor that evening, I do now.

In my second consecutive Wimbledon junior final I came up against yet another Swede, Henrik Sundstrom, and this time I really felt the pressure on me: the Australian media were beginning to take serious notice of me, and their interest felt like a lead weight on my back. The situation was complicated by the fact that I really did not like Sundstrom: I really did not approve of some of the things he got up to on the court, such as trying to call lines, and arguing that shots were in when they were clearly out. To me cheating was, and for that matter still is, one of the worst crimes a sportsman can commit, and my natural reaction was to rip the culprit.

Fired right up by the mere presence of my opponent, and determined not be thought of as a failure by losing the final two years in succession, I came back from a service break down in the final set, to win.

Once again my dad was there in the Wimbledon locker room afterwards, but there was no need for any apologies this time, and he came up to offer me his congratulations. I looked up at with a big smile on my face and told him: 'I've won the little one Dad, now I'm going after the big one!'

Chapter Three

MAYBE NOT JUST A
CRACK IN THE WALL

So what should be paramount in the thoughts of most fit and firing eighteen-year-old males? The answer shouldn't be too hard to come by, although priorities may differ slightly. Besides the obvious, some of the more academic amongst my peers could have focused some of their attention on the prospect of furthering their education. For me, that had long since ceased to be a factor in my life, and the course of my future seemed pretty well charted. Otherwise it's usually a case of girls, cars, girls, rock music, girls, having a few beers and then back to girls.

Sure, sport also fits in the equation, especially if you come from Melbourne. Footy is tantamount to religion, cricket is thought of as a national treasure, and the MCG is akin to a cathedral. The traditions of Australian tennis were also a matter of intense pride for the older generations, even though my sport had been through the doldrums and yachting had overtaken it in prestige, with a win in the Americas Cup.

So imagine the pressure brought to bear on this still juvenile and somewhat fragile mind when Australia reached the Davis Cup final for the first time in six years. The match was played in my home town and I, having been out of junior tennis little more than five minutes, was expected to go and win it. It is also worth remembering that the opposition included the player who had won the Australian Open a matter of weeks previously, standing that prize next to the French Open title he had taken eighteen months earlier. And just to help along that pressured feeling, one of my own countrymen, who just happened to be both a tennis legend and a national icon, was doing his best to publicly undermine my confidence and convince me I had about as much right to be out on court as Ivan Lendl would have in attending a convention of the world's most humorous men.

Playing Mats Wilander was a challenge I believed I could handle. I'd known and liked him for a couple of years, ever since I had first run into him as a talented Swedish kid with a mop of hair and ears like a koala bear, on the clay courts of Milan. There was no denying he was a supremely gifted tennis player. To win the French Open title at the age of seventeen, and then follow it up with the Australian while playing from the baseline on Kooyong's grass, and beating McEnroe in the semi followed by Lendl in the final, is a superhuman achievement.

Mats won the French at his first attempt in the grown-up world, and took the Aussie at his second, having lost in the first round in his only previous appearance two years earlier. Though our paths would cross numerous times in forthcoming years, we both had a mutual respect for one another that blossomed into a good friendship. In addition, neither of us was really sure whether we wanted to be the world's best tennis player or the next great rock star, and we both took the odd walk on the wild side in later years.

John Newcombe's barbed criticism was considerably harder to

Maybe not just a crack in the wall

take, and rankles to this very day; it really made one wonder whether he was as patriotic an Australian as he made himself out to be. I certainly knew of a different John Newcombe! Captaincy of the Australian Davis Cup team, which came a couple of decades later, seemed to change his attitude to young players who maybe needed the occasional arm around their shoulder. Why this change? Perhaps advancing years helped generate a little more understanding; maybe he was just thinking to enhance his own reputation.

A couple of years ago, in the very last match of Newcombe's term as captain, Australia played Spain in that tempestuous final in Barcelona. Australia had won the trophy a year earlier against the French in Nice, and what a story it would have been for Newcombe to go out a winner!

Lleyton Hewitt was selected to contend one of the coveted singles slots and Hewitt was not a person who behaved on court in the pristine and time-honoured Aussie ways of a Sedgman, a Laver or a Rosewall. He is prepared to bounce a racket now again, question an umpire and antagonise an opponent by brandishing his fist and letting rip with a loud and vociferous 'C'mon!'. Alex Corretja made his feeling clear on the matter before the final - though as far as I'm concerned, good on you for acting that way, Lleyton. However, it was just the sort of behaviour that Newcombe attacked me for, back in 1982. Yet more than eighteen years later, he was defending a players right to behave in that way!

Back in the early 1980s Fraser was captain, and his thinking suited me in two significant ways. For a start, he was no lover of Newcombe. I'm told they had their clashes when Frase took over from Harry Hopman, because Newcombe liked to go out partying at night and then turned up for practice whenever it suited him.

Whenever Newcombe's name came up in a conversation with Frase involved, there would be something pretty negative muttered from the captain's direction.

Much more importantly, Frase had a great belief in my ability, and had known about me from way back. His brother John used to take me on those early morning training sessions when I was at school, and Frase was around when I was just a kid at Grace Park, beginning to play local competitions against grown men. Then we used to go on week-long tennis camps with him on Phillip Island, where he learnt a bit more about my game and personality - although to my mind he didn't always have the right ideas about my technique. For instance, for a long time he insisted I should flatten out my forehand, which wasn't totally beneficial in the long run.

If Ian Barclay was a second father to me, then Frase was like an uncle. He knew grass court tennis as well as anyone: you don't beat Laver in a Wimbledon final if you don't know a trick or two! Frase wasn't to everyone's taste, however, and John Alexander and Kim Warwick had their differences with him; but I always held the guy in tremendous respect. Contrary to some popular thought put around over the years, Frase and I had hardly any clashes at all.

Nevertheless, there was one occasion when I *did* call him all the names under the sun. As Davis Cup captain, he took a few of us up to play an exhibition match in Geraldton, Western Australia, which isn't a place exactly overburdened with comfortable five-star hotel rooms. On arrival it became apparent that we were going to have to share, and some of the older guys must have known what to expect because they decided we would draw lots for room partners. I drew the short straw, which meant sharing with Frase, and I don't think I had a minute's sleep because of the volume of his snoring - it was like an earthquake.

Maybe not just a crack in the wall

Some used to say the Australian Davis Cup team in those days was a Melbourne mafia, with Paul McNamee, Peter McNamara, Frase and myself. It's hard to argue the case, although there was also John Fitzgerald who came from the little outback town of Cockaleechie in South Australia. Fitzy was acceptable because he was a Catholic, and at least they play footy, rather than rugby, in that state! Another thing we all had in common was Irish descent, except for the odd man out, Mark Edmondson: he was from Gosford, New South Wales - and anyone who has ever met Eddo knows he is a real odd man out!

Following my win in the Wimbledon juniors, and in the doubles in partnership with John Frawley, I went on to win the US Open junior event as well, beating Guy Forget in the final. The tournament was frankly not that memorable, but the final was staged on the grotesquely huge Louis Armstrong Stadium, so at least I had the chance to play on that; now the stadium has been more correctly cut down to size. Needless to say, the handful of spectators who arrived to watch in a stadium built to take an audience of something like 30,000, didn't exactly make for a great atmosphere.

By that time I was playing regularly on the full tour. I'd made my Australian Open debut at the age of sixteen, although I was well beaten by Edmondson. However, things went considerably better in the Frankston indoor tournament on the outskirts of Melbourne, when I defeated another Aussie called Syd Ball: his main claim to fame was that he was once engaged to Sue Barker, my current day colleague on the BBC.

All that said, the Davis Cup was something different. Playing for your country must be the ambition of any Australian who picks up a tennis racket (with just one exception, namely Mark

49

Philippoussis) and I was certainly no different. I was born in 1965, mid-way through a run when Australia won the Davis Cup four years in succession; indeed, between 1950 and 1967 we held it all but three years, which is some going. Anyone who knows anything about the game can reel off the list of all-time greats who cemented that legend.

Tennis had been not just an Australian sport, but an Australian property, and I wanted to recapture some of the past glories. Sure, I watched our yacht beat the USA's to win the Americas Cup a few months before the final; as I recall it was required viewing, albeit in the middle of the night, because the climax took place when we were all together in Sydney for the Davis Cup semi-final against France. However, I didn't get too carried away by it all; to be honest, I really didn't give a toss about sailing.

So frankly I couldn't see the point of having the boat's skipper, John Bertrand, in our locker room before the final. I think it was Frase's idea, to encourage patriotic motivation, but to me, Bertrand wasn't particularly special; and I wasn't too keen on letting outsiders in to what should have been the team's domain - and I didn't want some guy who probably didn't know anything about tennis, lecturing to me before the biggest match of my life.

In retrospect, I was so young I probably didn't fully realise the enormous significance of the achievement at the time. Whatever the circumstances, I was still extremely nervous, and anything that added to the already considerable pressure seemed unnecessary. I had served my apprenticeship as the teams orange boy a year or so before, behind Alexander, McNamee and McNamara when the United States thrashed us 5-0 in the semi-final on an ill-chosen Perth court that was supposed to be a slow Greenset surface. McNamara had beaten Ivan Lendl, the world's top player, on a

Maybe not just a crack in the wall

similar surface six months previously. Unfortunately for us, the top crust had worn off during the practice week, and the court became so quick it was perfect for McEnroe and Co.

By the time of the first round against Britain the following year, Frase decided a young Cash was ready to face the Poms in Adelaide. I can remember him coming up to me and saying, I want to play you, what do you think? As I recall he didn't mention my age, but I thought it was strange for a guy who was that experienced, to be asking a young buck his opinion. In fact I was the youngest player to represent Australia for more than fifty years.

To say I was apprehensive was understating the case, and my anxiety probably contributed to the fact that I broke almost all my rackets in practice. I had to send an SOS to one of tennis's great Mr. Fix-its, Stuart Wilson, who worked for Slazenger at the time. It was impossible to make any to my specific requirements in time, so they jetted out some of the same model manufactured for Guillermo Vilas. I used to like a heavy racket, but Vilas' were more than 35g heavier, which was a significant weight. Consequently, Ian Barclay's task for a day or so was to bevel the edges down and make the rackets lighter.

I was drawn to play John Lloyd in the opening rubber, though the first day was a total washout, which only served to make me even tenser. I think Frase gave me the nod because I had beaten John (or Flossie, as everyone in tennis used to call him - and still do) in the Victorian Open a few weeks earlier as I made way towards becoming the youngest player to win a tour event at the time. Flossie may not have been the most powerful of players, but he was still talented and extremely experienced, and he came back a lot stronger and more determined after our previous meeting.

Despite losing the first set and not playing anything close to what

I regarded as well, I managed to hang on and win in five sets. However, the victory was not without its cost, and by the end of the match my elbow just felt numb from using that heavy Vilas racket. Fortunately for me, Paul McNamee played a blinder in the second singles, and a doubles team of McNamee and Edmondson made easier work of things.

Luckily we had an unassailable 3-0 lead when the time came for me to play Buster Mottram in the fourth rubber. That particular confrontation was dead, and so was my right arm: I could barely raise it from my side, and not surprisingly went down to Buster pretty tamely.

Tame isn't quite the word anyone who had anything to do with the Australian camp would use to describe the match preparations that year. Nevertheless, we still managed to get through a couple of potentially rough ties against the Romanians and the French. The problem with playing Ilie Nastase in those days wasn't his talent - even he, one of the most argumentative men ever to walk onto a tennis court, would struggle to deny he was past his best by that time.

Nasty's speed between the lines may have disappeared, but his ability to distract his opponent by using the most blatant gamesmanship remained as legendary as ever. I was ready for him, having been beaten as a bit of a naive rookie in Bristol England on grass the previous year: on that occasion, no sooner had we walked on the court than Nasty had started to work at my concentration. I was sitting down, pulling on my wristbands and testing the tension of my rackets when a commotion broke out from the other side of the umpire's chair. With ascending volume and increasing feeling, my opponent was just yelling: What is this shit? What is this shit?? WHAT IS THIS SHIT???

Maybe not just a crack in the wall

The match was being televised, and even in those days the effect microphones couldn't help but pick up Nasty's outbursts. Officials were running everywhere, and the crowd, which looked as if it were made up of predominantly more senior citizens, looked shocked by his antics. His teenage adversary, unused to what this man had been getting away with for years, had forgotten about his routine pre-match preparations and was transfixed by the exhibition. Finally the tournament referee felt brave enough to walk up and ask the exact nature of the problem. Nastase, with that impish grin on his face, looked the guy squarely in the eye, picked up the pretty sizable towel that had been left for us to wipe away our sweat, and said: What is this sheet? It is not a towel. It is a sheet.

Without doubt, the object of the whole exercise was to create sufficient mayhem to unsettle me, and he was 100 per cent successful, going on to win with ease. Before the tie in Brisbane, Frase told Mark Edmondson, the other designated singles player, and I what to expect. Personally I didn't need any warning, and as it turned out, there was no real need to worry because the tie was won by the time I faced Nasty. I lost only ten games in three sets against Florin Segarceanu, and then, determined not to be lured into Nastys web twice, I ignored all his antics, although he went through the entire repertoire. Not one wisecrack endangered Australia becoming overwhelming 5-0 winners.

Unfortunately I wasn't quite so focused in the semi-final against the French at Sydney's White City. There were specific reasons for this, which will soon become clear - but for the time being, suffice it to say that I lost the opening rubber in straight sets to a lithe, agile and big-serving Yannick Noah. He may not have liked to play on grass as much as the French clay, but that afternoon he seemed to capitalise on every mistake I made. Fortunately Frase's decision to play John Fitzgerald instead of Edmondson or McNamee proved inspired, and Fitzy produced two of the performances of his life to beat first Henri Leconte and then Noah, even taking a leaf out of the Jimmy Connors playbook by revving up the crowd's support with his pumping fists.

Ironically the French returned to exact revenge against Fitzy, who is now Australia's Davis Cup captain himself. In his first year in charge he took the team to the final, only to suffer some traditional home criticism after losing last December's final to Guy Forget's team at Melbourne Park. With Hewitt, the new world number one, Rafter making a determined farewell and the match played on grass, it was supposed to be the final that Australia couldn't lose - but things didn't quite turn out that way, and Fitzy ended up carrying the can.

Being 12,000 miles away in London I wasn't too sure of the rights and wrongs of the issue, but I do know plenty about Fitzy. Primarily he has the reputation of being one of the tightest men around: thus even though he made about $1 million one year from doubles alone when he and Anders Jarryd were top of the pile in doubles, he still insisted on flying economy everywhere he went.

On one long flight across the Pacific he was rammed right in the middle of a line of four seats, with quite a prim and proper lady sitting next to him. Maybe it was the airline food, or perhaps it was just the confined space, but Fitzy suffered a terrible bout of flatulence. Recognising that action needed to be taken, he went to the bathroom; but within a few minutes of returning to his seat the problem had returned. Fitzy decided he would let out a little sampler, just to judge the extent of his dilemma - and it absolutely reeked.

Glancing to his left, he was confronted by the obviously offended

Maybe not just a crack in the wall

female, and then quickly averting his gaze, he saw that the man on the other side of him was fast asleep. Realising he could pass the blame, Fitzy commiserated with the woman about the anti-social aromas. She admitted she had been suspicious about the sleeping man, and declared she thought him totally disgusting. Safe in the knowledge he had got away with it, Fitzy eased back in his seat and let off all the way to Los Angeles.

Australian tennis players clearly have a problem with their wind. Rafter was a notorious culprit, although he earned the incredibly apt nickname of Skunky for a different reason: namely the streak of white hair in the midst of his otherwise dark scalp. But on one particular occasion he incensed the fastidiously clean Andre Agassi by visiting his particular corner in the locker room and, well fed and determined to pollute the atmosphere, letting rip. Agassi furiously demanded a bit of respect from Rafter, but was promptly told where to go - and that, believe me, was why there was always a certain edge to their many confrontations. Lesson one: don't piss off a determined Aussie.

The Aussie teams preparation for the 1983 Davis Cup final at Kooyong was almost compromised by the feeling of pressure, stirred up, it has to be said, by Fraser himself. All four potential singles players were very evenly matched: Fitzgerald, McNamee, Edmondson and myself. Nobody knew who would get the nod from Frase, and consequently he prepared us for the final with a series of what could best be described as trial matches.

Practice became so intense that it was frankly unhealthy. It was almost like playing an Australian Closed Championships, where the prize for the winners would be a place on the team. Most teams' preparation would be based around the style of the opponents, and with Wilander and Joakim Nystrom the potential Swedish singles players, it just might have been an idea to get in some concerted hitting time against guys playing predominantly from the baseline.

But Frase didn't think along those lines, he wanted us toughened up and determined. Off the court we might all have been a group of mates, but there were times on it when the ferocity became too much. Word had leaked through to the Australian media that our sessions were often pretty heated, promising the makings of a good story for them. As it turned out, the reporter from *The Melbourne Age* zeroed in on McNamee, saying his behaviour was a disgrace to the honour of representing Australia.

Macca may have thrown a few rackets, but he clearly wasn't the worst violator, and was frankly mild tempered compared to me. He hadn't enjoyed the best of years and this was soul-destroying for him. Meanwhile the rest of us were beginning to think the press just wanted to hinder us, and that they would have been happier with Sweden winning.

It has been said afterwards that sitting on the courtside benches at that time was like perching on the brim of a volcano. At one stage, Frase got so concerned about our behaviour that he called in a psychologist named Laurie Hayden. From the moment of this mans arrival, I wasn't happy about him being there.

Later life has revealed to me the benefit of psychology, but back then I thought it was just something to treat basket cases. In retrospect that's exactly what I was at the time, along with the three other guys who wanted to be on the team. Nevertheless, Hayden sat us down and told us to be more self-congratulatory over our good shots rather than furious about the bad ones. He insisted that throwing rackets, swearing and cursing wouldn't improve anyone's game and said we should acknowledge the winners hit by our teammates.

Maybe not just a crack in the wall

At the end of his speech, we all tried to take on board what he had said as we headed back out to the courts. For a while, everything was lovely: it could have been the church courts on a Sunday afternoon. Frase was sitting courtside with a nice contended smile on his face as cries of 'Great shot, Fitzy!', 'Well done, Eddo!', 'Keep it up, Macca!' and 'Good on yer, Cashy!' echoed around Kooyong.

The match was scheduled to start on Boxing Day, and here we were in the lead-up to Christmas with a mood of goodwill to all men gloriously abundant. At a conservative estimate I would say it lasted no more than half an hour, as gradually tempers began to fray again - and before long the rackets were flying, with the swearing and cursing as savage as ever. By now Frase's expression had changed, and he just shook his head, muttering that he could not believe his luck. ✓

Things really came to the boil with a notorious practice match involving John Fitzgerald and I, just two days before the draw. Folklore states that Fitzy was getting the better of me, that there was a dispute over a line call, I bounced my racket which flew into the stands, and Frase had to send me back to the locker rooms to cool down. Frase is supposed to have said after the tie that he had reprimanded me for disruptive practice, and considered leaving me out because my behaviour was not conducive to the interests of the rest of the team. However, I don't remember it quite that way.

Certainly I was pissed off because Fitzy was beating me, and admittedly I bounced my racket like I did with great regularity but this time it bounced with a life of its own! We were on one of the side courts at Kooyong, where a little hill goes off towards the stands: after giving the racket a bit of a heave, it cartwheeled about five times and careered over a wall before landing about three rows

57

back close to where my Uncle Brian was sitting.

I can honestly say I'd never seen anything like it before, and if I hadn't been so angry, I could have burst out laughing. The embarrassing thing was I had to go and retrieve it from in front of my uncle, just like a naughty little kid. I do recall Frase calling a halt to practice, and he did have a quiet word with me, saying that was enough for the day - but I don't remember him sitting me down and delivering a lecture.

The next day I was a different character in practice, as it had suddenly come home to me that I was really pushing things too far. So when our captain named the team on the morning of the draw, it was a moving occasion. I remember Frase stood up and said, We're going in with Cash and Fitzgerald in the singles, followed by McNamee and Edmondson in doubles. I was smiling, and so was Fitzy; it felt like a great honour after all the criticism from Newcombe. Then I looked across at Macca and there were tears rolling down his cheeks. He was disappointed at not getting a singles place, and it showed - but in effect it served to bring the team together just at the right moment.

Australian team spirit to me is a wonderful thing. Maybe it's because we live so far away from everyone else, and are often so far away from home that togetherness and comradeship is really important. Quite possibly it is born out of an inferiority complex because, as our critics love to remind us, we are all just descendants of a bunch of convicts who were shoved off to the other side of the world.

When things calmed down after the draw, I went up to Macca and asked if he was OK. Right from the start of my career he had taken me under his wing and acted as something of a mentor, and I cared about him; I knew he was still decimated, but he said he was fine.

Maybe not just a crack in the wall

Macca is such a fiercely patriotic Aussie that he wanted to give everything for his country, and he assured me he was going to kick the Swedes' arses in the doubles. Something like forty-eight hours later, he was as good as his word.

First up I suffered against Wilander's skill, consistency and accuracy. He just seemed to carry on the form that had won him the Australian Open three weeks before, and serving sixteen double faults didn't exactly help my cause. Neither did too many errors, that I kept making when going for outright winners because I was so fired up. All was far from lost, however; next was Fitzy against Nystrom, and we had always viewed Nystrom as the potential key to victory.

In the second singles Fitzy came through in four sets against Nystrom to level the tie, making the doubles pivotal, which is so often the case. In previous years we could have called on that great partnership of McNamara and McNamee, who had won Wimbledon a couple of times. Sadly, however, McNamara had missed the whole year following major knee surgery - but Eddo and McNamee went into the final unbeaten. Eddo was no mean doubles player, having won the Australian Open title four years out of five. Alongside Macca, the pair of them were just too damn good for the Swedish team of Anders Jarryd and Hans Simonsson.

So then it came for me to play Nystrom, and involuntarily my memory flew back the month or so to the press conference after our match at the NSW Open, where Newcombe's mouthpiece Thirsk had been blatantly supporting the Swede. Afterwards he had had the audacity to ask why a lot of the fans were against me and wanted Nystrom to win. I kept my cool, saying Joakim was a very good player and that Swedes were popular around the world because of Bjorn Borg's exploits.

Apart from that brief conversation I always refused to speak to Thirsk. I always acknowledged him, and that was about it. He regularly tried to take the conversations further, but I would just tell him I wasn't saying anything, and then turn around to chat with another reporter.

I knew exactly what was needed when I walked out for the match. We led 2-1, and I knew Fitzy would have his work cut out beating Wilander if it went to a fifth rubber. I had gone to bed early the night before to make sure I was well rested, but I hadn't been able to sleep that well. Breakfast was a very brief affair, as I forced myself to push something down amongst all the butterflies. Fortunately once I was out on court for the match, all my nerves seemed to drain away, and I benefited from my experiences against Mats two days earlier.

Unquestionably we should have had some practice against baseline play, rather than those full-out matches against each other; but Nystrom played the game in a similar way to Wilander, though without quite as much brilliance. Within just a couple of points I realised the fast court was really playing to my advantage, and that Nystrom couldn't handle my attacking game.

Controlled aggression is the term I like to use in description of my performance that day. One thing I was determined to achieve was a consistent first serve, and I was all over the net. Before too long Wilander, sitting on the Swedish bench, realised there was nothing he could to affect the outcome: Australia were on their way to recapturing the Davis Cup, and I was proving a few of my critics wrong. I remember match point so clearly.

Apparently Nystrom won only two of the last twenty points. To close out the match I attempted a lob that he wouldn't be able to properly reach and sure enough, the ball just flew harmlessly out of court off his racket frame. The photos show that I punched the sky with a deliriously happy right-hander, before falling into the arms of captain Fraser. It was just a wonderful feeling. Not only had my crucial 6-4,6-1,6-1 victory been the second fastest live match in Davis Cup final history, but I was also the youngest player ever, at eighteen years and seven months, to win a deciding rubber.

Within a matter of seconds Macca and Fitzy were jumping over the wall to get to me, and the real festivities had begun. But somebody was missing. It goes without saying that voices were raised - I've never been one for silent celebrations - and we all started noisily questioning the whereabouts of our fourth team member who had played such a distinguished part in the doubles win the day before.

Onto the court swaggered Mark Edmondson with that rolling walk-cum-jog, and the crowd just roared. He's built like a brick dunny and looks like a mean old grizzly, but at that moment he was flashing the unusual sight of a big wide grin. Eddo had never exactly been a crowd favourite, but at that moment he looked like a rock and we just climbed all over him.

This is a memory that will live with me until my dying day, and to win a Davis Cup final so early in my career was a tremendous achievement. But it wasn't without a price, and I wasn't to learn the full extent of the toll it had actually taken until much later in life. For a while I thought it was an experience I didn't want to repeat, not because of the glory, but because of the intensity of the whole thing. I was really feeling the weight of national expectation.

Little did I know that many of us would be back on exactly the same court for a re-run in three years time - although there were a great many highs and lows to experience before then. Some things I would never change, some of which brought so much pain, agony and heartache. Unfortunately my family had already suffered one terrible blow, the scars of which will never properly heal.

Chapter Four

DISTRESS AND DOOBIES

My half brother Ralph was a rebel, to put it mildly. He was a tortured soul who had taken the break-up of my mother's first marriage very hard. By the time he was in his twenties he had lost his way in life; he got involved in the biker scene and also developed quite a drug habit, and trouble just used to follow him around - and then one day he killed himself.

Ralph was nine years older than me and hadn't lived at home for a long time. Nevertheless I still feel a horrible cold sensation when I remember the police coming to our house early in the morning to break the news. It's something you never forget, and I still find it extremely hard to talk about the memory. However, after the initial shock and subsequent grief, none of us in the family could really say we were surprised. Earlier in life I'm told he was a really sweet kid who was very popular with all his mates; but becoming a biker seemed to change all that. He never really had a proper job, although did a lot of mechanic jobs on cars and motorbikes.

I couldn't really say I knew him that well because there was a generation gap. I was probably closer to my other stepbrother Craig, who first stoked up my interest in music by playing the

Beatles' A Hard Day's Night all the time. But I remember having a loose tooth when I was six years old, and Ralph said he would fix it; so he took a step back, swung his fist and punched me right in the mouth. Naturally I was pretty upset - but I didn't have a loose tooth any more.

Ralph did the Easy Rider thing and went on the road, riding around Australia on his motorbike. He came back with a lady called Linda who had fallen pregnant, and they had a beautiful little son named Lee who was just two years old when his father died. Both Ralph and Linda were heavily involved with drugs, which made their life very unstable. They moved around, living in flats and squats. Then one night when Ralph was having a fine old time drinking in a bar, a guy he thought was his mate turned out to be a psycho, and slashed Ralph in the face with a broken bottle. My stepbrother lost one eye and was fortunate to keep his sight in the other; and apparently the only crime he had committed was to say he was going home to the missus.

It's not difficult to imagine the psychological torment he suffered after such an attack. Added to that Ralph also suffered from depression, which is often the case with people dependent on drugs. In the end it all got too much for him, so he just pointed a gun to his head and pulled the trigger. I was eighteen at the time, and unusually was spending a few weeks at home. Having just played Wimbledon, I was getting ready to head off to the United States. I had already represented Australia in two rounds of the Davis Cup - but that morning I don't think tennis even entered my mind.

Renee, my sister who is two years younger than me, was distraught, and my younger brother Daniel was very upset. After a while my parents tried to be philosophical about the whole thing. My dad was always very supportive of Ralph, and got on with him as a stepfather; but I think it's the hardest thing my mum has ever suffered in life.

Just a day or so after the tragedy I was due to jet off across the Pacific to continue my promising tennis career, but needless to say, I didn't want to go: how could I leave my family at such a grief-stricken time? My parents sat me down and stressed it was important to them, as much as it was to me, that I went and played the US Open. I'd just got through to the last sixteen of Wimbledon, and earlier in the year had followed up my win in the Victorian Open by winning the title in Brisbane; I was therefore ranked comfortably in the world's top fifty. Even so, they almost had to drag me to Tullamarine Airport; and somehow I got on that flight, which meant I could not attend my brother's funeral.

Subconsciously I must have been wracked with guilt. There I was, thousands of miles from home in New York, and supposedly concentrating on tennis when my mother was burying one of her children. It would have been a test for the best adjusted of minds, but at the time I was regarded as something of a wild boy - and I just got wilder. For instance, a week before the US Open began, I was thrown out of an exhibition event in upstate New York at Port Chester for three code-of-conduct violations. More trouble with officialdom followed at the Open when I was fined $1,750 for twice throwing a racket and abusing the umpire during my second round match against Canada's Glen Michibata.

Even more heinous deeds were to follow in the next round, when I took on one of USA's favourite sons, Bill Scanlon. In my opinion, American umpires are without question the worst in the world, and are quite prepared to give their player the benefit of the doubt in tight situations.

Another official who didn't seem to have a proper grasp of the rules was Georgina Clark of England. At the time of writing she is one of the top executive supervisors on the WTA Tour, but back then she was just an umpire - and she got everything wrong. I hit a first serve that was clearly a fault, but my opponent broke a string trying to get the ball back so he had to halt play to change his racket. Anyone knows I should then have been allowed another two serves, but she stubbornly insisted I could only have one. It was laughable.

I felt I had been the victim of some abysmal decisions in my match against Michibata, and then it soon became abundantly apparent that the Americans wanted Scanlon to beat me at any cost. I lost, which was hardly surprising, and suffered even more dreadful line calls. Looking back throughout my entire career, I can honestly say that this was the only match I lost by being so angry.

The rage provoked in me by their blatant favouritism was so intense that I could not recover my composure. The American officials just wanted their guy to win: it was as simple as that. So after the match I walked to the net, shook hands, and then, turning my back to the umpire's chair and bending forwards, I gave its resident a clear view of my backside. I didn't go the whole way by dropping my shorts and giving him the full moon, but the intent was obvious.

So was the outcry afterwards. My actions were termed un-Australian behaviour, and apparently the reaction at home was almost apoplectic - and guess who was leading the torrent of criticism? A well known admirer of mine called John David Newcombe.

To say that my shocking conduct was in reaction to my stepbrother's suicide would probably be overstating the case. I've never properly processed it in my mind, but I certainly seemed to

Distress and Doobies

step up my rebellion. I'd been saddled with the wild boy reputation two years previously when I was world junior champion and had been regularly getting in trouble on court. To this day I really don't know if I was over-reacting; but the whole episode following Ralph's death certainly wasn't a pleasant experience.

Given the choice, I would have preferred to have kept my suffering within. However, when I came home for the Davis Cup semi-final against France, I did attempt to apologise for my actions, and told the press I had been a little up tight after a stressful month. I didn't go into things any deeper than that, but anyone who knew me must have been aware of the reasons for my below-par performance against Noah in the opening rubber at Sydney.

Pressures were also building on me in Australia, and rather than improve after the Davis Cup victory, they worsened. As a result, every time I touched down in Sydney or Melbourne I felt a mood of apprehension overtake me. Whether it was a Davis Cup tie or just a regular tournament, I felt I was playing for the whole of the nation, and that everyone was watching my every action.

To a certain extent they were, because around that time we were devoid of many great sporting heroes. It wasn't just tennis: we had just lost the Ashes in cricket, Australian swimming wasn't going through the golden period it is enjoying at the moment, and I think we won just one gold medal in the 1984 Olympics (if my memory serves me correctly, that was won by my old mate John Seiban). Basically there was Greg Norman, Wayne Gardner and myself doing really well in world terms, which clearly wasn't enough for a sports-mad society. ✓

Outsiders have to understand that Australia is a country consumed by sport, and the media mirrors that interest. Nothing but glorious victory is good enough, and sometimes even then there will be plenty of people willing to pick faults.

It would be hard to admit that I don't have a fiery Irish temper. Then you can add a streak of stubbornness that comes from the Chicago blood I inherited from my mother, add the trauma of my stepbrother's suicide alongside my generally volatile reaction to criticism, and it might just explain my somewhat explosive personality at the time. Well, that's my excuse, anyway.

I was a perfectionist, and didn't like losing. Indeed, show me a world-class sportsman who does. Yet even at my worst, in my opinion none of my behaviour matched the sort of things John McEnroe was getting up to on court. Sometimes I would get fined $500 for bouncing a racket, and though I wasn't defaulted, it still made big news. If I argued a call during a match it would be on the television news that evening, and that's all people saw: whether I won or lost became irrelevant. Some of the treatment I received still takes some believing, and I remember reaching the finals in Brisbane only to be called a spoilt brat.

My dad was so incensed he caught up with the journalist who wrote the offending article in the *Courier Mail*, grabbed his notebook, and ripped it up and threw it in the rubbish bin. The headlines the next day weren't Pat Cash Wins Title but Cash's Father Attacked Me. I became so confused, and didn't know whether I was a good guy because I was winning things for my country, or a bad guy because every week there was some kind of criticism. This tradition for critical vendetta carries on to this day: you only have to look at the investigations current-day players such as Lleyton Hewitt and Mark Philippoussis are forced to undergo. It gets me thinking, is it really any wonder that Jelena Dokic has turned her back on Australia?

At the time, nobody was a greater help to me than Paul

Distress and Doobies

McNamee. He was my mentor, and showed me so much about being a globetrotting tennis player. He was always quite a hyperactive individual who taught me about the training, the traps and the girls.Another experienced player who was an influence in my formative years was John Alexander; he was also much calmer than Macca, which for me was an advantage.

JA was the guy who very early on singled out Jimmy Connors as a player with many strengths to emulate. One of the most important Connors lessons he taught me was always to be a magnanimous winner and praise your opponent. If you win, and then bad mouth the other guy without showing him respect, he will be doubly determined to come back and kick your arse the next time. If you are nice to the people you beat, and really resolve to get the better of those you lose to when you next meet in competition, then you'll become a better player.

So said JA, quoting the gospel according to James Scott Connors; and while the likes of McEnroe, Lendl and Becker were bad mouthing all and sundry, I always took heed of those words. Therefore it came as an acute disappointment when JA wrote an article berating me for losing my temper. By then, of course, I had stopped reading the newspapers; but as I said before, word gets around, and in many ways it's even worse hearing about people criticising you at second hand. So to hear that somebody I liked and respected as much as John Alexander had given me a spray was hurtful, even though it was probably warranted.

I had a much better reputation in Britain. I just got my head down and got on with things, letting Johnny Mac take most of the flak in his guise of Superbrat. I suppose that was one of the reasons I began looking for a home in London, though most sporting Aussies like to establish a base in the Northern Hemisphere because the travelling is so time-consuming and downright tiring.

Anonymity is another thing I enjoyed about being away from Australia. Fame is not something that I have ever relished, and I always felt a level of notoriety went with me in my homeland. I hate walking into places such as restaurants and maybe even just shops, in the knowledge that people are turning around and pointing at me. Some people enjoy being stars, others like me really don't want to be public property, and I felt the tall poppy syndrome whenever I was back home in those early days. Towards the end of my playing career I would find bunches of young blokes coming up to me and telling me I was a sporting legend. Quite frankly I'd be embarrassed, and wouldn't expect such adulation.

After a while I realised these people were kids and young teenagers when I was winning Wimbledon and the Davis Cup. They remembered me for my achievements in the game, and not for what my *persona* was supposed to be. Sometimes I would almost be expecting a fight because of all the negative stuff which had been said about me, but all these guys wanted to do was shake my hand. It took a very long time for this feeling to sink in.

There was, however, one aspect of fame which I did find useful. Music had always been a big part of my life; I suppose it is in my genes, because my grandfather Thomas was a wonderful classical pianist. My aunt and sister Renee both sing in the national opera, and music is always being played in the family house, although it isn't necessarily to my taste. I always liked the Beatles as a little kid, and I remember some rock albums my stepbrothers played: Led Zeppelin's Physical Graffiti and Lou Reed's Transformer.

Every music fan can distinctly remember the first record they ever bought, and mine was by the Electric Light Orchestra. The second was by Cheap Trick, and that was it: I was eleven years old,

Distress and Doobies

and I was sold.

Cheap Trick became my band. I tried to join their fan club; I got their albums; I read everything I possibly could about them, and later on went to see them play at Melbourne's Festival Hall, which ironically was the venue of my first ever tour final several years later. Their name was scrawled all over my school books, which is a natural thing for a young kid to do, but they are still a major part of my life now, and I have good reason to think about them every time I walk onto a tennis court.

Once I started playing tennis seriously I quickly discovered how freely I sweated; my clothes would always be drenched within a couple of games of starting a match, and I needed to wear a headband to stop the sweat pouring down into my eyes. For a couple of years I made do with what my sponsors gave me, but then I began to think it would be pretty cool to have my own personal design.

So was devised the black and white check headband I still wear today. Many people have thought it was based on the chequered flag in motor racing, which is waved to signal the winner. In reality it was all down to my idolising Cheap Trick, and in particular their guitarist Rick Nielsen. Everything he wore was always black and white, often in a chequered design, and the headband was my attempt at a tribute.

Just a few months ago I finally got to meet Rick for the first time. Time and again they had played in Melbourne, but try as I might, I just couldn't get back stage. Then one of my buddies called Malcolm Dome, a legend in the London hard rock scene who happens to work at the Total Rock radio station based in The Kings Head pub near my house in Fulham, was the deliverer of some good news.

Malcolm reported Cheap Trick were playing a concert at The Garage, Islington, and then asked if I wanted to interview Rick Nielsen. Did I ever! I got to meet all the members of the band as well as Nielsen, and went to the concerts where they performed all their early stuff, the music of my youth.

I could not have been happier, and then on the second night Rick dragged me up on stage. I thought he was just going to say something like 'This is Pat Cash, the tennis player, and he's such a big fan that he even wears a black and white checked headband'. Instead he presented me with his guitar strap (black and white check, naturally) and then made me give a speech of thanks. At that very moment I can honestly say I saw the benefits of fame.

Going back to my youth, I soon got into much heavier music as well. Thin Lizzy's Live and Dangerous was one album I loved, and that great band reminds me of another strange story. Paul McNamee and I were practising at Queen's Club in London before playing doubles in the Stella Artois tournament, which is a part of the build-up to Wimbledon. I guess I was about eighteen or nineteen at the time, and very much a rocker. It was quite early in the morning, long before the gates opened, and I saw this long-haired guy watching us from a distance. I can remember thinking the person looked distinctly like Scott Gorham, one of the guitarists with Thin Lizzy and another hero of mine. But what would somebody like him be doing hanging around a tennis court so early in the morning? I concluded it must have been a long-haired groundsman or something, and gave the subject no more thought.

At the time, Prince had these new graphite rackets on the market and Macca was contracted to the company. He had a few of them, which was quite something as they were definitely state of the art, and I was allowed to give one a try. Later on we were in the locker rooms and Macca happened to say there was something he had forgotten to tell me: earlier on this guy with really long hair had gone up to him and asked him if he thought I would like to swap my pristine new racket for a guitar. He said he was from some band Lizzy something - but that didn't mean anything to somebody like Paul McNamee, so he had told him to piss off.

Hearing the story I looked at Macca with an expression bordering on the horrified. The thought of one of Gorham's Gibson Les Paul Sunbursts in exchange for something as mundane as a tennis racket made me feel weak: what a deal, and he had told him to piss off? I hollered at Paul that it was Scott Gorham - but he just came back with the question, Well, who the hell is he? But by then I was out of the locker room having grabbed one of Macca's rackets, almost leapt down the stairs, and was running around Queen's Club in search of one of my guitar heroes who had turned out to be something of a tennis fan.

Sadly he wasn't to be found, but several years later I met Scott when he played as part of the band in a gig to raise money for my charity GOAL. Naturally I asked him if the story was true, and he confirmed it was. By then I owned my own Gibson guitar, along with several other models, but it was still a case of what might have been.

Many a rock musician nurtures a dream to be a top line sportsman in the same way that so many tennis players have yearned to be guitar heroes: John McEnroe, Mats Wilander, the late and great Vitas Gerulaitis, and myself, to name just a few. There is no question that my being a top-line tennis star opened the way for some introductions to big names in the rock business, which otherwise would have remained just heroes.

Reminiscing a little bit, there was a store in the middle of

Melbourne called Central Station Records, really no more than a hole in the wall; the girl who worked there was always dressed in jet black, and she used to sell all the English heavy metal stuff: Deep Purple, Black Sabbath and of course Led Zeppelin. These were pretty well known names by then, but other bands such as Judas Priest, Saxon, Motorhead and Iron Maiden also caught my interest.

At the age of fifteen I can remember being in London for the junior tournaments, and going to see Whitesnake and Motorhead at what was then called the Hammersmith Odeon but now goes by the name of the London Apollo. Even though I had to buy a ticket from the touts outside, it had a lasting impression upon me. It was one of those legendary rock venues I had long been reading about, and when the time came to buy a home away from Australia, I made sure it wouldn't be too far away from Hammersmith. In the end, I bought a place less than half a mile away down the Fulham Palace Road, and I still try to get up to the Apollo when my kind of band is in town.

When I first started creating a bit of interest on the tennis court, several management companies began to joust for my business. One was owned by a guy called Glenn Wheatley, who also managed the Little River Band with John Farnham as well as Australian Crawl, which were very big back home at the time. Glenn promised me all kinds of stuff, and there was never a shortage of tickets for rock shows. One of the bands he arranged tickets for me was Iron Maiden who, over the years, I have probably spent more time watching and listening to than anyone else. Back then I used to stand right in front of the speakers so my ears would be ringing for a week afterwards because the music was so loud. I had the time of my life.

Distress and Doobies

The support band at that particular gig was an Aussie outfit called Heaven. Later on I was invited back to the bands' hotel for a party, and can remember sitting in the corner until the early hours of the morning. It turned out a few of Heaven liked their tennis, and I was Wimbledon Junior Champion at the time so we had mutual interests. One guy in particular was interested, the guitarist Mick Cocks who was earlier in the band Rose Tattoo, another of my all-time favourites. I did a deal with Mick, that I would help him with his tennis if he taught me to play the guitar.

We both kept our words, although I think I got a lot more out of the agreement than Mick. He was meant to be a real wild one, but to me he seemed quite tame, and a really fun guy. He showed me how to play, and got me a cheap guitar on which to practise. Being something of an obsessive character, I did so with great regularity, and almost immediately my guitar was just as important a part of the Cash luggage as my tennis rackets.

Steve Harris, the founding member and vocalist of Iron Maiden, became another really good mate. We kept in contact wherever we might be in the world, and I'd give him a call whenever I was in England. They were just beginning to sell records, I was starting to win tournaments, and we broke through at much the same time. We had something in common, and if I wasn't wearing my tennis gear at the time, it was fair bet I was decked out in an Iron Maiden T-shirt.

Several years later a couple of the band came over to watch me in the US Open, with hilarious results. Heavy metal hadn't really taken off in the States then. Admittedly there were bands like Styx, Heart and Kiss, but they weren't exactly what I would call rockers. It was the time of Michael Jackson and Lionel Ritchie, so you can imagine the stir created in the Flushing Meadows' players lounge and restaurant by a couple of English guys with tattoos all over their arms, cut-off black T-shirts and extremely long hair.

People used to mutter about them, say they were friends of that Pat Cash, and wonder what kind of drugs they had in the pockets of their leather jackets. The irony of it was that, whatever their appearance, both were clean-living family men. But just to add a bit of steam to the joke, they walked in the next day wearing T-shirts they had had specially printed: across their chests in big, glaring type was the message: NO, WE ARE NOT A FUCKIN' ENGLISH ROCK BAND BUT HAIRDRESSERS FROM MONTANA!!!

Gradually I was getting my act together musically. I could play three or four chords, which prompted mates to suggest I could now play the whole Ramones catalogue and was eligible to join Status Quo.My mate Mick Cocks had put a band together with another Melbourne boy, former AC/DC bassist Mark Evans, and they did old blues covers. Pretty soon my guitar and I were appearing on stage for the first time at a pub in Manly - though I admit I had to get drunk beforehand because I was so nervous. I can remember playing Gloria, the old Them song written by Van Morrison.

Both Mick and Mark had one major personality flaw in that they were Carlton supporters; but other than that, they were top guys in whose company I used to have a great clean-living laugh. Mark would regale me with tales on what it was like to be on the road with a top flight rock and roll band like AC/DC, and told many a story of the crazy antics of Angus Young, the guitarist who used to go on stage dressed as a schoolboy, complete with short pants and a cap.

In 1984 I caused a few raised eyebrows at Wimbledon, and not just by reaching the semi-final only a matter of weeks after my nineteenth birthday. The All England Club is not the most liberal place in the world when it comes to the wearing of outlandish clothing - and I'm not talking about the predominantly white rule, which is still rock solid for anything worn on court. Not too many guests are spotted with hair down their back, tattoos all the way up their arms, and wearing several of the other accoutrements of rock and roll. So when Iron Maiden's Steve Harris pitched up as my guest, a few murmurs of incredulity were heard amongst the conservatively clad members in their grey suits and club ties.

They would have been even more shocked to learn what had put me in such an unperturbed mood in my earlier rounds, which included an impressive four sets win over Mats Wilander. For a while I had been enjoying the occasional puff of a joint. Nothing too serious, and certainly nothing addictive, but extremely relaxing. The smoking of marijuana was pretty commonplace amongst tennis players at that time; cricketers drank vast amount of beer, and we smoked a joint now and again. Of course there were rumours about guys taking things considerably stronger, and it's no secret that Vitas Gerulaitis got increasingly into cocaine, and several other Americans were thought to do a couple of lines. As for the rest of us, it was just a little bit of grass, which to this day is not a substance on the ATP banned list.

Walking through Wimbledon village one evening, I bumped into somebody I knew who asked me if I wanted a joint. Sure, I said. Why not? So I took it back to the house I was staying in at the time with Neale Fraser, Wally Masur and a couple of other Australians. I kept the joint under my pillow because, as well as I got on with Frase, I don't think he would have been quite liberal enough to tolerate drug taking of even the very softest kind.

Several nights when I went to bed I had a couple of puffs, and I have to say it gave me the most restful sleep I have ever enjoyed in such an otherwise stressful environment. My views on marijuana have changed nowadays, but one of my favourite comedians Sam Kinisen explained 'when guys drink there are fights, but when you are stoned you just can't be bothered'. Of course, this was all happening around the time that one of cricket's greats, Ian Botham, made headlines about his grass smoking. And then there was former United States President Bill Clinton, although of course he didn't inhale!

Speaking of marijuana does remind me of another extremely funny story involving one of the most amusing characters to figure in my life, my Uncle Brian. A highly educated man, he is one of the most respected criminal lawyers in Melbourne. He is also a man who believes in enjoying life to the full; therefore he does not believe in sipping just a small sherry when seven or eight cognacs is a much better idea.

Uncle Brian is extremely proud of his Irish roots, and he gets back to the old country as often as possible. He says it's because of his interest in horse racing, but others in the family believe it's the only place in the world where people can keep up with him in the drinking department. He's not married, but he's had several girlfriends over the years.

More than once he has been an embarrassment to my father, although the two brothers were regularly inseparable at my matches. Indeed, it was Uncle Brian who sat near to my dad during the Wimbledon final and relieved me of my headband when I made it up to the players' box. But this story is not about Wimbledon: it centres on the 1986 Davis Cup semi-final against the United States in Brisbane, when both Paul McNamee and I came from behind to beat Brad Gilbert.

I had a bunch of mates up for the tie: Dean Barclay, the son of my

Distress and Doobies

coach Ian; Mark 'Piggy' Zucker, son of my physio David; and Mark Bertalli. All three are now godfathers to my twin sons, Jett and Shannon. As Australia won the tie there was quite a celebration in the bar of the hotel afterwards, and the guys came fully prepared to party. They had rolled a few joints beforehand and stuck them in a cigarette packet along with their regular smokes; they could then sneak off outside, have a puff, and not cause too much fuss.

Midway through the evening Piggy asked Deano the whereabouts of the cigarette packet so they could go and enjoy a joint. The reply came that he had given them to Uncle Brian who had asked to borrow a cigarette and had then gone up to his room. The question immediately arose about what a prominent criminal lawyer would do if he found himself in possession of some illegal drugs.

The answer soon became apparent. The lift, or elevator, arrived on the ground floor by the bar. The door opened, and out stumbled a particularly tranquil and happy looking Uncle Brian. Stumbling and wobbling his way across the room, he flashed a huge grin at everybody he passed before finally slouching against the bar. Finding himself next to Dean Barclay, he looked up with extremely glazed eyes. Trying to focus, he enquired in that deep gruff voice of his, cultivated by far too many late nights: Hey Deano, got any more of those special cigarettes?

Getting back to Wimbledon, just one of those special cigarettes was sufficient for me, and after a superbly relaxed eight hours between the sheets, I still got sufficiently fired up on court to go further than ever before in a Grand Slam tournament. My confidence on grass (the courts, that is) had naturally been boosted enormously by the experience of the Davis Cup final, and though Mats was seeded fourth in the tournament, I really fancied my chances in our second round match - and what is more, proved that my optimism wasn't ill founded.

With Peter McNamara still recovering from his knee surgery, I played doubles alongside Paul McNamee - and as I recall, every round but one was a draining five set encounter. However, I followed up my win over Wilander by beating Brazil's Cassio Motta, the big-serving Kevin Curren who reached the final the following year, and Ecuador's Andres Gomez, who took title celebrations to an art form when he won the French Open in 1990.

By the time it came to facing McEnroe in the semi-final, I was frankly exhausted. Though I don't feel he played that brilliantly to beat me, I wasn't able to offer much of a fight and went down in straight sets, setting up a McEnroe v Connors final. In the press conference after the semi-final, I was asked who I thought would end up champion, and I must admit I was tempted to go for Connors because I hadn't been that impressed by Mac, even though he whipped my two mates McNamee and Masur earlier in the tournament.

Don't ask me why, but I decided to keep my thoughts to myself and sat on the fence, which was just as well, because that was the year Mac absolutely annihilated Connors, 6-1, 6-1, 6-2. I can remember watching with Steve Harris and thinking how wrong my prediction would have been. In the end the match was so one-sided, we left early to get to the bar.

Well, if you are a rock and roller and move in those circles, you have got to act the part as well.

Chapter Five

MR. SHOEBREAKER

Ivan Lendl, John McEnroe and I are all sons of lawyers; though without doubt there are plenty of people around the tennis scene who would probably have good reason to call us sons of something else. We were also extremely good players, and had a burning desire to succeed on the court. There, the similarities between the three of us ends.

McEnroe and I have plenty more in common. For instance, we both have Irish blood coursing through our veins, which could explain some of the more tempestuous outbursts. Well, that's my excuse anyway. We've also both nurtured a long-standing desire to be good at playing rock music, and enjoy the company of people who have attained such excellence. The two of us still do our bit to entertain and compete on the Senior Tour; and finally we both commentate on the world's big events.

Away from a tennis court I think we also both possess a sense of humour - and this is a characteristic not typical of Ivan Lendl. Johnny Mac still hates him with a passion, as in fact most people do and its nothard to see why. Arrogance was always his style, and amazingly, for a Czech guy who went to live in the United States and actually took on American citizenship, Lendl was unquestionably a racist.

Around the mid- to late 1980s we had quite a few black players on the tour. Arthur Ashe had long since retired, but from America there were Chip Hooper, Lloyd Bourne, Rodney Harmon, Todd Nelson and Bryan Shelton. Of course there was also Yannick Noah, and from Nigeria, though he was educated in Texas, there was Nduka Duke Odizor, a legendary cheat, but off court a lovely guy. Lendl would say the most offensive things, and didn't care if any of them were within earshot. Sitting in the locker room or players' restaurants, he used to make the cruellest racial jokes, all with not the faintest sense of remorse.

Homosexuals were another brunt of his jokes. For instance, there was an Australian guy who once worked for the ATP and is now a journalist; I'm not 100 per cent sure whether he was gay or not, but if he was, it certainly wasn't any of my business, or indeed Ivan Lendl's. Yet day in, day out, this poor bloke used to take a fearful hammering from Lendl's idea of humour. What could he say back? If he had told the world number one to piss off, then he would have lost his job.

But the day Lendl decided to have a joke at my expense was the day he made a big mistake. Not only did he run into somebody who didn't give a damn about his reputation or his ranking, he also earned himself a fierce enemy who would take great delight in getting even with him at a place that really mattered a few years later. As I recall, the incident happened very early in my career, when I was only just eighteen years old, and fresh from the junior circuit. Even though I was Wimbledon boys champion and junior world number one, in terms of the full tour I was still very much a new kid on the block.

Mr. Shoebreaker

Lendl had taken over the world number one spot a couple of months earlier and quite rightly thought of himself as a big star. Nevertheless I was feeling kind of special as well. I had just signed a deal to wear tennis shoes made by the Italian firm Diadora, and had been given a very unique gift. One of my great sporting heroes of the time was the legendary 400m hurdler Edwin Moses, who was another, but much more celebrated, Diadora client. In honour of Moses, the company had made him some special crimson red leather jogging shoes. Nowadays there are all different types of coloured athletic footwear, such as Michael Johnson's golden spikes and David Beckham's silver soccer boots. Back then, however, red leather jogging shoes were unheard of, and to make their new signing feel wanted, Diadora had presented me with a pair.

They were my pride and joy. I loved them, and one afternoon I was sitting on a bench in the Monte Carlo Country Club locker room talking to Paul McNamee. I had already lost in the qualifying rounds of the tournament but was hanging around because Monte Carlo in the European spring is not an unpleasant place to spend a few days training. The actual setting of the tennis courts is one of the most beautiful in the world. They are terraced, climbing above the clear blue Mediterranean, and if you look across the bay there is the designer Karl Lagefeld's villa standing on the headland.

I was minding my own business when in walked Lendl, and he instantly took huge amusement in the red shoes on my feet. He bent down, pulled the laces and ripped the shoes apart. There was no other way to describe it, he totally destroyed the things, and the little plastic bits that held the laces in place were pinging all over the locker room.

Lendl thought it was absolutely hilarious. Like a great big bully at school, he was having a good time at the expense of one of the younger kids. But he didn't realise that this new boy wasn't going to take any of his shit, and I absolutely flew at him in a fearful rage. He looked totally stunned as I grabbed him by the throat, and if Paul McNamee hadn't intervened very smartly, who is to say what would have happened. Never mind red shoes, for me the red mist had come down, and I wanted to kill the world number one.

Macca had his arms around my chest, pinning me back, but I was still shouting at Lendl, yelling what a despicable bastard he was, and how I would punch his lights out once I got the chance. All through it, Lendl was looking at me with the expression that suggested, you cannot do this to me because I am the number one. He really did think he could do anything he wanted. There were a few players in the locker room who just missed the incident, and several of them have since told me that they truly wished I had given Lendl a really good hiding.

From that day on I disliked the guy intensely, and always referred to him as Mr Shoebreaker. He was always so conceited, so superior and always used to put people down; he would regularly berate me about my game, and say I possessed so many technical and fundamental faults. To me, he was too unfunny for words, and I always wanted to make him really suffer. That was why I enjoyed beating him at Wimbledon so much. It was the one major title he never won, but craved so much.

History shows that 1987 was his last real shot, although he did reach the semi-finals in the two following years, and got beaten by Boris Becker both times. Was I upset that I had denied a great player the thing he really wanted? Was I hell! I loved every second.

Several years beforehand, Lendl seemed to have the measure of me, although I still maintain I was dealt a cruel injustice in one of

Mr. Shoebreaker

our biggest confrontations. Following on from my Wimbledon semi-final against McEnroe in 1984, I found myself at the same stage of the US Open a couple of months later.

I was still a teenager, but had been around the scene long enough to develop a distinct dislike of Flushing Meadows, which meant I had something in common with 95 per cent of the men's tour. To my mind the home of the US Open stank, and I mean that literally, since it had been built on an old refuse dump. I think it was Kevin Curren who once said the best way to treat the place would be to nuke it, and he wasn't far wrong.

Considering my obsessive dislike of people shouting during matches, it's amazing I didn't completely lose my cool, because the place was a zoo, pure and simple. I remember once a group of us were sitting around the locker room, when in walked David Dinkins, New York's mayor at the time. He stood there, like the politician he was, and bold as brass insisted that we must all agree that the US Open was the greatest tournament in the world.

To a man, we were all sniggering at the guy. The greatest tournament in the world? If he wanted honesty, we would have to tell him his tournament was a downright shocker: it was right up there vying for the ranking of the worst tournament in the world. Some afternoons you could be playing on court whilst being choked by the smoke coming off a hamburger stand. Juniors couldn't get a practice court for love nor money, while the locker rooms and players' lounges were pitiful in comparison to others. But the very worst thing was the total disregard demonstrated by the spectators for the players. Do they honestly go there to watch the tennis? Or are they there to buy the T-shirts, eat the burgers and hotdogs, and most importantly, make a lot of noise? There is no denying that it had its own atmosphere and energy, but so much of that was pretty negative, as many people who have visited New York know.

I'm sure you don't need to be told that the average New Yorker makes more noise than most other human beings. They don't know the meaning of the word whisper. Wally Masur was playing a match one day against Aaron Krickstein who was an early graduate of the Nick Bollettieri academy, a little bit before the likes of Andre Agassi, Jim Courier and Monica Seles. A fact of life at Flushing Meadow was people walking around the courts during rallies; if you didn't like it, you soon had to learn to live with the problem. However, people blatantly shouting out was another matter. On this particular occasion, Wally was about to serve on centre court when his concentration was interrupted by somebody bawling: Hey, hey, hey, hey!

Wally pulled out of his ball toss, and looked up and saw this spectator (I use the term loosely) directly behind him in the second row, waving his arms and yelling at the top of his voice: Hey, hey, hey! Hey Frank. I'm over here, he shouted. I'm up this end, not down that end. I'm up here. Can you hear me?

Hear him? I'm sure his voice was audible in Downtown Manhattan about twelve miles away, let alone at the other end of the court while somebody was trying to serve and concentrate on doing his job. Wally just glared at the guy, who did not show the faintest touch of embarrassment. Walking back to the service line, Wally was just about to have another attempt at actually the getting the ball in play, when Frank himself took over. Hey, Buddy! I see you! Just wait there, man, and I'll be with you as quick as I can. This ain't much of match anyway, the guy can't even serve!

Thankfully, neither Frank nor Buddy came to watch any of my matches. Or if they did, they were sitting side by side and didn't feel the need to yell across the court at each other. However, I had to overcome two of the noisiest opponents in the first couple of rounds: Ilie Nastase and then Brad Gilbert. Brad, who is an encyclopedia of sporting facts, and is happy to tell them to you.

I'm convinced that Gilbert has never managed to stay quiet for more than five minutes in his life - although this doesn't surprise me, since every day for him is a caffeine overload, starting with four or five coffees at breakfast. Maybe that's why Agassi finally got rid of him as a coach - you would have to feel sorry for Andre, with a new baby crying all night, and then BG talking like a man possessed over the morning wheaties.

Carrying on the sort of form I showed at Wimbledon, I next beat Todd Nelson and Greg Holmes, before registering another important victory against Wilander in the quarterfinals. Next up was the prospect of facing the black-eyed, brooding foe called Lendl, who may not exactly have been a firm friend, but was still an opponent to respect.

For a start, he was the defending champion, having scored a straight sets win over McEnroe in the previous year's final. He was also still world number one, and would go on to remain top of the rankings in an unbeaten run of 157 weeks. And New York was clearly his kind of town, as he seemed to have a monopoly on the year-ending Masters, played at Madison Square Gardens. Add to all that, he always took great delight in beating me after our Riviera altercation a few years earlier.

Louis Armstrong Stadium was packed. In those days the stands used to climb above the court like mountains, and though it wasn't particularly attractive, the sight was certainly impressive. Now the United States Tennis Association have brought some semblance of respectable order to the place, building a new stadium court and taking the top level off the old one. Then it was big, brash and brutal, and perfect for New York.

That Saturday was awesome and so, courtesy of the American media who love a trademark, was born the name Super Saturday. The penultimate day of the tournament is still regarded as the greatest day of tennis in US Open history, although CBS's television coverage has everything to do with that. The men's final on the following day often seems like a postscript.

My semi-final against Lendl turned into a classic that swung both ways and then, after almost three and a half hours, came to a climax in the tensest of fifth sets. I really did produce a great performance. I played like there was nothing to lose, charging the net any time I could. We both had match points, though the way I lost mine still gives me nightmares to this day. I've relived the volley I hit down the line so many times.

My heart stopped, I was convinced it was a winner but somehow Lendl managed to get his racket to the ball and hit a perfect lob, right onto the baseline in the corner of the court. I still had the energy to chase back and get the shot, but it was an impossible task and my retrieving effort only steered the ball out of play.

Next point I hit a perfect ace, no question. It flew straight down the middle and curved at just the last fraction of a second. I knew then it was good, and I stand by my belief all these years later. Video evidence certainly backs up my case, and Tony Trabert, commentating on American television, certainly felt it was a legitimate clean ace.

Unfortunately the line judge - with the easiest line on the court - thought otherwise, and the umpire wasn't about to overrule. I could not believe what was happening. I argued and shouted and gesticulated, but none of my actions did any good: the guy in the chair was not going to change his mind, and I had to suffer for one of the shittiest calls I was ever given. To this day, sitting in the commentary box myself, I still give a hard time to linesmen who miss calls when stationed in the central position.

With my spirit hugely dented, if not broken, Lendl quickly broke back my serve. The match proceeded into a fifth set tiebreak that I didn't play well, and ultimately, I ended up the loser. Then just to make matters worse, as I was sitting in my courtside chair trying to get my head around the disappointment of defeat, I heard somebody in the crowd behind calling out to me.

They are not backward in coming forward, these New Yorkers. He was asking if he could have my racket, and, not being a sentimental sort of person, I didn't exactly want to keep it as a souvenir. So I just tossed the racket over my shoulder and up to the guy. The result? I got hit with the heaviest possible fine, the authorities thinking I was venting my anger rather than answering the request of a spectator. I don't know whether the umpire heard the call through all the other noise and hubbub; though in my opinion he hadn't been aware of too much that had been going on that afternoon.

Never mind the quality of the match, the racket throwing made all the headlines, as well as television and radio news. Once again Pat Cash was the tempestuous sinner and the bad loser. The afternoon did teach me one lesson, however: in future if the fans wanted something to remember me by, it would be nothing more than a soaking wet headband. Tossing away rackets was far too expensive.

I was getting fined all the time. It was around the same time that McEnroe was going mad, and I'd written a bunch of letters to the powers that be, asking just what was going on? The ruling body at that time was the Men's International Professional Tennis Council (MIPTC), and the man in charge a certain Mr Marshall Happer III.

Uncovered

He was yet another lawyer from North Carolina, and my dad used to joke that he and Happer became bosom buddies. So regular was their correspondence in those days, I honestly believe they established something of a rapport. Perhaps it even extended to Christmas cards.

My problem was, I couldn't make any sense of what was going on.I was being heavily fined for just bouncing rackets. Nowadays players break them all the time and just get warnings. Remember the case of Goran Ivanisevic at the tournament in Brighton a few years ago? He didn't just break one of his rackets, he broke all of them. Consequently he couldn't continue playing and denied the paying public entertainment. I know everyone loves Goran, but did he get slapped with a hefty fine?

The thing that annoyed me more was getting fined for swearing - that used to really piss me off. Being a hot-headed kind of young man, the problem was only to be expected, and I landed myself in trouble as a teenager because of a heated conversation with someone whom I view as a long-term mate. Colin Stubs was the Australian Open tournament director back in 1983, and had a big say in the scheduling of matches. One night I scored an extremely late win over Brian Teacher, only to be told I had to be back on court the next morning at 11am to face John Sadri. Totally infuriated, I marched into the tournament director's office to confront Stubsy.

We were pals, but I was swearing at him and he was swearing back at me. As far as I was concerned it was a private conversation, but standing just outside the door was an Italian called Franco Bartoni who sat on the MIPTC. Taking the law into his own hands, he reported me for insulting the tournament director, and I was landed with a huge fine. After that I used to swear under my breath most of the time - though that was still too loud for some supervisors.

By the nature of their title, supervisors are guys who are supposed to attend tournaments in a supervisory capacity. They are supposed to monitor the umpires and line judges, as well as step in as arbitrators if things needed sorting out. Some of them weren't too bad, and went about their job in a sensible manner. They realised we were men playing a very energetic game at a high standard, often with great sums of money involved, and so they treated us accordingly. Kurt Neilson was a decent guy, and Bill Gilmour was reasonable enough, although being a fellow Aussie I think he was stricter with me than he was with many of the other players.

In contrast there were other supervisors who loved to flex their muscles and exert a little bit of power; in some ways their behaviour brought back all my negative memories of the teachers from my schooldays. Without question the worst culprit was Ken Farrar. He was a shocker, a vindictive American from New England who quickly became widely despised amongst the players.

Apparently he was quite a sportsman at college, and excelled at soccer, ice hockey and lacrosse, which can all be quite violent games; yet he seemed to want tennis players to act like little choirboys. He once fined me so much at one of my comebacks in the 1996 Australian Open that the figure amounted to more than my prize money: I was fined $10,000, when I collected only $9,000 for winning. It started with me allegedly swearing at a lines judge who had foot-faulted me at a crucial time in the match. Farrar was immediately on the walky-talky. I went up to the linesman and asked which foot had caused the problem.

Farrar, up in the stands, was talking to me, saying the calls were correct. But how could he see? He was sitting at a completely different angle, and it wasn't as if he had seen every serve. I told him to shut the fuck up, and that was another fine. A female lines judge next thought I was talking to her, so that became a point penalty. Then at the end of the match the umpire insisted I had shaken his hand too forcibly, and I got another fine for that. Can you believe it? I always thought a firm handshake was the mark of a man, but it cost me more money. Afterwards I went absolutely nuts at Farrar and Peter Bellinger, the tournament referee. The outcome? You guessed it; another fine for swearing at them.

There was a theory that Ken Farrar had a hit list, and it won't come as any great surprise to learn that McEnroe and I were right at the top. He convinced ATP officials around the world that the best thing to calm a player down was to warn him early on in a match for any borderline behaviour. Calm down a tense, fired-up player by warning him? Was this guy an idiot, or what? Other players were getting away with things, but there came a point when Farrar made my tennis a misery. I can understand the problems of somebody using really foul language when there are kids and ladies around, but we are talking about professional sport here.

Top tennis players do what they do for the money, make no mistake about that. So when mega-millionaires like Sampras and Agassi maintain they play just for the thrill of glory, ask one question: if a big, prestigious tournament, say something as grand even as Wimbledon, suddenly declared there would no longer be prize money at stake, would those guys turn up to play? I don't think so.

Therefore, when the line judge ruled that my perfectly good ace was wide against Lendl in the US Open semi-final, he was potentially costing me hundreds of thousands of dollars. What is the natural reaction of most people when they are dealt that sort of injustice with such immense financial ramifications? They resort to what has become known as industrial language.

Study other top sports. What do Shane Warne or Glenn McGrath do when they have a perfectly good leg-before-wicket appeal turned down? Are you telling me they don't make a few curses under their breath? And when top soccer players like Stuart Pearce or Gareth Southgate miss crucial penalties in World Cups, do they just mutter something about better luck next time?

With a few exceptions - and I'm talking about really God-fearing sportsmen like Michael Chang or Bernhard Langer - the natural reaction is to let rip with a time-honoured curse. Yet even when I did it under my breath, dear old Kendall Farrar delighted in hitting me with a fine. Even the normally calm Andre Agassi received a point penalty at Wimbledon because Farrar had lip-read a swear word directed at him.

To make matters worse, we players had no support from the people who were being paid to do that very job. As long as I can remember there has been a guy around called Weller Evans. You still see him at tennis tournaments to this day, and whereas most of the tour guys dress in either suits or shirts and trousers, Weller is always dressed up as if he is a player.Is he trying to tell us something?

Back in those days he was employed by the ATP and got a seat on the MIPTC as a player representative. Did he represent my interests? No way. I had a furious argument with him just before the Australian Open in 1985 when a journalist was trying to dig up some dirt on me. Evans was more than helpful, aiming opinions all over the place and saying he had never seen anyone so young being fined so regularly. Given half a chance, I would have told him there and then what I thought of his ethics; but my dad thought it was best if he had a quiet word in Evans' ear. To no avail, because Weller told him I could go and complain to whoever I liked, but he felt absolutely justified in saying whatever he liked about me.

In saying that, he doubtless knew he could count on the support of the people in charge because they wanted to crack down on us in a big way. I can distinctly remember speaking to Marshall Happer and saying: You are fining us for doing next to nothing, so does that mean you want us all to be like Bjorn Borg? If that ever becomes the case, the men's tennis circuit is going to become an incredibly boring place, and that won't do any good for the marketability of the game.

You can call me a clairvoyant, because there and then I predicted the future. Every time you read some criticism of tennis these days, there are the same old questions. Where are the characters in the game these days? Why are there no McEnroes or Connors? Noahs or Nastases? Why are the players all such dull personalities? Getting on for something like twenty years further down the line, you can lay much of the blame firmly at the feet of Marshall Happer III, Ken Farrar and their like.

Back then I was beginning to suffer other problems that had nothing to do with officialdom and people who got a buzz out of exerting a little bit of power. The problem was my body, and the first of a long catalogue of injuries that were to trouble me for the rest of my career.

My style of play was always very stressful on the body, and particularly the back: I was always stretching for those high smashes, throwing myself around the court, and contorting myself into various shapes. Maybe if I had stayed back and played from the baseline like so many of the other guys, I might never have had a problem. However, if I had done that, I would never have won

Mr. Shoebreaker

Wimbledon or a couple of Davis Cups - so everything is relative.

In retrospect, the trouble really started when my legs began to get sore early in 1985. I had spent a lot of time training with the Hawthorn footballers during what masquerades as the close season for tennis, attempting to improve my cardiovascular fitness and stamina. This involved a lot of distance running, which was hardly my strong point, as well as a lot of sprint repetitions. After four hours of hard work with Barkers, I would go and run up hills and around golf courses.

The upshot was, I felt very tired quite early in the year; even though I was playing well, my back was stiff and my legs were extremely painful. Knowing so much more about my body now, I have come to realise that as soon as your legs get sore, you move differently, and compensate for this in other areas. And so the trouble starts.

As far as I can remember, the first time I felt something seriously wrong in my back wasn't during a match. Paul McNamee had a place at Harry Hopman's old Floridian tennis complex at Bardmore. Like most Aussies, Paul needed somewhere as a base when he was in the Northern Hemisphere, and being such a good mate, he let me stay there, so we could practise together. A few of the travelling Aussies used to pitch there too, such as Charlie Fancutt and Kim Warwick. I used to go out regularly with Ian Barclay between tournaments for spells of hard training during the day and a little fun at the weekends. My mates from Iron Maiden spent quite a lot of time in the Bahamas, which was only a short flight, and I made that journey quite a few times.

Aches and strains are an everyday part of being a professional sportsman, and you quickly learn to live with them. Up to that point the only problems I had suffered was a bit of tendonitis in the knee, which is just a sign to any athlete that the leg has been working a tad too hard. A little rest and the pain disappears, it's usually as simple as that. On this occasion, I was doing my routine stretches on the floor to warm up for a hit with Macca; I just pulled my legs up to my chest, a really simple exercise, and felt something twinge in my back. I can remember thinking, That seems strange, as one side of my back went into spasm. The sensation was nothing like anything I had previously experienced, but after a couple of days rest, it seemed to go away.

My regular physiotherapist David Zuker was thousands of miles away in Melbourne. Even the tour guys like Bill Norris were at a tournament somewhere else, and I didn't think too much more about it. I might have mentioned the twinge to Ian Barclay and Macca, but neither of them had qualified as chiropractors.

I carried on practising, and soon headed off to Houston to play in quite a lucrative Lamar Hunt-owned WTC tour event at River Oaks. But while I was there, the twinges in my lower vertebrae returned and seemed to be getting worse, and I grew increasingly worried. I was beginning to realise that something needed to be done, though I didn't know exactly what.

Somebody recommended me to undergo some treatment from a local chiropractor called John Rice, but this helped only marginally. The following week I got to the quarterfinals in Atlanta, though I could barely move, and couldn't serve properly. The ATP trainers weren't as knowledgeable as they are these days; they were basically just 'patch 'em up and get 'em back out there men, and they told me I was suffering with nothing more serious than a simple back spasm. I was not convinced, however, and feared there was something seriously wrong.

I was advised to go back and see the young back specialist in

Mr. Shoebreaker

Houston, who was also something of a man about town. He was quite into the balancing of muscles, and gave me some manipulation treatment at the base of my spine that seemed to do the trick. Physically tended, mentally reassured, and soothed by another week's rest, I was sufficiently confident to head off for Las Vegas where the Caesar's Palace-staged Alan King Classic used to be one of the richest events on the tour.

Nobody in their right mind wanted to miss that one; it was really big, in terms of both prestige and money. I was one of the top seeds, but almost as soon as I started playing, the back started to hurt again. One night a guy was despatched to drive over the state line and get me a special chemical that was supposed to help. It was called DMSO, and is basically used on racehorses when they have muscle spasms. I may be no thoroughbred, but it seemed to do the trick for a while - until I played a match against the American Jimmy Arias, one of the first off the Nick Bollettieri production line.

Jimmy was a very good player - and still is, as a matter of fact. He and I battled out an extremely good seniors match in Naples, Florida only a month or two ago. However, back then he was struggling in a bit of a slump, and was just outside the list of seeds. Seeing his chance, he lured me into going for a high smash, I landed awkwardly on my heel, and just felt so much pain I could hardly carry on.

At that moment I knew I had big problems, and realised something had to be done. Two days later when I tried to play doubles with John Fitzgerald I couldn't walk properly, couldn't bend, and found it painful even to sit in a chair.Amazingly we managed to get to the final. I think the DMSO was doing its stuff, but on the morning of the match I could barely get out of bed. Yet somehow we beat Paul Annacone and Christo van Rensburg - though I have to say, most of the credit must go to Fitzy.

Had sense prevailed that would have been the moment to say time out to get the whole thing sorted; but I was young and *not* overly sensible. I underwent X-rays in Houston, which showed no bone damage and only a slight curvature of the spine, caused by the spasms pulling my back muscle to one side. I therefore considered that with a bit more rest I would be able to make it through the European season, and most relevantly, get to Wimbledon's grass courts, which were once again appearing on the horizon. I wasn't due to go home to Australia until July, and I tried to bluff my way through a couple of months play, making regular visits to Bill Norris' various treatment tables around Europe. But in my mind I knew things weren't really getting any better.

The clay court season could best be described as a glaring error. I passed on the Italian Open in Rome, much to the dismay of my sponsors Sergio Tacchini and Diadora, and instead played the World Team Cup in Dusseldorf. Soon it was confidence as well as an aching back that took a hammering, and I lost tamely in a match screened on national television.

On harder courts I could get traction from my push-off, but clay just gives way under your feet. One vicious but probably fair critic likened my movement to that of a newborn giraffe that had just wandered onto an ice rink. I was completely unco-ordinated, and the former German player Claudia Kohde-Kilsch, commentating on that televised match, insisted that even she could have beaten me.

I didn't like criticism at any time, but when it was made mockingly, it really angered me. She knew what I had achieved in the past, she knew I was a good player, and if she was anything like as perceptive as former tennis players should be, she cannot have missed the fact that I was playing in pain. So when she saw me missing balls that beginners could have returned, she should have shown more respect, rather than take cheap shots.

Not many people knew the actual extent of my injury, but anyone could see I was in trouble. I was sliding on the clay with no control over my back and legs; it didn't feel as though my legs were part of me, and when I tried to change direction, it seemed to take ten minutes to turn around. Not surprisingly a few rackets were bounced and line judges barked at as I vented my anger. Then, when sense temporarily prevailed and I pulled out of the French Open, some people even shrugged off the suggestion I was hurt and dared to say it was because I was scared of clay.

If that was the case, why did I also pull out of the opening grass court tournament at Beckenham? Instead I practised for the Queen's Club event, and was given regular treatment from an osteopath called Terry Moule, who came recommended by Paul McNamee. I thought that Terry's work might have done the trick until I hit a serve the day before the tournament and my back just went crack. My immediate thought was, I *have* done it, now.

I could barely walk off court, and couldn't bend to one side. Barkers just bundled me into the back seat of a car where I lay with my legs up in the air, and we were driven to Terry's place, which wasn't exactly just around the corner. The journey seemed to take forever, and I felt so much worse when I got there. Amazingly a few cracks of the back, a rub and some hot cream, and I was ready to play the next day.

In retrospect I shouldn't even have considered walking on court, but I managed to beat three reasonable grass court players in Mark Edmondson, Vijay Amritraj, and a fellow Aussie called Peter Doohan before losing in the quarter-final to a kid called Boris

Becker. For later reference, take note of the two last names.

My serve was just about the only thing functioning. Though I didn't really know who this ginger-haired German youngster was, in truth I was utterly hopeless against him, and got beaten in straight sets. At the time it was viewed as a big upset, because the extent of my injury was still pretty private. So the question on everybody's lips at that tournament was, Who is this Becker kid? Trust me to be the one who started it all for him!

The pain meant I got no real practice before Wimbledon. Despite reaching the semi-final the previous year, I was horrendously below par, and only got through one round in the singles. Seeded sixth, I needed five sets to beat Todd Nelson, although regular rain delays helped my cause. Then I went down in another five-setter to the Chilean qualifier Ricardo Acuna, after fighting back from two sets down.

If I was being totally honest with myself, I could not have expected very much more - but there was some consolation in the doubles. Teaming up with John Fitzgerald, I got to the doubles final for the second year running. We even beat the defending champions John McEnroe and Peter Fleming on the way, which was no mean feat.But in the end, the combination of Heinz Gunthardt and Balazs Taroczy, added to the rigours of playing both the semi-final and the final on the same day, proved too much.

Finally I headed home to Australia, determined to get the back problem sorted out. It wasn't even possible for me to play the Davis Cup quarter-final against Paraguay in Sydney, so I made my debut as a television commentator, not knowing that I wouldn't be hitting another competitive tennis ball for eight months. First I rested, then I had traction and electronic muscle stimulation under the supervision of my physiotherapist David Zuker; but unfortunately nothing seemed to work, so it was clear there was only one place for me to go: hospital.

Melbourne's Epworth Hospital has a place in tennis history because it is the place where the legendary Fred Perry passed away almost a decade later. On a summer's morning back in 1985, the Epworth was the place where I had my worst suspicions confirmed after undergoing a CAT scan. Going for the results I found Zuker already sitting down in the office, and his words had a chilling edge to them. Sit down, you won't be going anywhere for a while, he said.

For those of you who understand this kind of thing, I had suffered herniated discs L4 and L5 in my lower back. For those who don't, something like the bubble you blow with gum had pushed out through a crack in the discs and was rubbing against a nerve. Whatever your level of chiropractic understanding, it was bloody painful and urgent attention was required.

Very quickly I was presented with two options. The first was surgery, as several specialists advised. The second was a considerably more radical treatment that had a high-risk element and was still very much in the experimental stages. It involved a single injection into my spine of chymopapain, a drug containing extracts from the paw paw fruit. If it failed, then it was dubious whether I would be able to jog properly ever again, let alone play top-flight tennis. Previous patients undergoing the treatment had suffered bad consequences, and their entire discs had dissolved because too much of the drug had been injected. To ease my concern, I was told that only a small amount would be put into my spine, just enough to dissolve the troublesome bubble of fluid.

Guys I trusted, such as David Zuker and Gerry Moran, advised me to go ahead, and I took their advice. Was I frightened? Of course

I was, but I knew something had to be done if I was to achieve the rest of my ambitions.

For the first time, but most definitely not the last, my career hung in the balance as my body seemed to be waving the white flag of surrender in front of my fierce determination to succeed. It was a confrontation that reappeared with great regularity over the next twelve years. Meanwhile a whole new aspect of my life was about to begin.

Chapter Six

Happy Birthday Daddy

Answer me this: who in their right mind enjoys pain? I know that's a pretty stupid question but over the years I've proved myself good at those. Admittedly there are some who get some perverse enjoyment out of agony: however not too many are professional sportsmen. Long before that great big needle was being aimed into the base of my spine, the suffering from my back resulted in far too much concern.

As many must be aware, one temporary remedy for teenager with something to worry is to go out and party. In that respect I was fortunate because, as one of the eligible young men on the world's tennis circuit, I could enlist the help of the ultimate party animal to help me forget my ailments for just one night. Little did I know a party hosted by Vitas Gerulaitis would be an evening that changed my whole life.

To me at the time, Vitas was quite simply the man. I'm sure that would be the case to any single young buck who played hard, both on and off the court. Nowadays many view him as something of a tragic figure, but I have to disagree. Some people want to have fun their whole lives, and there can be little argument that the boy from

Uncovered

Brooklyn packed 80 years into the 40 he spent on this earth.

He knew everybody that it was hip to know. He did everything. He hung out with rock stars like the Rolling Stones and Van Halen. He went to every rock concert. He was a magnet for the world's beautiful women and was welcomed warmly at the door of every nightclub. With the possible exception of Ronald Agenor, he could play guitar better than any tennis player.

If he liked somebody, he became extraordinarily generous - he once gave me his guitar as a gift. He had been on stage with some of the world's top bands and jammed with the very best musicians. He was the leading light in those Hard Rock Café rock parties we used to stage before Wimbledon, which led to a hundred other stories. He was indisputably a star.

A regular criticism of Vitas, usually by the duller people around tennis who didn't really know him, is that he played too much off the court and not enough on it. There is definitely a grain of truth in that assumption, but the records show how gifted he was at the game. Vitas won the Australian Open in 1977, beating John Lloyd in the final at Kooyong. I was twelve at the time, smitten with tennis and quite an impressionable kid. Maybe that's why I always viewed the guy with such admiration. He had also been runner-up at both the French and US Opens, and had that legendary match against Bjorn Borg at Wimbledon.

Like me, he regularly fell foul of officialdom and was forced to pay the price. Back in 1981 he was suspended for three weeks after the US Open as the fines imposed upon him exceeded the $5,000 limit. Just a few months later, again in his hometown of New York, he was fined another $1,750 after losing the Masters final to Ivan Lendl.

By the time I came onto the scene, Vitas was past his best. Before long he was heavily addicted to cocaine and when he died, accidentally and so tragically in 1994, he didn't have any money (to be brutally honest he had snorted most of his winnings.) I remember him a year or so earlier. People weren't coming to him for television work any more because he couldn't breathe properly: he had no nose, his sinuses were shot and he was perpetually sniffing. To many people who saw him, he looked so sad; but Vitas didn't require pity because his condition came as a result of choices he had made. Basically he lived to enjoy himself.

One story that readily comes to mind dates back to the aftermath of one the first Hard Rock Café Wimbledon jams. I was a co-organiser, after involving my good mate and tour manager to the rock stars, Billy 'Bush' Barclay. Vitas was heavily into cocaine by then. Through Billy, he had established a relationship, partly out of friendship and partly out of requirement, with a drug dealer who for the purposes of this book we shall call Smithy. That's not his real name, and people who know him might recognise the character when I mention the absence of his two front teeth. Drug dealing is not the most praiseworthy of occupations, and I'm not going to condone the people who ply the trade; however, because Smithy is still around to this day, I think it's better to preserve his anonymity.

Following the jam at the Hard Rock that had appearances from Rolling Stone Keith Richards, Roger Waters of Pink Floyd, various members of Bad Company and my old friend Bruce Dickinson from Iron Maiden, Vitas' lust for life was far from satisfied for the evening. His Wimbledon playing days were behind him then, but he was still very much part of the scene. Consequently he invited everyone back to his suite at the St. James Court Hotel, which was very much the place to stay in town. By then a lot of the top players were into hiring houses out at Wimbledon village. It was quiet, they were near to the practice courts, and there was none of the hassle of the West End.However, that was never the Gerulaitis way, not even at the peak of his playing career: he was a city boy, and loved to be in the middle of the action. He needed to have fun and party.

Smithy, being the procurer of some required substances, was naturally invited back to the St. James Court, and got into his car parked nearby in a side street off Piccadilly. Not surprisingly the police were keeping an eye on who was around, and they immediately started tailing Smithy because his occupation was quite well known. Unbeknown to the boys in blue, but very much on the mind of Smithy, a sandwich bag containing about a kilo of cocaine worth a few thousand pounds was nestling in his possession.

Luckily for Smithy, traffic was quite heavy in the West End of London that night and the police got jammed behind a couple of other cars. Pulling up at some traffic lights, Smithy spotted a couple of tennis players he knew from the party in an adjacent taxi cab who were making their way to Vitas' little soiree. He signalled them to wind down their window and shouted he would see them soon at the hotel soon.

I doubt whether they even knew who Smithy was, he didn't look the most wholesome of characters. But with perfect timing and accuracy of a Michael Jordan drop shot, Smithy tossed the bag of cocaine through both car windows and right into one of the player's lap. Apparently the guy looked down in a state of shock, yelled something beseeching the Almighty and rapidly shoved the bag up his sweater. Within a minute or two Smithy was pulled over by the law, but to their great disappointment, he wasn't in possession of a single gram of any illegal white powder.

Subsequently the party went ahead, and Vitas and his many of his guests got their coke. However, I will go on record here and insist nobody playing at Wimbledon that year took a single sniff. Everybody knew the rules and though more and more people were viewing it as incredibly fashionable to snort a line or two, you were mad if you took anything like that just before such a big tournament.

Eventually Vitas also saw the consequences of his ways. Before his death, he had cleaned up and was coming back. Any form of therapy teaches you that it is necessary to reach rock bottom before you can get back up and I'm sure that's something he experienced. Things got pretty bad and desperate, and for a while Vitas was wasted. Then he got his act together and his appearance improved. He put on some weight and developed a passion, bordering on an obsession, for playing golf every day. He had even contested some tennis exhibitions and with the Senior Tour in its formative stages, there was a great chance of making sufficient money to get himself back on an even keel.

Then tragedy struck. Before hearing the facts and circumstances, I'm afraid to say that my immediate reaction was the same as everybody else who knew Vitas: very wrongly, as it turned out, I thought he had gone back to the cocaine, had one big last fatal binge and killed himself. Instead he died of carbon monoxide poisoning from a faulty gas heater at the house of a friend where he was staying after the US Open.

To me, the day of his death was one of those occasions when you always remember your whereabouts. Everyone knows where they were on 11 September or the day Princess Di was killed. For me, you can add 17 September 1994 to the list. I was playing a tennis exhibition in Ibiza, and I can't ever remember being more upset about the loss of a great friend. I didn't go across to New York for the funeral, though in retrospect I wish I had. However I did write a letter to his mother who was an admirable woman.

I can remember telling her that her son was a wonderful person and a friend to everybody. All the people who knew Vitas only had magnanimous things to say about him, and throughout all his problems he remained a loving, generous and friendly human being. It was such a shame that somebody so good as he was, had to die. By nature of his big-heartedness, all Vitas' friends have something by which they can remember him, and I am probably luckier than most: I have two of the most beautiful children because it was at another Gerulaitis party, back in Houston when I was in the midst of all my back problems, that I met their mother.

Wherever in the world Vitas found himself, he thought nothing of hiring an entire floor of a top hotel, or paying out to reserve an exclusive nightclub for a whole evening. He was so open-handed nobody else had to pay a cent and though he resorted to narcotics, I think he still got an immense high at the sight of other people enjoying themselves.

On this particular night, Vitas and a friend who was acting as co-host seemed to have lured every good-looking woman in the whole of Texas to Houston. I'd like to say I knew a lot of them but I would be lying. Dr. John Rice, who had been treating my back, persuaded me to go along, insisting that a little relaxation would be beneficial. Shy and reserved as ever, I just made small talk with a couple of Aussie guys before somebody introduced to this stunning Norwegian model by the name of Anne-Britt Kristiansen. Straight away the bells started ringing in my head big time.

In my opinion she was the most beautiful girl in the place: tall, slim figure, wonderful blonde hair and eyes that lured you into their trap. Not surprisingly she had been surrounded by other guys for hours, most of them Scandinavian. Later on it transpired she was really enjoying herself in their company because it was the first time she had spoken her native language in almost a year. That's what she insisted, anyway.

Although I was totally smitten, I was not one of those really up front guys when it came to chicks. Natural bashfulness meant that I resigned myself to having to wait well back in the queue for her attention, so on this occasion I just blended into the background and admired her from afar. Leaving the party on my own that evening, I could only speculate on what might have been.

Committed to other tournaments, I never even expected to see this Norwegian vision ever again. However, the continuing back problems meant I headed back to Houston to revisit the same young doctor. As well as giving me treatment of the traditional kind, he decided another night out would be remedial, so we headed for a nightclub.

It must have been fate, because one of the first people I saw was the girl who had so caught my attention a couple of weeks earlier. Unfortunately she was in the company of Vitas' buddy who had co-hosted the party. Again I was too shy to make an approach but the doc must have taken pity on me because he decided to break the ice. Marching up to her, he interrupted her conversation and said Mr Cash would like a word.

Not knowing much about tennis, she didn't have a clue who this Mr Cash was, and speculated it must be some sort middle-aged oil millionaire with a cowboy hat, a beer gut and a cigar. So I don't know who was more surprised when I got a tap on the shoulder from my medical friend, and spun around to be confronted by the lovely Anne-Britt.

Apparently she wasn't there with Vitas' friend after all; they were just chatting, after recognising each other from the previous party, and she had come along with a couple of girlfriends. From that moment I realised she was available, and was determined to make an impression. We carried on talking for the rest of that evening and made a date for the next.

We saw a lot of each other until I headed for Europe. Parting really was sweet sorrow, and though she was doing really well as a model in the United States, she admitted her interest in the job took a dive when I boarded that transatlantic flight. I was missing her too, and telephoned nightly to invite her across to England - on one condition: trying to be the consummate professional, I insisted she stayed with a girlfriend when the time for Wimbledon came around.

Who is kidding who here? Love really blossomed in London, and Anne-Britt ended up staying five weeks instead of two; but then we were parted again, as I had to head back to Australia and get my back sorted out. We spoke on the telephone all the time, and when the diagnosis was bad, she was the first person I thought of telling. I needed her with me, and although she had a lot of modelling jobs in her diary, I begged her to fly to Melbourne.

After much persuasion, she agreed, and arrived the day after the Davis Cup match against Paraguay, at which I was reduced to a mere spectator. Being head over heels in love, I wanted her to meet the Cash family straight away, which she did in great style. They liked her, she got on well with them and I couldn't have been happier - except for the knowledge I was soon to have that enormous needle aimed into the base of my spine.

Throughout the course of my career I was unfortunate enough to suffer quite a lot of agonies. Laying my hand on the Bible, I can honestly swear I had never experienced anything as painful as that injection. Basically they doped me up, wheeled me down to a theatre and then, under an X-ray machine, injected the chymopapain into the herniated disc.

Think of me as strange if you like, but I have always been fascinated by surgery and the workings of my body. I still possess a video on an Achilles tendon operation I underwent several years later, not to mention the knee and the back operations as well. The specialists would use the X-ray machine to check that the needle was where it should be: lying there in my anaesthetised state, I could actually see the injection going into the disc.

Suddenly any form of morbid interest disappeared. Pain is not a sufficiently fierce word to describe the feeling I then experienced:I thought I was about to breathe my last. I was moaning, and could feel my back go into spasms straightaway. Because I was under sedation the whole thing seemed like a nightmare, but I can remember thinking: 'Thank God it's finished.' Then to my dismay, I heard a voice say: Right now we are going to put the stuff in. Can you imagine the pain when the chemical went in? Yet in truth, I was more than happy to put up with the agony because the treatment wasn't even a gamble, as something had to be done. The bottom line was that I hadn't been able to play anything like properly for months, and now the problem was being rectified.

I stayed in hospital five days. Of course there were some initial scary moments, but there always are after operations. I can remember trying to ease myself from the hospital bed and negotiate the ten feet to the bathroom but my legs would not listen to my brain, and I for a few seconds I felt panic. However, I was told it wasn't an uncommon reaction, so I guess nearly every patient who has undergone some sort of back or leg surgery feels the same way.

Nevertheless, I had never known anything like this before and I was on my own. Did I call out? Should I collapse?Somehow I made it to the toilet, but it had taken me something like five minutes, and during that time, so many negative thoughts went through my head: I was convinced something had gone wrong, and feared I might have been rendered a cripple. Never mind getting back on the tennis court, I couldn't even walk a dozen short steps.

Eventually things stabilised, and I was assured that everything was perfect, but a long period of convalescence was required. I was ordered to relax after the treatment and take things extremely easy. However I also felt the need to get better acquainted with Anne-Britt. We headed up to the then secluded beaches of Northern Queensland near Cairns. The intention was to chill out, soak up some sun and if my recuperating back allowed, indulge in a few other pursuits. Tennis may have been out of the question but I was still a hot-blooded young man in the company of a very attractive woman. And during our stay, two very significant things happened.

Firstly we got back from the beach one day to find a letter pushed under the door. I was amazed because I didn't think too many people knew of our whereabouts. Opening up the envelope, I was intrigued by what I read: Hi Pat, I hope you don't mind me disturbing you, but my name is Lew Hoad and I used to play tennis in the Davis Cup for Australia. He continued by listing a couple of titles he had won - as if I needed telling. There were Australian, French and Wimbledon wins in 1956. Another Wimbledon title against Ashley Cooper a year later in a final that was supposed to be one of the all time greats. Three Davis Cup victories in four years, between 1953 and 1956. He was a legend, an all time great himself.

Hoad wrote that he had seen Anne-Britt and I walking around this sleepy old seaside town. He said he was with his wife Jenny but she had gone off somewhere for a day or two, and he would love to talk me. He finished up by saying he would be in a certain pub and invited me to go down for a drink.

Initially I was tremendously honoured. I felt a flush of pride sweep over me. Lew Hoad, somebody you can put right up there with Laver, Rosewall and Emerson, wanted to meet me. I held him in tremendously high esteem, because so many people had told me I played the game in a Lew Hoad way. I moved like him, I struck the ball like him and possessed the tendency to be a little 'hit and miss'. And Hoad even suffered with a bad back, too.

Of course Anne-Britt didn't have a clue about Lew Hoad when I proudly showed her the letter. Then I started to ask myself whether it was somebody playing a prank. Did Fitzy or Wally know where I was? They are always looking to even the score. But it wasn't the sort of thing I would joke about. I had heard all the stories, mostly from Neale Fraser, about the great Australians. I felt I was following in the dynasty, and I didn't want to make a fool of myself.

So I came to a decision that has since caused me much soul searching: I didn't go to the pub. Somebody barely twenty years old and trying to climb the tennis ladder had the audacity to ignore the invitation of the legendary Lew Hoad and leave him standing alone at the bar. If some young kid did that to me now I know what I would think.

At the time I put it down just being so young, and the fact I never drank in pubs (I didn't go into that kind of establishment because I wouldn't have felt comfortable after my stepbrother Ralph was almost blinded by that psycho with a broken glass). In addition, I didn't want to leave Anne-Britt unaccompanied in the room, or take her somewhere she would be bored and not involved in the conversation. Deep down however, they weren't the reasons for my no show: it was because I was totally in awe of Lew Hoad. I would also be intimidated by his drinking reputation, fearful that I wouldn't be able to keep up and that I might do something stupid.

I was really mixed up about the whole thing, but in retrospect, I suppose I was also thinking what somebody of his status would say to me Would he end up being like Newcombe, and therefore critical of some of my traits? That would be too much to bear from another hero. I just had so much admiration for him that I chickened out; it was that simple.

I never received another invitation to speak to the great man and nine years later, just a few months short of his sixtieth birthday, he lost his fight with cancer. Words cannot describe the tremendous sense of regret I feel nowadays. I would have loved to have known Hoad and benefited from his advice, but I just tossed away the chance. It was unforgivable.

The other memorable occurrence of that Queensland holiday had an equally lasting consequence, and although it was something I initially regretted at the time, I have now realised it was one of the greatest things to ever happen to me. Barely four months after meeting Anne-Britt, and with our relationship still very much in the formative stage, she became pregnant.

Now you might say, even in those distant days, there were ways and means to avoid accidents like that, and you would be right. The last thing either of us needed at the time was a baby. I was only twenty and my tennis career was hanging in the balance - although if everything went well with the treatment, I would be jetting around the world for the next ten years.

Likewise Anne-Britt was a highly successful model with a promising career beckoning up and down the catwalk and in front of the camera. Unfortunately you don't see too many pregnant women showing off the latest creations during the Paris Fashion

Week.

Going back to Melbourne, we decided against Anne-Britt visiting the family doctor, the father of my old childhood team-mate Mark Hartnett. Instead she went to be examined elsewhere. Meanwhile I waited outside in the car, which says a lot for my commitment to the situation; all the time I was thinking that we just didn't need this. When she walked out of the doctor's office, I stared at her with a questioning look and she responded by just nodding her head; the thought flashed across my conscience: 'Oh shit!'

When you think of some of the lengths, expense and heartache countless couples go to conceive a child, perhaps my behaviour at the time was unforgivable. But I just couldn't see it. Then, to make matters worse, Anne-Britt burst into tears and seemed to spend the entire next week crying: she felt alone in a strange country, thousands of miles from her parents, and her life was about to change forever.

Telling my parents was no easy matter, either. There is only one thing, I have found more difficult to break to my father and we'll come to that later. It took a couple of weeks to build up the courage. Knowing he viewed my tennis career with so much importance, I was frightened a heart attack might ensue when I broke the news. He had the business head, and we had spent so much time planning the future.

With a deep breath I blurted out the news. I was convinced Dad would go absolutely nuts. In the event he was very calm. He just smiled at me, said OK, got out of his chair and gave me a great big hug before shedding a few emotional tears; as would any family loving Irishman knowing he is about to become a grandfather. We discussed whether I had sufficient money to support a young baby. Obviously the answer was yes, and so my mind was now clear on the subject.

Mum's immediate reaction was to ask if we were going to get married. I replied that we weren't, and she asked why. I told he we didn't want to, and she simply walked out of the room. To add to a distinctly uneasy atmosphere, my sister Renee was screaming at the top of her voice after greeting the news with hysteria.

Dad issued orders for her to pull herself together and give me some support. As a future opera singer, she possessed quite powerful vocal chords and her message was she thought I would be trapped. I don't think Anne-Britt ever truly forgave Renee for that little outburst. In retrospect the most reassuring thing was the reaction of my father. After that I just knew he would be there for me through thick and thin. Looking back he has always given me unconditional support, and that is all any son can ask.

So many people insist that true strength is born out of adversity, and those months after my back treatment saw me change in so many aspects that were to benefit me in years to come. Imminent fatherhood is, of course, something that promotes increased maturity in a paternal sense. Meanwhile I was also beginning to realise my own body also needed considerably more attention.

Previously I had never been too fussy about what I ate, so long as it tasted good. Soon I had altered my diet to improve recovery and began consuming a lot of high protein, which aids muscle strength. This interest became a way of life, and to this day, I still put huge importance of eating some particular types of food and ignoring others. The mindset of tennis players, and indeed top sportsmen in general, has changed so much in this respect over the last couple of decades. You used to hear stories about the legendary Aussies drinking crate loads of beer and devouring huge portions of steak and eggs. That sort of thing would be regarded as absolutely mindless now, and I remain one of the most fastidious people about food.

A chance telephone call while I was in Sydney watching the Paraguay Davis Cup match made another huge revolution in my life. A guy called Nigel Websdale rang me out of the blue in my hotel room; I didn't have a clue who he was, but started to listen when he said he could fix my back. Initially I was sceptical; was he just another one looking for a bit of publicity?

Deciding to give him the benefit of the doubt, I agreed to meet him and he immediately struck me as a funny sort of guy. He was a surfer, and was extremely muscular, but walked with a bad limp. He wore a tracksuit and had lost one of his front teeth. He appeared nothing like the physiotherapists I had previously dealt with, but we went for a drive whilst he told me his life story.

He had suffered with polio as a kid, and had devised a set of exercises to overcome his disability. Ever curious, I asked for a demonstration and we stopped at a kids' playground where he began showing me these exercises that required incredible strength. They included leg lifts while he hung from a bar high above his head. The basic idea was to strengthen up the stomach muscles will under a natural traction from hanging.

At that age you are easily influenced: the exercises looked brutal, and I was extremely impressed. But first I had to check out the theories with people I trusted back in Melbourne like David Zuker and a friend who soon was to become my long-term fitness trainer Ann Quinn. Given the go-ahead, I temporarily moved to Sydney to work with Nigel, and bumped into the former Australian test cricketer Michael Whitney who taught me the important lesson of not trying to come back too early. He had undergone three knee operations, the second two because he was too impatient to get back on the field. It was great advice that I still follow and recommend.

The Australian Open was looming large in my sights, but I had to accept the fact I wouldn't be able to play. It was a tough thing to come to terms with. I was getting stronger all the time, but to rush back into action would almost certainly have meant all the good work was wasted. Naturally there was a lot of interest in what was happening with me, but I tried to keep everything a secret from my friends in the press. Nobody knew anything about the Websdale exercises or Anne-Britt's pregnancy.

I can remember my Dad being extremely dubious about Nigel. It was a real guru situation, and we went into so many aspects of what works the body. I have never been so clean in my life, having three hot baths a day because Nigel believed in keeping the back warm. He also had me doing so many of these leg raises as I hung from a bar about eight feet off the ground.

Basically you just gripped the bar with your hands and hung, so you stretched your back out and hold it in an extended position like traction. Then you build up to bringing your knees up to your chest. Eventually as I developed strength you get your feet right up near your hands, which was really tough. And I was doing sets of thirty as much as eight times a day.

Years later, when the air of secrecy had died off, I showed the Australian cricket team the exercises. I said it would do their stomach muscles the power of good, and certainly there were a few beer bellies in that side needed a little toning. The likes of David Boon and Merv Hughes, both great athletes it has to be said, looked at the bar and straightaway said words to the effect of 'not me, mate!' I think Allan Border managed two, and that was the sum total.

I developed quite a friendship with AB: I think we had mutual respect for one another. In my view, and many other peoples' as well, he was the guy that held things together for Australian cricket during the bad phase after we lost the Ashes. John Fitzgerald and I had dinner with AB and Ian Chappell in London after we had been beaten in the Wimbledon doubles final. During the final we had a bit of fun when I smashed a real sitter up into the Royal Box on Centre Court and AB made a perfect catch. No real surprise I suppose.

Over the dinner table it was time for a few friendly barbs, and I was giving cricketers a hard time, saying they were grossly unfit in comparison with us tennis players. Fitzy kept whispering into my ear: I can't believe what you are saying, Cashy. You can't tell great captains like Border and Chappell that all cricketers are wooses and wimps.

Looking me squarely in the eye, AB had the perfect riposte: Look mate, he said. It's like this. We get one chance when we are at the crease and if we make a mistake we are out. Look at you guys. You even have two goes at getting a serve into play.

Fair point I reckon. As for Anne-Britt's pregnancy, we managed to keep that under wraps for about five months until she appeared in a bikini beside a swimming pool in Palm Springs, California. I was there to give my back its first real test by playing doubles, but the press were focused on something else: my girlfriend's unmistakable bulge.

Ian Barclay and I fended off queries, but the hounds were on the scent of a good human interest story and I telephoned my Dad for advice. The signs were pretty obvious and by now I was so excited about the baby. So we decided to approach Richard Evans, an experienced English writer who had penned a very complimentary John McEnroe's biography. Anybody who can be that diplomatic with his pen clearly possessed the ability to put my situation into the right perspective.

I wanted the Davis Cup tie against New Zealand to be my proper comeback but by the time I arrived in Auckland, nobody was talking about anything other than the baby. Even Paul McNamee curiously took me to one side and asked for a discreet but frank run-down on events.

Tennis-wise, I was so keen to be with my mates again that I got off the flight from the United States and went straight out to practise for four hours. What a smart move, I couldn't even get out of bed for two days afterwards. I was so exhausted. I was also physically sick and needed to be cajoled into just playing the doubles with Fitzgerald.

After repeatedly telling everyone I still felt bad, I ended up on court alongside Fitzy again. It was 8 March, exactly eight months since I had last hit a tennis ball as the two of us lost the Wimbledon doubles final. This time we won, beating Kelly Evernden and Russell Simpson in straight sets. Australia were through to the next round, and I was back after the most harrowing experience of my young life.

Yet everything was by no means clean cut. Although I had family matters to think about, there was a conflict of interests because my ranking down in the 400's after such a long lay-off.I couldn't keep off court any longer, and went to play back to the play in the United States. However, I was nowhere near my best, and walked off court one freezing night in Chicago with a match poised at one set all.

Despite playing indoors, I felt the cold conditions were endangering my back. Added to that I was playing dreadfully, and was in a filthy mood with myself. It was just one of those nights when I wanted to be anywhere else. I thought things had been going well, but I suddenly realised there was such a long way to go. My good tennis was months away, not just days. So I simply walked off, handing the match to a fellow rock fan from Houston called David Dowlen, who should be eternally grateful to my charity.

My head, rather than back, was the root of the problem. But slowly things got better, and I even proved myself on the European clay, on which I had been rendered almost helpless a year earlier. Tomas Smid and Jakob Hlasek were top flight performers on the slippery red stuff, and I beat both at the World Team Cup (although I'm not sure if my critic Miss Kohde-Kilsch was in attendance).

By then the date of the birth was getting closer, so I resisted the temptation of a wild card entry into the French Open and instead booked a flight to Oslo under an assumed name. It was a good job I did. Anne-Britt started getting contractions late at night and at 2.03 am on the morning of 27 May, 1986, after no more than a quarter of an hour of labour, I became a father for the first time.

Amazingly it was my twenty-first birthday, and Anne-Britt could not have presented me with a better present than our son, Daniel Patrick. Like his dad he was somebody in a rush, he didn't want to hang around, and came straight out. And nothing has ever given me as much satisfaction as actually being there at the moment of birth. It's scary, but it's wonderful. Then and there I developed a tremendous respect for Anne-Britt and for all mothers.

The sun never set that night as a beautiful glow was seen on the horizon. It's a common occurrence in Norway at that time of the year, but it seemed so strange, and somehow magical to an Aussie. To me, as I'm sure it is to every father, Daniel was the most beautiful thing I had ever seen: I just couldn't stop looking at him, and life seemed so wonderful. You feel a wonderful contentment, and think that nothing else really matters.

Uncovered

As my mates called to congratulate me on my twenty-first, they got a shock and we all celebrated something more special. For a day or two I was ecstatic. And then little more than a week later I honestly thought I was dying.

Chapter Seven

WHAT AUSTRALIA EXPECTS

Several years ago I vowed that never again would I make myself ill by drinking too much. That was back in the days when my tennis career was lurching to a frustrating close, and I was spending too much time in nightclubs with a glass of Jack Daniels. As I recall, the evening in question was spent in the company of some members of Iron Maiden, and we resorted to those ridiculous drinking games. I repeat, never again!

Back in my younger days I led a far more temperate lifestyle - though even that took a slight detour immediately after Daniel was born. How many people can claim to have celebrated their twenty-first birthday while becoming a first-time father? And of those, how many can claim to have completed the day sober? As I recall a bottle of Bailey's cream was used to wet my son's head - in retrospect, not a concoction I would readily recommend.

After shaking off the hangover, it was time to get back to work: there was a tennis career to resurrect. So while Anne-Britt stayed in Oslo with the baby, I headed for London to prepare for the grass court season. Rocky Loccisano, a Melbourne mate trying his luck on the satellite circuit, was coming to stay with me; as my dad had requested a Wimbledon wild card on my behalf, Rocky would be a good practice partner.

Fate proved he would have other uses. Soon after arriving in London I suffered a couple of pretty severe stomach cramps, and put them down to having eaten something that disagreed with me. But the pain got worse until it became all but unbearable, and I was forced to ask Rocky, in no uncertain terms, to get me down to St Stephen's Hospital pretty damn quick.

I didn't know what was wrong but I was extremely concerned, not to say scared. Surely it couldn't have been related to the injection in my back, but I wasn't sure. One thing was for certain: I had never felt more ill. The stabbing sensation was agony, and increasing all the time. So many questions were racing around my head: what was the matter? Was it as serious as it felt? Was I going to die?

Initially the problem was diagnosed as a swollen oesophagus, which was kind of strange as the pain was in my guts, and not my throat. Then tests were carried out for gallstones, as well as an ulcer. Finally somebody had the bright idea of ramming their finger right up my backside. I must admit the feeling came as something of a shock, but it proved that two things needed to come out: the finger and my appendix, and you can make your own decision as to which was more important.

With Wimbledon so close I wondered whether there was any way of stalling the operation. I was told it was possible, but that I would have to play on medication, which was a risk. In addition I wouldn't be able to prepare as strenuously as I would have liked. So after the usual consultation with my dad, I decided to go ahead with surgery straightaway.

The surgeon Dr Charles Akle was magnificent. Out of admiration

What Australia expects

for my extremely well developed abdominal muscles (thank you, Nigel Websdale), and mindful that I was a professional sportsman, he employed the keyhole method that was still very much in the pioneering stage. Making his dissection through a tiny hole in the abdominals, he pulled the appendix through it and hardly left a scar. Such was his skill that within a day, I was on the hospital's exercise bike and even doing gentle sit-ups.

Thanks to the optimistic support of another fellow Aussie player, Charlie Fancutt, I realised Wimbledon was still a possibility. Still, to receive a wild card, I had to prove my fitness to the Championships' referee Alan Mills. I had missed Beckenham and couldn't play Queen's, so what could a good Irish boy do? I tell you what this descendant of County Wexford did: he headed across to Dublin and played in a special charity event with McEnroe, Wilander and a guy called Matt Doyle who was educated in the United States but actually hailed from the Emerald Isle.

It was a notable trip for several reasons. After some considerable initial trepidation, I realised I could actually stretch into hitting three-quarter hit serves, and my stomach felt fine. The upshot was, I was on my way to Wimbledon - and Daniel, aged two weeks, saw his father on court for the first time. I also met a character called John O'Shea who involved me in the charity GOAL, which I support to this day.

O'Shea is a typical Irishman: he drinks, swears and then drinks a bit more. Yet in my view he is something of a modern-day saint which is amazing, given my prejudice against the notebook-welding fraternity, since he is a sports journalist who allegedly gives many a subject of his columns an exceedingly hard time.

For almost two decades he has dedicated himself to this charity, which gives support to third world countries. Basically O'Shea and

GOAL have taught me so much about life, and have given me a form of purpose that was lacking before. After hearing the Davis Cup horror stories, I avoided India at all costs for most of my playing career. But then, desperate to get into any tournament, in 1995 I went to play the Chennai event, and the reasons for which the charity was working were immediately brought home to me. Nobody could have prepared me for the shock of suddenly recognising how poor the quality of life can be in the sub-continent.

I was shocked. People were sleeping in the street just around the corner from the tennis - though sadly that happens in most of the world's big cities. I asked the driver to pull the car over so I could take a closer look at this terrible poverty, and was then subjected to an even more overwhelming experience, when a man tried to give me his daughter. She must have been about thirteen years old, and was a pretty, giggling thing; but women aren't regarded too highly in that country. This guy was desperately trying to force her into the car, and I had to get quite physical with him to stop him succeeding.

More recently I made my second visit to Calcutta for GOAL, and that city was even more appalling. I saw kids playing at the riverbank with a film of horribly polluted grease on top of the water. Pigs were literally eating human excrement and running around people's houses, while a woman was washing her pots and pans in that filthy river. The germs must have been outrageous, with the likelihood of disease almost unavoidable.

Right in the heart of all that squalor was a little shack where GOAL had built a classroom and medical base. It made me feel worthwhile, and that I was doing something for these poor people. You go there and it's terrible, but then you see the things provided that are keeping kids alive - admittedly only a drop in the bucket, but it's helping. Furthermore, GOAL's administration costs are only

What Australia expects

4 per cent (I don't want to criticise UNICEF, but theirs are 80 per cent).

I do what I can, and dedicate as much time as possible making trips, videos and television programmes. It's important that an individual sportsman, who by necessity must be selfish all the time, can give something back to others less fortunate. Indeed, sometimes the utter selfishness of tennis players is hard to comprehend. We become totally self-centred to the point where nobody else seems to matter. There is little room for negotiation. Everything has to revolve around you, and it can be a horrible situation for others who, more often than not, are loved ones.

I suppose that is why I get a tremendous sense of atonement from my work for GOAL. So many other top players have causes they support, and I believe that if you have got morals and see somebody sick, diseased or just under-privileged, you should do something if you can. It doesn't make all that necessary self-importance right, but it helps. Perhaps it's just a way to ease the guilt that I, personally, have carried as a Catholic.

GOAL has reached twenty million people with medical support and educational services in India alone. Good work has also been done in Ethiopia and Rwanda, as well as the Honduras, Brazil and Papua New Guinea. And a school for 1,000 pupils has been built in Kosovo, the first erected since the war there.

O'Shea has involved many notable Irish sportsmen, such as snooker player Ken Docherty and athlete Sonia O'Sullivan. Yannick Noah has done his bit, Mats Wilander does his by being US president for GOAL, and Johnny Mac, in spite of his inhumane on-court behaviour, is extremely generous when it comes to charity.

One of the greatest honours I have ever received was bestowed on me during a big London rock night I arranged for GOAL with my wife Emily and Nathalie, the wife of Adrian Smith from Iron Maiden. Led Zeppelin's Jimmy Page and Robert Plant used the occasion as their pre-tour warm-up gig. In addition, a band formed of the support from Jack Lukeman (an Irishman with one of the greatest voices in rock), Adrian Smith, Scott Gorham (I finally caught up with him years later), Kim Mazelle and myself got up on stage for a bit of a loose jam.

There was supposed to be another band member: John McEnroe, or big Mac as I sometimes call him, was due to join us on stage. But the warm-up band consisted of rock legends such as Led Zep's Page and Plant, and their presence proved too much for McEnroe: stage fright got the better of him, and he made a swift exit - which shows he is not the bold, brash loudmouth most people think.

I was also the Masters of Ceremonies, the one who persuaded people to put their hands in their pockets, and on this occasion to donate more than £30,000. During the evening John O'Shea made his way to microphone, and I feared the worst. Doubtless he had been drinking, and earlier he had openly admitted complete ignorance of what or who Led Zeppelin was or were. The last time I had introduced him to a rock star was at Wimbledon. The man was Mark Knopfler of Dire Straits, and he had dressed decidedly low key so as to avoid excessive attention; and O'Shea poured on the pity, thinking this poor guy was a struggling musician who scratched out a living busking around the London tube stations! Instead I had to tell O'Shea that he was one of the most successful record sellers of all time.

As it happened, my fears of another grade one demonstration of rock music ignorance were horribly off the mark. All O'Shea wanted to do was announce I had been appointed the UK's president of GOAL. As the announcement was so public, I couldn't possibly turn the job down.

However, we have inadvertently jumped forward more than a decade, so let's get back to Wimbledon in 1986.In all honesty I was expecting to be dumped out of the tournament in the first round. Despite the exhibition match in Dublin, I frankly had little hope of success after such limited preparation; let's be honest here, two weeks earlier I was lying on an operating table having my appendix removed.

I can now admit that the first time I actually managed to serve properly in practice was on the Saturday before the Championships began two days later. Fortune certainly favoured me through the early rounds.First I played Guillermo Vilas, who by then was aged thirty-three, and hadn't even played Wimbledon three years out of the previous five. The former French Open champion was still a formidable opponent on clay, but there have never been too many Argentines who like playing on grass. Vilas may have been seeded 15th, but he took his leave in three straight sets without too many complaints. I needed four to beat the Kiwi Russell Simpson in the second round, and went the same distance against Jay Lapidus in the third round.

By this time I had really surpassed my expectations, and was so pleased that the now customary donations of my chequered and sweaty headbands to the crowd had begun. But an even bigger surprise was to come for me. Admittedly Mats Wilander was probably at his least competitive on Wimbledon's grass, despite having won the Australian title on Kooyong's soon-to-be-dug-up lawn. However, I had a good record against the Koala Bear, and a few rounds earlier he had been extended to five sets by Britain's Andrew Castle. Even so, if somebody had told me a couple of weeks earlier that I was destined for the quarter-finals, I would have questioned their sanity; but I produced one of my most determined performances to come back from losing the first set to beat second-seeded Mats in four.

The win could not have been better timed, as the people who were paying me to use their clothing and rackets were beginning to ask questions about my worth. In their eyes it had been a year since I had won a worthwhile match, and some were getting ready to dump me. I can't say I blamed them - you don't sell too much in the way of goods if your great advertising ploy is ranked down in the 400s and never on court.

Beating Mats and getting to the quarters didn't exactly return me to the world's top ten, but I went up more than 300 places on the rankings to 102nd spot. Things could have got even better had my fitness not finally fizzled out against seventh-seeded Henri Leconte. Exhausted by all the play immediately after surgery, I realised I needed a good start. I took the first set, but then finished second best in the next couple of sets, both in tiebreakers, and just fizzled out in the fourth set. No excuses, I very simply just ran out of legs - but that defeat was another of those crucial formative moments in my career. It was on that afternoon that I committed myself to possibly the greatest challenge of my career. I knew I had the game, the talent and the speed; by now my back was fine, and I had proved a lot to myself: to have progressed so far, with limited preparation after the appendix operation, was some feat.

Up to that point I had got by on natural ability. Sure I had done some fitness work under the guidance of Ian Barclay around the circuit, and Neale Fraser at Davis Cup get-togethers. The things I'd learnt from Nigel Websdale about diet and exercise had caught my interest - but now it was time to step things up a level. I decided I would spare nothing to become, quite simply, the fittest tennis player in the world. Mind you, there were some distinct contenders for that honour. For instance, what Ivan Lendl lacked in personality, he more than made up with conditioning and body strength. Then there was Boris 'Boom Boom' Becker, who that year won a second Wimbledon title before his eighteenth birthday. Stefan Edberg was also beginning to make his presence felt, and it's still arguable whether there has ever been a finer athlete on the tennis court.

I believed I had an ace up my sleeve, however: Ann Quinn. Ann was somebody I had known in Melbourne for a while. She was Australian, in fact she even started playing tennis on the same church courts in Deepdene that spawned Peter McNamara and myself; but rather than pursue a playing career, she had moved into specialist training. She possesses a Master's degree in biomechanics and exercise physiology, and she worked for a long time at Nick Bollettieri's tennis academy in Florida. In fact she had basically written his fitness books for him, and became the mother of specialist fitness training for tennis. Agility and movement were two of her big things, and she had all kinds of wacky ideas to improve my game.

Initially she was supposed to come to London and begin work before Wimbledon, but the appendicitis had caused her to cancel the flight. After a quick return to the grass of the All England Club and the pretty straightforward task of beating Britain in the Davis Cup quarter-final, it was time to get down to work.

We hadn't dropped a set against the Poms until the tie was effectively won after the doubles. Using the little gap in the calendar before the start of the American summer circuit, I immediately noticed the benefits of working with Ann. However, it did cause considerable embarrassment. We used to go right out to the very back courts because people found huge entertainment in my running backwards, throwing big medicine balls, touching different lines and picking up strategically placed tennis balls, and trying to sprint against the resistance of huge elastic bands. Nowadays you see players doing that kind of training all the time, but back then I was regarded as something of a freak show. Mates such as John Fitzgerald and Wally Masur didn't require any prompting when it came to having cheap laughs at my expense, and they just loved my new training regime. A racket was nowhere to be seen most of the time, and they found the whole thing hilarious.

We began to work in increased secrecy. I used to keep a lookout for spies, because I've never been one to share my training techniques with other people. Why give yourself a boost and then share it with everyone else? After a while Fitzy and Wally had to find something else on which to vent their humour. Anyway, away from Davis Cup duties there was every chance they could be adversaries on any given week, so I didn't want them to know too much about me. A while later Fitzy asked me for some guidelines about my fitness routines. He was my doubles partner and one of my best mates on the tour, but I wasn't going to be helpful. I can't remember my exact reply but it was pretty curt, and went something along the lines of mind your own business. Before long he and Wally were to appoint their own fitness adviser, so my example can't have been so ludicrous after all.

Nigel Websdale made me aware of the importance of the right foods, but Ann took things a step further: she monitored everything I ate, and kept me on an extremely low fat diet. It's commonplace now, but back then, somebody who only consumed vegetables, fruit, grilled meat and fish, and minimal dairy products, was unusual. The physical results soon made impressive reading, however. My body fat was registered at 4.2 per cent, compared to

What Australia expects

10 per cent that was the average amongst other top athletes of the time. For an average male the percentage rose in excess of 17 per cent. Years earlier, when I was just sixteen, I had proved myself stronger and faster than a group of far more experienced players including Peter McNamara. Now I was surging ahead.

During one of our pre-season fitness tests, I was clocked over a 10m standing start sprint between laser beams at 1.71sec. I remain convinced I could have done better, but it was still the fastest 10m sprint ever recorded. I don't know how many of the worlds top sprinters have tried, but none has beaten my time. Although I had never been a slouch exactly on the court, I was becoming far more athletic, and my confidence was growing all the time. I took the view that increased fitness might only make the difference between two or three points every match, but they could be the points that really count.

There is no doubt that after a while I became totally obsessive about my fitness and developed a paranoia that everything had to be exactly right. Practice had to be done at a certain time; meals needed to be consumed in precise relation to when a match was likely to start; the stringing of my rackets had to be perfect. At times it went too far and I made myself look ridiculous. Did I realise it at the time? Probably not, but I wanted to be the most professional player out there - I now know there is a fine line.

On occasions I used to go nuts over silly things.If the food did not turn up on time, or Ian Barclay had forgotten to do things, I would rant and rave. And if a courtesy car didn't arrive smack on the designated minute to take me to practice, I would go freaking barmy. Anyone who knows me, and my sense of punctuality these days, will find that absolutely hilarious. It even got me in trouble with Bjorn Borg when I was still playing. In 1991, seven years after his retirement, Bjorn was attempting to make a comeback, still playing with the wooden racket that won him all those Wimbledon and French Open titles.

Our careers didn't really cross but I viewed him with enormous respect. He was the first in the line of modern players operating almost exclusively from the baseline and employing that double-fisted top-spin backhand. Now they are a dime a dozen, while there isn't anybody who plays like Jimmy Connors or Johnny Mac. Nevertheless he was a great, and when I got a request to hit with him in practice, it was an honour.

Andrew Castle and I used to alternate practice with Bjorn in London, and on one occasion I got horribly held up in traffic. Finally arriving something like fifteen minutes late, I dashed to the court and found he was gone. I telephoned him and asked his whereabouts, only to be told he had got fed up with waiting. I apologised and pleaded my innocence, maintaining fifteen minutes isn't really that long. Back came the reply: That is too long. I came to practise as well.

Standing there with a telephone in my hand, I was taken aback. Clearly he was under serious tension, and the pressure of making a comeback after all his years of greatness must have been a huge burden. In fact history has since proved that his comeback was financially motivated, and I don't know whether he was going through all his problems with drugs and women at the time, although I've heard the rumours and I'm sure they're true.

I've talked to guys who have been out partying all night with Borg. They would be totally shattered, but he would play a match, running around like a hairy goat. He was another guy who was totally obsessive, be it in his training, his playing, his partying or his women. It was all or nothing, and absolutely flat out all the way.

What Australia expects

All the players at the time heard the stories of three or four chicks in one night along with bottles of champagne and God knows what else. I don't doubt them.

My obsessive nature initially just manifested itself in the desire for supreme fitness on the court. Later on, it got to the point where I would rather train in the gym than play - but that wasn't for a while. I just realised that fitness was my real chance of attaining my true potential, and I wanted to give it a 1000 per cent. So Ann Quinn was on the team to make sure the body was working properly, and Barkers had long been around to fine-tune the game. The next priority was the mind, and I had to answer the question of whether I wanted to bring a psychologist on board. To an outsider looking in, the answer should have been obvious, given some of the moods and mental traumas I had been through.

Though I was becoming a little more liberal in my attitude, I still harboured the feeling that psychologists were the first step for people on course towards the lunatic asylum. I may have been slightly highly strung and prone to throw a tantrum, but I was no basket case. However, my dad had long held the view that I needed some sort of psychological help- though I suppose there are millions of fathers around the world who have thought that way about their offspring. Nevertheless, not all of them had a son who was ranting and raving his way around the tennis courts of the world. In the end, I reluctantly agreed to meet a guy called George Jenko.

The overwhelming thought in my mind was a desire to show this guy I wasn't some sort of nutcase, but I found myself actually listening to him, which did come as something of a surprise. Before the Davis Cup semi-final against the United States in Brisbane he got me to unwind in a manner I had rarely managed previously.

After establishing a 2-0 lead on day one, with Paul McNamee beating Brad Gilbert, and me also registering a win over Tim Mayotte, we could have been accused of being over-confident. Because then, Paul Annacone and Ken Flach delivered a shock to Fitzy and I in a marathon doubles encounter when they won in five. All ended fine, though, as I recovered from a first set deficit to beat the verbose Gilbert and send Australia through to their second final in years.

My performances in the singles, and more so my attitude, were convincing enough to finally sell me on psychology. I don't think I had ever been so calm for a big match, and a lot of that was down to George Jenko. However, in terms of relaxation I didn't even come close to the state of Uncle Brian after smoking his special cigarettes at the celebration party.

As I wanted to be the top player, I wanted the best to work with me, and although I had some good results with George, I set my sights on a specialist in the sports field. My physio David Zuker had been to the Australian Institute of Sport in Canberra for a sports conference and was impressed by the resident psychologist, Jeff Bond. Taking note of David's recommendation, I contacted Jeff and was equally impressed. So we reached an agreement based on him splitting his attentions between the athletes at the AIS, and me.

Jeff quickly became a great help, and was the perfect complement to the team. Almost immediately he helped me to handle every kind of disappointment and distraction that can happen during the course of a match. He soothed my distrust of umpires and line judges by telling me I had not played a match in my life without making some sort of mistake. With officials being capable of human error as well, what was the need to yell at them as if they had committed murder?

We struck a deal. If I felt I had been treated badly by a call, I would simply talk to the official at fault sensibly, rather than attack him with a hollered verbal outburst. It seemed to work, and Jeff's importance became increasingly obvious as the weeks went by. The ultimate test of my new-found serenity was the 1986 Davis Cup final. Or to be more precise, the traditional Aussie preparations to yet another confrontation with the Swedes on Kooyong's grass. And it was very much a case of second verse, same as the first: once again captain Neale Fraser threw all the prospective singles players into trial matches rather than practice sessions, and once again sparks flew - and the fiercest came in a match between the two regular doubles partners.

I don't know what it was between Fitzy and I during the build-ups to Davis Cup finals. Jeff had calmed me down no end in the weeks leading up to the team meeting together, and my ranking had been improving nicely. Then as soon as I got to the team base in Melbourne, all the old nerves and anxiety returned. Everything blew when Fitzy was leading by a set and a break. Not that it mattered one jot to me in the context of the week, but to me, he was so frustrating to play against. He looked like he could beat the shit out of anything I served, and was volleying so well, too - which was only to be expected of a world-class doubles player.

Being the supposed number one singles player manifested itself in a ton of pressure on my shoulders: the thought kept going through my mind, I should be beating this guy. Two rackets had already been broken, and when I served a double fault, something just fused. I walked off the court, packed up my gear and told Fitzy he was too good, therefore I was bagging it for the day. Pretty impressive stuff from a country's top player in his home city just days before a Davis Cup final, wouldn't you say? But the shit had not even begun to hit the fan. Still fuming, I walked back to my car and was confronted by the task of having to pack Daniel's pram away in the trunk.

Many fathers will appreciate that this is not always a straightforward exercise when the temper is a little frayed. Add to the scenario a television news crew, complete with camera and news reporter who will not take no for an answer. Yes, you are right, light blue touch paper and retire: the fireworks were about to start.

The Channel 9 reporter was called Tony Jones. I don't know the name of his cameraman, but the guy just got closer and closer, almost poking his lens in my face. He must have been getting some brilliant pictures because I was grimacing, moaning and swearing under my breath. Half the problem was the cameraman's intrusion, half was the fact I just couldn't work out how to collapse that goddamn pram. Once again I was convinced all the media were just looking for negative stories. I'd suffered four years of it and I'd had enough.

Get that fucking camera out of my face, were apparently my precise words before the cameraman alleged I struck him. In fact I only grabbed him and pushed him out of the way before adding: Turn that fucking thing off.

Once again the television viewers of Australia would have some choice evidence on which to base their opinions of the nation's best tennis player, just days before a huge match. I could almost imagine John Newcombe racing into the studios to give his viewpoint. But amazingly the cameraman did as he was told, and I don't think that would be the case nowadays. today they would keep the film rolling to get the sort of footage directors like. In retrospect I felt sorry for the guy because he was only doing what he was told to do. Maybe he realised he was over the top, and that what he was doing was not appropriate. Perhaps he had even experienced similar problems with a collapsible pram. I maintain I didn't punch him, but only pushed him, and at the time I wasn't faintly embarrassed by my actions; but I do regret the suggestion that I resorted to violence.

Perhaps mindful that he received a bad rap in our previous final, Paul McNamee took on the role of diplomat. Surrounded by the nation's media, he insisted our team spirit was good, and that nobody cared more passionately about Australia winning the Davis Cup again than Pat Cash. I'd like to think I proved that in the match.

It was the last final ever played at Kooyong. The newly renamed Tennis Australia were building their new national tennis centre next door to the MCG in a much more central position for the people of Melbourne. It was also one of the last finals played immediately after Christmas, which probably upset Frase because he took great delight in annoying the Swedes by keeping them thousands of miles from home over the festivities. Mats Wilander wasn't in the Swedish team - he had announced himself unavailable because he was getting married - but even without him they had the better line-up, with far better rankings than us Aussies. Stefan Edberg, aged twenty and semi-finalist at the US Open a few months previously, was their number one, with Mikael Pernfors, an unseeded runner-up at the French Open, the second string.

I may have been playing in my home city, but for the first time in my entire career, I suffered with having the sun in my eyes as I began proceedings against Edberg. Possibly it was down to nerves, but I dropped my serve twice in succession. Stefan was also feeling the pressure, although it was his third final in as many years and the Swedes were going for the hat-trick of victories. He definitely got tighter as the match progressed, and I hung in there to give Australia the lead with a 13-11,13-11,6-4 win. Then the crew-cut Pernfors, who both looked and sounded more American than

Swedish and was educated in Georgia, immediately struck back by humbling McNamee.

Determined not to repeat our sub-standard showing of the semi-final, Fitzy and I beat Edberg and Anders Jarryd in the doubles to re-establish Australia's lead. I can distinctly remember a conversation in the locker room during the mid-match break: we'd lost the third set but led by two sets to one, and Jeff Bond told me to pump myself up again because I had gone a little flat. Jeff was very good at analysing mood swings, and used to flash me the odd illegal signal with the umpires not watching. Barkers tried the same, but they kept a closer watch on him during the regular tour. And Frase? Well he was never really one for big conversations at the changeovers, and neither was I, so that suited us both.

Barkers and Frase would sit down before a match, my coach filling in my captain on matters that required concentration. Frase had quickly come to the conclusion that Barkers knew more about my game than he did, and the liaison worked well. Frase was also not a great one for travelling the circuit in those days, and so he didn't know much about the opposition or his own players little quirks; but he was prepared to take advice. Some Davis Cup captains still insist on being in total charge, which is stupid and doesn't work. The players' coaches should always be involved if possible, and Frase ushered in a new era in this respect. Harry Hopman had always stressed it was his way or the highway, and that was the situation both Frase and his successor Newcombe played under.

Newcombe went back to the old Hopman theory and soon came to the realisation it didn't work. When I had been working with Mark Philippoussis for more than a year, I was left in complete disbelief after asking his full-time coach Gavin Hopper how often

What Australia expects

Newk had enquired about Marks form. How *often*? How about never, said Gavin in reply.

Never! To borrow the words of somebody else, you cannot be serious? Not surprisingly, Philippoussis - or Flip as he likes to be called by his friends - opted to take the highway, and after that Newcombe would always make his life as difficult as possible. Some people never change.

On the opening day of the 1986 Davis Cup final I did not see a ball hit between Macca and Pernfors. I was on the massage table having a rubdown, but I put the result down to Paul just having a bad day. In reality he got absolutely chopped, and I was in ignorance of the red-hot performance Pernfors produced. He may have been something of a novice on grass, but I was in for a shock. Nowadays I would have faced him on the opening day with the two number ones meeting in the fourth rubber, but back then it was all down to the luck of the draw. Luck was something I didn't experience too much of in the early stages, as nerves played their part and a couple of volleys got pushed wide.

Pernfors was simply magnificent. He covered the court far better than the supremely athletic Edberg. He lobbed and hit some passing shots which to this day stand as some of the finest ever played against me. He was wrongfooting me and passing me at will, and no matter where I tried to place the ball, he was there to hit a winner.

I was in big time trouble. The first set left me completely shell-shocked, and the second wasnt any better. Trailing by two sets to love, I can remember walking towards the Australian bench and saying to guys like Peter McNamara, John Fitzgerald, Wally Masur and Mark Kratzmann that I just couldn't beat this guy. He was just too good.

To a man, they all replied that I could, and their faith in my ability seemed to give me confidence. If I was going to win, it would require one of the all-time great comebacks. Once again I pumped myself up, and the 12,000 strong spectators were great with their support - a support that any one playing a final on home turf would never underestimate. The crucial break of serve went my way early in the third set and from that moment the tables were turned.

In my view, this was a perfect case of my improved fitness, both physically and mentally, really coming into play. I was locked in my imaginary cage that Jeff Bond and I had created in response to the extreme chanting of the Swedish supporters, the same cage that would serve me so well at Wimbledon. I played some great tennis in the fourth set, and stupendous stuff in the fifth, to finally win the trophy 2-6,4-6,6-3,6-4,6-3. It will always stand as one of my greatest performances, and winning the Davis Cup a second time gave me as much joy and satisfaction as the first.

Later on I found it was again historic. In spite of our magnificent Davis Cup tradition, no Australian had ever recovered from a two set deficit to win a deciding rubber in a final. Neale Fraser praised me at the dinner that evening by saying he didn't think the cup had ever been won in greater circumstances, and I was touched by those words. Then it was my turn, even though speech making was not exactly my forte at the time: with no prior warning, I was called upon to respond to the toast given to the team by Prime Minister Bob Hawke. I think I can pretty much remember what I said as I leaned against the top table in my smart light suit:

People say that *I* won the Davis Cup, which is not true at all. When you look back on the year it was very much an overall team effort. Macca (Paul McNamee) played in every match; Peter Mac (McNamara) set up the win in New Zealand, playing the best I have ever seen him; and Fitzy (John Fitzgerald) and I teamed up to win every doubles [my elation had made me forget about the United States semi-final]. It was very much a team effort, and I was able to look good to finish it off.

Sergio Tacchini brought out a T-shirt that said 'Pat Cash, Twice Davis Cup Winner'. It also said 'Pat Cash, Davis Cup, Australia', but the 'Australia' was small and it was obviously designed to be recognised as me being a twice Davis Cup winner. I never wore that T-shirt, and gave all mine away. I didn't like it all - I thought it was in bad taste, and I told them so, too.

I ended my momentous year of 1986 as a team man through and through. And now I was about to start 1987, which could not have been a more personal and individual experience.

Chapter Eight

THE SUN SHONE ON SW19

Not surprisingly, during a life in tennis that now extends to close to a quarter of a century, there are several things I've grown to dislike with utter contempt. Right at the top of the list must come agents; with a few exceptions - and I can probably bring that number down to just a couple - agents are merely parasites who promise so much, only to leave you totally let down. They feed off the blood of tennis; they live well; they fly at the more comfortable end of the aeroplane, enjoy the best hotels, and know the finest restaurants in all the world's big cities. Nevertheless, 99 per cent of them are the epitome of sleaze.

I have experienced the extremely good and the really bad. Throughout my career, my father kept a sharp eye on everything, and thank God for small mercies. For the most part my agents were Mark McCormack's International Management Group, yet in all that time I only felt comfortable with one of their employees, Jim Curly, who was based in the States and now works as the tournament director of the US Open. Cream does rise to the top in this case. He was a truly honest, nice guy who would always tell the truth and never try to deceive me in any way. Otherwise, in my experience there was always something untrustworthy about so many other people I dealt with.

For example, nowadays my involvement in the Seniors Tour means I am constantly coming into contact with a certain Sergio Palmieri, an Italian on the IMG payroll, and I have to say that he is one I have always found hard to trust. He has more fingers in more pies than you can imagine. He is a players' agent, but he is also running the tour, and consequently can skip back and forth across the fence. For the players he is all but unobtainable - it isn't uncommon for a player to telephone Sergio twenty or thirty times with no return call and he is also greedy at their expense, a characteristic of which I have personal experience. Let me explain: the London senior event, held each December at the Royal Albert Hall, is now a five-day tournament, whereas most others on the Senior Tour last only four. There is almost no such thing as prize money with the seniors, you only get paid for appearing at the tournament, each player having his own set fee with the occasional bonus. So in effect, we were asked to play an additional day at the Albert Hall for no extra money.

Because of the current financial recession in which men's tennis has landed itself, the Senior Tour is not flourishing as it was a few years ago. In America they are now down to just one tournament, and the only thing keeping the tour alive on that continent is John McEnroe. My fee was originally $30,000 a tournament, but it has dropped to $20,000; I can't really afford a pay cut, but that's the way of life at the moment. However, IMG are charging the tournament directors around $100,000 just to stick the ATP logo on everything and negotiate a deal with the players. Senior tournaments are dropping like flies because the promoters cannot afford to pay players, hire venues, build stands *and* pay IMG that

The sun shone on SW19

$100,000. And guess who is negotiating on behalf of the players? Sergio Palmieri, who now works for IMG.

I asked him why I was only getting the same money for playing a potential five days in London, if I made the final, rather than four everywhere else. He said that's the way it has always been done, and it's non-negotiable. I pushed him for an extra day's pay and eventually, after much discussion, he agreed. But he insisted: Don't tell any of the other guys.

The man appalled me. Sergio, I said. You are being paid as the players' representative, and that means *all* the players. It is your duty and responsibility to be pushing for this payment to be made to everyone, not just me because I have made a fuss.

As it turned out, I did only play four days in London last year because I lost in the semi-final. However, the complete conflict of interests was truly atrocious. Basically Sergio Palmieri cares about just one player on the Senior Tour, and that is John McEnroe. My patience with IMG finally expired after I had been living in London for more than ten years and the only bit of business they put my way - as an ex-Wimbledon champion - was one Golden Wonder crisp commercial. For a while I decided to go on my own, but now I am with a completely different sort of person called Duncan March of Blue Summit, who used to work with Ian Botham. He is considerably more proactive, and we are talking about a breath of fresh air in an otherwise malodorous atmosphere. For a while it appeared I needed an agent to talk to my agents.

Duncan is in the process of helping me to change my mind about agents. However, the root of my dislike for them stems back to a day of enormous disappointment at the beginning of 1987. Losing the final of a Grand Slam tournament is hard enough; doing it in your home city is even worse. And the sensation that your shoulder is just about to drop off hardly adds to the feeling of well-being. But walking back into the locker room at Kooyong after being defeated by Stefan Edberg in the final of the Australian Open, I had to contend with something extra: the spectacle of Edbergs agent, Tom Ross, shouting, screaming and leaping all over the place like some pubescent kid.

Ross worked for the management company that was responsible for Edberg, but in my view that was no excuse for his juvenile, unprofessional behaviour; even Edberg looked embarrassed by it. I have always believed that the players' locker room should be reserved for the sole use of the contestants themselves, their coaches and their physiotherapists, and no one else. Unfortunately, agents are allowed to ply their trade in the players' lounges and restaurants, but certainly not the locker room.

I just glared at Ross with such fury that he obviously thought his head would soon be ripped from his shoulders. Realising the error of his ways, or perhaps in self-preservation, he immediately backed away, letting me through to my bench; but despite his profuse apologies, I have never trusted or liked him any better since that occasion. Many years later our paths were to cross again when I coached Mark Philippoussis and he was the agent involved, and he remains heavily involved in tennis to this day. His prime client is the world number one Lleyton Hewitt, and you can't go much higher than that in the business; undoubtedly the percentages are racking up nicely. And although I don't have cause to go into the locker rooms at Grand Slam finals any more, Lleyton should be doing so for many years to come so let us hope that Tom Ross has learnt from his past errors.

Returning to Kooyong was always going to be an extremely tough call, barely three weeks after the triumph of winning the

The sun shone on SW19

Davis Cup final in such heroic manner. Many Australian fans believed it was a forgone conclusion that I would just carry on where I left off against Pernfors, and win the title with ease. But Neale Fraser, who had a better idea of the realities of the situation, has since admitted that he thought I would struggle to recapture my best tennis so soon after such an emotionally draining experience.

I almost proved dear old Frase wrong, and maybe I only came up short against Edberg in the final because of the intensive physical work I had put in beforehand. Seeded 11th, I got a bye in the first round, and then beat the Italian Claudio Pistolesi in four sets. A couple of Americans, Ben Testerman and Paul Annacone, should both probably have been despatched more quickly than they were, but I made it through to the quarter-finals to face Yannick Noah.

Then midway through the match, I miss-hit a couple of shots and felt a jolt of pain in my right shoulder. Immediately I saw the danger signs flashing, because I had been working hard on my serve and the joint had been taking a pounding. Fortunately I beat Yannick, rounding off the win to love in the fourth set; but I knew I was in trouble. The problem was simply over-use, and all it required was a week or so of rest. But of course that's not possible in a Grand Slam tournament.

My shoulder was killing me as I faced Lendl in the semi, and the fact that I won remains one of the miracles of my career. I only managed to serve at three-quarter pace throughout, and I got through to my first-ever final of a major because I volleyed so well; the grass court was dry and the ball bounced high, so just rolling my arm over generated sufficient pace.

I couldn't practise at all on the day before the final. My trusty physiotherapist David Zuker tried loosening up the troublesome muscles, but the shoulder was shot - and Edberg was in no mood for sympathy. I'm sure he felt a desire for revenge after the Davis Cup final, and he was playing me off the court. By courtesy of my half-paced serve, he rapidly took a two set lead.

Stefan knew the route to the title at Kooyong, having lifted the trophy two years previously. Throughout the tournament he had been in supreme form and had only dropped one set on his way to the final, in his opening match. Miroslav Mecir only managed to take nine games off Edberg in the quarter-final, Wally Masur fared just marginally better in the semi, and it appeared that I was next in line for the treatment. But somehow I managed to get myself back in the match, and levelled the score at two sets all.

However, I knew I was undoubtedly still the underdog. The shoulder pain became unbearable, and serving for the fourth set, I hit three successive double faults. There was no pace or stick on my delivery, and as I tried to find a little extra power, I lost my rhythm altogether. I managed to grab the set after losing my serve, but I had lost the momentum. Edberg broke early in the fifth, and recaptured the title he'd won as a teenager. My hopes of a perfect Australian summer had fallen at the last obstacle, and my dreams of Grand Slam glory were forced back on hold.

After the match I was not in the best of moods - I defy anyone to be a good loser in those circumstances. Even before being infuriated by the sight of Ross in the locker room, I'd got myself into trouble on the awards podium. As is normally the case at the Australian Open, the runner-up is asked if he would like to make a short speech before the winner is presented with the trophy. Naturally I said well done to Edberg, because I've always viewed him as one of the finest players ever to grace a grass court. Then I said something along the lines of 'I'm supposed to thank a load of people like the sponsors Ford and all that junk. But I won't do that,

I'll leave it to Stefan.'

And the outcome of those innocent words? You guessed it: immediate outcry. I got totally slated and Ford were apoplectic, thinking I'd called their cars junk. Hands up in all honesty, that wasn't my intention at all. Cars aren't something I've ever thought particularly strongly about; to my mind they get you from one place and to another, and that's it, and I'm certainly no Mark Philippoussis who used to collect Ferraris. But one of Ford's top Australian bosses was really sounding off about what the country's top player had said about their product, and I was informed by Paul McNamee that Tennis Australia were at risk of losing their major sponsor.

A year later I again made it through to the final, and once more ended up the loser, this time to Mats Wilander. Brian Tobin, then head of Tennis Australia but subsequently president of the International Tennis Federation, asked me forward to make a speech. I declined rather forcibly, making certain the spectators didn't hear a word of what I said to Tobin - which went something like: No, fuck it. Guys like you didn't stick up for me last year. Why should I say something on your behalf now?

As far as I was concerned, Tobin never seemed a particularly good leader. Apparently he was quite amusing company at the bar and liked a drink or two, but I felt he was ineffectual when it came to matters that counted to his players and history was certainly to prove me right. Nevertheless I quickly regretted my actions, because the crowd weren't to blame; indeed, they'd been really supportive, and unquestionably merited my thanks. It wasn't their fault I had lost two finals in succession. Neither were they involved in the situation with Ford, which really came back to haunt me. Little did I know that IMG had stirred themselves into action, and were actually near to agreeing a sponsorship deal with Ford; however, an overly sensitive managing director finished that idea off.

My mood was slightly more philosophical as I faced the press after losing to Edberg. The disappointment was immense, but the anger was subsiding and I was reported as saying: I have proved I can come back up, and that's what champions have to do. I think I can do it now.

The belief was indisputably growing. As far back as early 1986, when I had just returned from the back surgery, I had begun to think winning Wimbledon was a distinct possibility. Once I even mentioned it in a press conference, but was subsequently berated by my dad who insisted I shouldn't go around coming out with boasts of that magnitude. Nevertheless, after winning the Davis Cup for a second time, that conviction grew. I knew that all the support components were in place, with Ian Barclay, Ann Quinn and Jeff Bond. The shoulder problem at Kooyong was just a blip, and I was certain my fitness was improving all the time; and my game was just right for grass. Most importantly, the motivation couldn't have been stronger, and everyone I met seemed to share my confidence.

After the Australian Open we beat Yugoslavia reasonably easily in the opening round of our defence of the Davis Cup, although Wally slipped up in the second rubber against Bobo Zivojinovic. John Fitzgerald was injured for this tournament, so I formed a new doubles partnership with Peter Doohan, who was to figure prominently in my life a few months later. Then I headed for Nancy in France where I took the title without dropping a set. But that victory was to take a slight toll because I hurt my knee whilst beating Wally in the final, and needed to take a month off following some arthroscopic surgery. Knee problems have continued to hinder me throughout my career, and genetically I blame my parents because we all have incredibly tight kneecaps with absolutely no give whatsoever. So that's another injury problem to add to my long list.

The operation wasn't a huge setback, and neither was losing early in the French Open to Jim Pugh of the United States. It just meant I could get to the English grass that much earlier and give myself even more time to prepare for the tournament that really counted. Anyway, clay court tennis was rapidly becoming a completely different game. It's dirty, it's slippery, and back in 1987 the balls were incredibly slow. Good volleying counted for next to nothing. Look at some of the players who have won the French and nothing much else: Sergei Bruguera, Andres Gomez and Thomas Muster. In turn, look at some of the wonderful players who were repeatedly frustrated there: Connors, McEnroe, Edberg, Becker and, in all probability, Sampras.

To my mind, nowadays it's tantamount to impossible to complete the entire Grand Slam by winning all four majors. I know Andre Agassi has collected them all in different years, but the French and Wimbledon are just too close together. Therefore Bjorn Borg's achievement of winning the two back to back three times in succession is a colossal feat. Even so, it did happen more than twenty years ago, and since then the game has evolved hugely.

Away from the tennis, the increasing number of disagreements and rows with Anne-Britt was becoming a problem. Everyone knows new mothers have a rough time, and by this stage Daniel was a year old and very demanding. Anne-Britt was still very young, and had sacrificed an extremely promising career as a model for the ties of motherhood. However, that wasn't the real problem: what she really resented was the presence of another woman, namely Ann Quinn. She just could not get her head around the fact that there was this other female who was giving me so much attention.

Being so immersed with my game and my aspirations for the next few weeks, I found it extremely difficult to rationalise the situation. I kept reassuring Anne-Britt there was absolutely no threat to her, and my relationship with Ann was purely professional. Much to my annoyance, some days I even had to miss training altogether so I could take Anne-Britt to the movies while somebody babysat Daniel.

Things got even worse when we headed back to a house in London, because with the natural exception of Ann Quinn, Team Cash all moved in together under one roof - Ian Barclay and I, with Jeff Bond. Much to her chagrin, Anne-Britt was required to fill the role of chief cook and bottle washer, which wasn't her forte. Little more than a mile away, my Dad and Uncle Brian were staying at the Gloucester Hotel, so everything was focused on me. I think it's fair to say that Anne-Britt was not amused. She felt extremely hard done by, having to do all the cleaning and cooking while all these guys just sat around and talked about tennis. Doubtless many will say that she had a point, and I can see that now; but like many a grown man, I compared my partner's domestic capabilities to those of my mother, who remains the greatest host, chef and taxi service for her kids.

At the time I was totally consumed with the prospects of Wimbledon, and viewed all the arguments and dissensions as an unnecessary hindrance, which were doing my chances no good whatsoever. It goes back to the fact that tennis players have to be 100 per cent self-centred if they want to succeed, and it is the loved ones who usually suffer the consequences. Look at the failure of relationships amongst so many top players of my generation: John McEnroe, divorced and remarried; Yannick Noah, divorced; Boris Becker, divorced; Henri Leconte, divorced a couple of times. More recently there's been Andre Agassi, while Pete Sampras had a couple of trial runs that broke up before he married Mrs Right. Then there is Martina Hingis, who for some reason can't find a steady boyfriend, although it's not for the want of trying. We are difficult people to love.

It's not just the selfishness: there are so many other aspects that come into relationships with sportsmen. There's the desolation that follows a defeat, and the bigger the match, the worse the feeling. In my case particularly, the struggle to recover from injuries is another sure-fire cause for depression. There's continual travelling, or enforced absences. Just everything is about the player, and everyone else has to fall in line. In retrospect I can see the error of my ways, and it really was an unpleasant period - but there was just one thing on my mind, and that fortnight of judgement was getting closer all the time.

First came the almost prerequisite injury scare, and nothing could be as terrifying as the twinges of back pain I suffered practising at Queen's Club. My dad was not in a mood to leave anything to chance, and immediately contacted David Zuker in Melbourne who booked himself on the first available flight to London. Imagine my surprise when I awoke one morning to find a guy standing at the end of my bed whom I thought was 12,000 miles away on the opposite side of the world! Soon Zukes was prodding and pummelling away, but thankfully found the problem to be nothing more than a little muscle stiffness.

Nobody should be too amazed that the English summer weather also presented a problem: in short, it rained for twenty days, and finding a dry grass court wasn't easy. Barkers and I really put in the miles, but I had to have somewhere to practise, because if you don't hit regularly on grass, you don't get the precise timing. The Queen's Club tournament was the usual rush between showers, but I was reasonably content with my form. Beating Kevin Curren boosted the confidence, and the subsequent win over Edberg stoked even more self-belief. Then I lost to Connors, but it was an excellent match, and I should have walked away relatively happy.

Unfortunately I wasn't. The domestic situation with Anne-Britt was worsening all the time, though thankfully Jeff Bond soon touched down from Australia to tend my troubled mind; he arrived the day before Boris Becker ominously won the Queen's title for the third time in four years. I concentrated on daily meditation with Jeff, and then every night spent an hour before bed in conversation with him for relaxation and reassurance.

A timely 'foot-in-my-mouth' article criticising women's tennis caused a minor scene, and an Australian female reporter saw the need to sit next to Anne-Britt during one of my matches at Queen's. Anne-Britt was quite distressed when she told me about it afterwards, as the woman was constantly barraging her with questions such as: 'Is Pat a chauvinist?' and 'Does he change the nappies?' - I was being painted as Pat the Pig, and I was angry.

Once again I felt the press were trying to damage my chances, so I sought out the reporter and told her that I would never talk to either her or her newspaper again. I wasn't abusive and didn't swear, but was firm and not exactly friendly. It was certainly a distraction I didn't need, because I was trying to block out all the problems at home and build up a focus and intensity about the tennis.

Champions have that trait. You see it with the likes of Agassi and

The sun shone on SW19

Sampras, and Jim Courier was another who zeroed in on the task in hand. He was an extremely bright guy who taught himself to speak different languages and play various musical instruments; but when he rocked up for the big tournaments, he was just so focused and call it what you like, putting on the blinkers or going into the tunnel, it is a formula that works.

Jeff was also adamant that I should enjoy my tennis. He said I should appreciate the good shots I hit, almost patting myself on the back out there on the practice court. He insisted I work hard on a particular goal every day, and by the time everyone was ready at London SW19, I was calm and perfectly prepared.

Annually the build-up to Wimbledon is huge. To many people in Britain, tennis doesn't seem to matter for fifty weeks of the year, but come the second half of June and everybody is voicing an opinion as to who is going to win. Naturally Becker was the favourite this year, after two successive titles. Although Lendl was still ranked number one in the world, Boris was named top seed, and his form in winning the Stella Artois title at Queen's only served to shorten his price with the bookmakers. Edberg also seemed a good bet after winning four titles on three different surfaces during the year.

I am sure that all my injury problems caused many people to view me with suspicion. The bookmakers were only quoting me at 16-1, which I thought was a very good bet. In addition I had opted out of playing the doubles, which might have sent a few imaginations racing. Though John Fitzgerald was fit again after his shoulder problems, and Bobo Zivojinovic asked me to play, I had decided to concentrate on the singles. Ian Barclay wasn't happy about the decision, but I thought the workload could be too heavy. There is always the possibility of playing a long, five sets singles match, and then having to be back out on court an hour or so later for the doubles. In theory you might have to play ten sets of tennis in one day, and though the rallies might be short, it's still an exhausting prospect. You could end up both physically and mentally jaded and it wasn't worth the risk. These days, with very few exceptions, you don't see the top singles stars playing doubles at Grand Slams.

A break in the rain just before the tournament gave me the chance to test my game against Tim Mayotte who was seeded one place above me at number ten. I wanted to face a big server so I could hone my returns. I came out on top against the big American and realised I was in good shape. So much so, I immediately went for a run over Wimbledon Common with Ann Quinn. As if Ann didn't know her job, Dad gave her the orders: Don't work him too hard.

Any Grand Slam champion will tell you they are most susceptible in the opening rounds, and therefore a favourable draw is imperative. You don't want to come into contact with any of the dangerous floaters. In 1987 there were names to avoid, such as big-hitting Zivojinovic, the athletic Frenchman Guy Forget who had been an adversary in the juniors, the talented Swedish volleyer Anders Jarryd, and the South African turned American Johan Kriek, who'd twice won the Australian title on grass. As a first round opponent, I couldn't have asked for anyone better than the diminutive American, Marcel Freeman. But in the second was somebody who presented considerably more concern, and whichever way I contemplated the match, the fact was inescapable that Paul McNamee knew my game better than anyone in the 128-strong draw.

For only the fourth time in tournament history a persistent drizzle meant there wasn't a single ball hit on the opening Monday. Although the sun came out in the evening, play had already been abandoned. More rain the next morning meant the action didn't begin until after 4pm, and Edberg rapidly posted an impressive start, needing only 61 minutes to beat his compatriot Stefan Eriksson 6-0, 6-0, 6-0. Word spread around the locker room that this might have been the fastest win in forty years. I didn't join in the speculation, however, and the nerves were jangling when I eventually walked out to face Freeman; I would have been concerned if they weren't.But I wasn't in a mood to linger, and needed just a quarter of an hour to win the first set, which gave me the impetus to go through 6-0, 6-3, 6-2.

McNamee presented a completely different problem, and I was extremely nervous. He might have been ten years my senior, but he was still extremely quick. He was a tricky, unorthodox player with a crafty game and a sneaky serve. He still had a great forehand volley, but most importantly of all, he knew every little thing about me.None of my fellow players had given me more assistance than Macca, and now suddenly he was out there to ruin my great dream. I always found it hard to play a mate, but there wasn't room for sentiment: the Wimbledon title was on the line.

Most alarmingly of all, Macca had beaten me three times in our four previous meetings, and I was acutely aware of the inherent dangers of him getting on a roll. I'm never usually that gregarious with the opposition just before we play, but I couldn't be like that with Macca - it would have been ludicrous. So we sat in the locker room and had a chat about the footy results back home. Gerry Williams, commentating for television, said it was almost like watching two brothers playing, and that's the way it felt to me.

Initially I couldn't get on top of Macca, and the first set was a prolonged affair; but once I got in front, things went better. Afterwards it was all smiles and bonhomie, which was only to be expected. To an Aussie, mates are important. Macca even took the piss by imitating my habit of throwing headbands to the crowd, and found a dirty old piece of towel in the bottom of his bag that he tossed into row two. But afterwards he told the press: There's nobody Pat can't beat. He's better prepared than ever, and his tennis is so much more mature.

Elsewhere sensation had struck. Not that I read the newspapers of course, but they were full of big news that morning: in a huge upset, Boris Becker had lost to my Australian Davis Cup doubles partner Peter Doohan. A second round defeat was the earliest exit for a champion since Manuel Santana had taken an early flight back to Spain twenty years earlier - and suddenly the tournament had taken on a new complexion.

Doohan's coach Michael Fancutt had previously asked me how the two of them should plan to beat Boris. Simple, I told them: just take the ball early, and attack the second serve. The fact that fifteen previous opponents had tried and failed on Wimbledon's grass was irrelevant, and though I believed Doohan to be a very good server and volleyer, I hadn't given him a hope in hell.

Boris was the only person I really feared, although I thought I could still beat him if I was at my very best. So when I heard he'd lost to Doohan, I did allow myself to think the big threat was gone. I was pleased, but not counting my chickens. Meanwhile Boris was coming out with his famous quote: I didn't lose a war. There's no one dead. It was just a tennis match.

Doohan went back to his £78-a-week room in the YMCA, and the tournament's main contenders started walking around with an added spring in their step. To this day he still maintains I owe him a percentage of my prize money; to which I respond by saying that his success was the fifteen minutes of fame that Andy Warhol insisted everyone would have. Doohan also won his next match against Leif Shiras, before going down to Zivojinovic. He hung around on the circuit until his ranking dropped, and now coaches at a Tennessee college. Maybe he tells the students his name will never be forgotten in Wimbledon history.

Then, after three weeks of rain, the sun came blazing through for my third round match against the big Dutchman Michiel Schapers. And so too did my notorious temper, albeit briefly. Jeff Bond had got my mind perfectly prepared, but for the only time during the entire fortnight I momentarily lost my cool after committing a couple of errors. The heat was exhausting, and I just got angry with myself. Though my shout wasn't directed at anyone but me, a baseline judge took offence and reported me to the umpire. A code of conduct warning rapidly followed.

I didn't want to lose my temper at all, because I had such a high respect for Wimbledon. One thing Ray Ruffels taught me six years previously was that the place is like a church, where people don their best white clothing. Fired up in the fourth set, I reasserted control and eventually walked off victorious in the knowledge I had played a match that had knocked me into form. Schapers was an awkward guy with a big serve and a huge reach, and although I cramped straight afterwards, the win was just the boost I needed because the next match was potentially a really tough one against Forget.

The Frenchman had a big game with a huge serve, but he was also prone to expensive errors, and four double faults in one game showed me how badly he was dealing with the situation. In contrast, my form was improving all the time, and Barkers insisted my performance in that straight sets win was my best of the fortnight. I begged to differ: Guy didn't play well and I nullified him, and in my opinion the way I beat Wilander in the quarter-final was better.

Statisticians later told me I dropped a mere nineteen points in sixteen service games on my first visit to Centre Court for the year. Apparently Gunther Bosch, the coach who had guided Becker to his two previous titles, insisted I would soon be the champion, and my game backed up the suggestion. When I played Mats at Wimbledon a year earlier, he had grown a little disenchanted with tennis, but now he was married and revitalised. A few weeks earlier he had lost the final of the French Open to Lendl, and a few months later it was the same story at the US Open.

Nevertheless he was getting back to his best; but I hit more aces than I did against Forget, and upped my game about 75 per cent on the performance against Schapers. I moved so well that Mats found it impossible to pass me, and it was that afternoon that convinced me I was close to my goal. However, my semi-final opponent was another huge obstacle.

To my mind I wasn't just taking on Jimmy Connors, I would also have the crowd against me. He knew every trick to get them on his side, and he would be doing everything possible to break my focus. It didn't matter that he was nearly thirty-five years of age and hadn't won a tournament since 1983. Zivojinovic hit twenty-five aces against him, but Jimmy had still won. A round earlier he had fought back from an abysmal start and a two set deficit to beat Mikail Pernfors. But first I had to contend with a pain in the butt, literally: practising against Brad Drewett, I had a strained a muscle in my right buttock which required immediate treatment with ice and an electronic stimulator.

Many people perceived Jimmy to be something of an arsehole, but in my opinion he was a great player. He had such an unusual style, nobody ever played like him and nobody ever will. He was a great athlete, but tough as nails in the bargain. Barkers and I regularly used to watch Jimmy practice and were amazed by his drive. Every point was regarded as the most important of his life: it was inspirational to see, and that was exactly how he played his matches. Maybe that's why he made so many comebacks and reached the US Open semi-final at the age of thirty-nine. I make no secret of the fact that I was a fan, besides which I never had any problems with Jimmy on court. Sure, he used to play to the crowd and joke with the line judges in a thinly disguised attempt at giving himself a little rest, but tennis is all about entertainment. The first time we ever played one another was at the Canadian Open in Toronto. I was told he was making faces at me for miss-hitting a ball; I didn't see him, so I don't know, and I will keep an open mind. However, it's fair to admit that opponents *can* certainly goad me.

Jimmy and I didn't really socialise. He never seemed to mix with the rest of the guys, but that's understandable - who would, if they were married to a *Playboy* centrefold? He had a certain style. In the States he played the true super star by climbing out of his limousine and walking straight onto the court. McEnroe doesn't hold his countryman in such high esteem as I do, but that's because he is consumed by a competitive jealousy.

The last time I ever played Jimmy was in a seniors event under some awful floodlights at San Diego, and he was just days away from his forty-ninth birthday. His serve had withered away into a dinky little shot, but his backhand was still unbelievable, and I swear he only missed about five all night. I could barely see the ball, but unusually there was $150,000 riding on the match and I needed the money. I won, but it wasn't pretty. Walking off court I knew the only way I'd beaten a guy looking squarely at the age of fifty was to run him into the ground.

I couldn't have made a better start in the semi-final, hitting an ace with the first ball. But Jimmy was intent on being no pushover, and fought fiercely to break back at five all, after I'd served for the first set. Walking back to the baseline to return, I knew this was a crucial moment. I was determined not to fold under pressure, and broke back immediately before taking control. This was again testimony to the work of Jeff Bond, who had instilled in me that following any loss of concentration, I should immediately snap myself back awake. Late in the third set the fire alarm went off, although I didn't pay attention. I had moved into a 5-0 lead, dropping just four points. The bell seemed too late to save Jimmy, but he was trying all his tricks with the crowd to disrupt my concentration. I knew he'd spotted I was tense, and I didn't want him to be inspired into another comeback as he'd managed against Pernfors. Summoning up all my focus, I managed to finish him off. The relief was immense.

On the Saturday between the semi-final and the final, things were on edge at home. Anne-Britt was bitching about doing the cleaning, Jeff Bond and Barkers were out in the garden mowing the lawn, and I was watching a movie in the lounge. It was Charles Bronson in Murphy's Law, which apparently is good but I can't tell you too much about the plot: I was visualising the next day's events on Centre Court. I went through everything, walking out behind Leo the locker room attendant and feeling nervous. Turning around to bow to the Royal Box. Playing the first point. Being break point up, and being break point down. Serving for the match. Winning the title. I still get butterflies in my stomach just thinking about that afternoon.

The sun shone on SW19

Previously I'd been down to the gentlemen's outfitters Moss Bros in Hammersmith to hire a dinner suit, just in case my presence was required for the Champion's Dinner at the Savoy Hotel the following evening. Then I'd gone for a hit at Surbiton with Darren 'Killer' Cahill. We'd fittingly started on the stroke of 2pm, and twenty-four hours later I would be walking out to face Ivan Lendl, Mr Shoebreaker himself.

Not surprisingly I didn't sleep too well, but getting out of bed in the morning verbally told myself: 'This is the day.' The preparations were meticulous. Although I didn't feel like eating, I forced myself to have a complex carbohydrate breakfast of cereal, fruit and grained bread. My special energy drinks were prepared, and an hour before the match I had another brief hit with Killer on Court Six. My game plan didn't differ from six months earlier when I played Lendl at Kooyong, and I can still hear Barkers endlessly repeating: Make him play every volley.

I felt good when I walked onto court. Lendl and I had just been standing in opposite corners of the corridor, but we hadn't spoken. I didn't want to wish him good luck or anything else insincere. The weather was sweltering. Somebody said it was close to 100 degrees Fahrenheit although I didn't think it ever got that hot in England. The male occupants of the Royal Box were allowed to remove their jackets. Straightaway I put the heat on Lendl, testing him for 13 minutes as he struggled to hold his first service game.

My service was working well. I dropped only six points in six games before the tiebreaker and then moved to a 6-1 lead, giving me five set points. Lendl managed to save four, and though a moment of self-doubt came into my head, I immediately pushed it aside. Lendl had a good block backhand return and a great full swing backhand, but couldn't play a shot in between. Could I tempt him to go for a full swing on a block backhand shot? I hoped so, and aimed at the spot on the court that wasn't too wide to give him room to swing, but was sufficiently far enough over to tempt him. Bang! My serve hit the exact blade of grass. He over-swung and directed the backhand out. I was set up, and knew I had the match won. I was loose: the nerves had gone, and my game had switched into overdrive. During the second set I didn't allow him a point on my serve, and with such an overwhelming lead, nothing was going to slip.

Because of all the rain in England that summer, I hadn't done as much endurance work as I would have liked; over my career it's the one facet of my make-up that has needed the most attention. Briefly I became concerned at the unlikely prospect of the match going to five sets, but soon suppressed such negative thoughts.

Lendl broke my serve in the third when I suffered a brief lapse in focus. This quite often happens if you are initially nervous and then relax yourself so much you lose some intensity. The body is slow to react to the brain, and it's a matter of finding that fine line. Thankfully all the work I did with Jeff once more paid off, and again I snapped myself back to break his serve twice in succession. I remember my last service game and match point like it was only yesterday: I went 40-love up for three match points. Thank God it was an easy game, and I finished it all off with a volley that got behind Lendl and into the open court.

GAME, SET AND MATCH, MR CASH 7-6, 6-2, 7-5. I was the champion, and pumped my fist in the air. Then I shook Lendl by the hand and he just said well done. I was polite, and I could see his disappointment; but I came out with no more than the standard reply of bad luck. There was nothing else to say, we didn't like each other, so there would be no sympathy. To me, some of these great shows of emotion towards a beaten opponent over the Wimbledon net are false. I think it's hypocritical to put your arms around each other and have a long chat. I know that's what Ivanisevic and Rafter did last year, but I don't buy that sort of show. Anyway, there had been other things planned for several months. I had some climbing to do.

Chapter Nine

Sorry Boris,
but I don't find that funny

Women's tennis has never been something I greatly admire, so I've long been top of the hit list for those who accuse me of chauvinism, and call me Pat the Pig. Nevertheless, I'm not going to start changing my mind now, and stand by my insistence that if anybody ever manages to get the female fraternity equal prize money with men, that person should be awarded a gold medal and then locked away for robbery!

I was one of the first to make my views on the subject known, and the predictable backlash followed. McEnroe and Connors have also said their bit (frankly it wouldn't be like them to keep quiet on such an issue). Of course Richard Krajicek came out with his 'lazy fat pigs' statement several years ago. In my opinion, no more than a cursory glance around the women's game is needed to tell you that the observation remains pretty accurate today. More recently Marcelo Rios took a couple of pot shots at this year's Australian Open, insisting the early rounds in any women's tournament are totally predictable and not competitive. So even before the likes of Jennifer Capriati, the Williams sisters, Martina Hingis and Lindsay

Davenport walk out on court, its almost a foregone conclusion that they are going to win with ease.

Let me say here and now, I applaud every one of those guys for their honesty: in my view, they are all absolutely spot on in their assessments. Right now the WTA Tour are repeatedly congratulating themselves, insisting that it is women's tennis keeping the game afloat. I don't deny there are currently some extremely good players near the top of the female ranks: but to my mind it is the rest who are just not up to standard, and who let the sport down by their lack of fitness. At times its an absolute disgrace. Thus, Steffi Graf was an exceptional athlete; Venus Williams possesses awesome power; Jennifer Capriati's comeback was inspirational. Martina Navratilova was also a player and competitor whom I viewed with tremendous respect - but there are other female players who should hardly be called professional sportswomen. It must surely be a reflection on the standard of women's tennis that Martina can still be competitive, albeit only playing doubles, at the age of forty-five.

Sitting on the top table of the Champion's Dinner in the Wedgwood blue opulence of the Savoy Hotel's ballroom, only the All England Club's chairman, Buzzer Haddingham, sat between Martina and myself. I feared some kind of confrontation. My admiration for her seemed irrelevant, as she had long been regarded as one of the most ardent feminists, and I'd already poured scorn over the cries for financial parity between the two sexes.

Fortunately peace reigned that evening. Martina and I just made our polite speeches, smiled for the cameras, and went our separate ways. We were both Wimbledon champions, me for the first time, her for the eighth, and it wasn't a time to argue. At a later date my practice time came after hers at an indoor court, only a matter of

Sorry Boris, but I don't find that funny

weeks after another article quoted me on the subject of equal prize money. This time I was convinced a row was about to erupt; but she just smiled, collected up her rackets, told me she had read the story - and then said that she agreed with what I had said!

I couldn't have been more shocked if John McEnroe, a fully paid-up despiser of golf and everything it stands for, had agreed to play eighteen holes with Ivan Lendl! In fact Martina proposed that I was being generous in my assertion that all the girls outside the world's top thirty were pretty poor, and thought it might have been more accurate to say outside the top ten. Not for the last time was I left in a state of total shock during my year as a Wimbledon champion.

Martina actually became a memorable ally some months later at the Australian Open. Tennis Australia were proudly about to unveil the new state-of-the-art National Tennis Centre on the banks of Melbourne's River Yarra, complete with sliding roof on the Centre Court. Kooyong's grass had sadly been consigned to history, and instead we played on a rubberised hard court surface known as Rebound Ace. Much to my dismay, as Wimbledon champion and the big Aussie hope, the organisers had also agreed to use the Korean-made Nassau tennis ball, a type that frankly decimated my chances. This ball was terrible: it was heavy, and used to fluff up in no time, anathema to somebody like myself who plays attacking serve and volley tennis. Heavy hitters like Lendl and Wilander would have been happy with that ball, but I felt it minimised my chances.

The company involved had paid Tennis Australia a substantial fee because they wanted the balls used at the Olympic Games in Seoul later that year. The International Tennis Federation rules decreed that any ball used at the Olympics first had to be used at a Grand Slam tournament. Money talks on a matter like that - but so did I, kicking up a real stink at the pre-tournament press conference. And I was fortunate in that Martina followed me into the interview room, and being told of my adverse comments, immediately stressed her total agreement. Though it might have had something to do with the fact that she, too, was a serve and volley player, I really didn't mind. Two Wimbledon champions speaking in unison had exerted enough pressure to get the rules regarding the Nassau balls changed.

Six months before this episode, the Wimbledon's Champion's Dinner was reportedly one of the more raucous in the function's long history. Uncle Brian and the gang had started to celebrate in true Australian style, so numerous glasses had already gone down when I stood up to speak. Neale Fraser, as an ex-champion, had given me a few pointers, but one of the most important things I wanted to stress was my gratitude for the familys support. A huge roar immediately erupted from my guests' table, rapidly followed by much polite but restrained laughter everywhere else in the massive room. I don't think many All England Club members had ever come across anything like the Cash clan in full flow before!

Soon we were all heading back home to Fulham, where many more friends were toasting my success. Killer Cahill and Paul McNamee were getting into the swing of things as midnight came and went - but Anne-Britt was upset because the noise had woken Daniel. Not wanting to start my first day as a reigning champion with a headache, I wasn't too bothered about the beer, and instead went upstairs to calm my little son. I must have lain there with him for more than an hour, enjoying the feeling of quiet, calm contentment. It's one of my most cherished memories.

So many other recollections from that year aren't nearly so gratifying; even my return to Melbourne ended in some unpleasantness. A big crowd had turned out at the airport to welcome their champion home, but the authorities grabbed me, and pushed me through a side door and into a waiting car. I was given no option, but the television news opened that evening with the story of Wimbledon winner Pat Cash shunning his fans. Naturally the newspapers followed suit the next day. The Mayor of Melbourne might have presented me with the keys to the city, but once more I felt like an outlaw in my home town.

I have many misgivings from that period. Initially I turned my back on a pile of money to play a tournament in Japan, because I preferred to go to Norway for a restful break with Anne-Britt and Daniel. The newspapers were way off the mark, claiming I was heading to Australia, the Caribbean and even the south of France to celebrate with my friend Joan Collins, who incidentally I've never met. Instead I ended up at an old caravan in a Norwegian national park, squashed amongst my in-laws. The press weren't the only people fooled, and I was a little surprised myself; but the experience helped me keep my feet on the ground. In addition I was able to spend some necessary time with Anne-Britt. Despite the fact that our relationship was under immense strain, she again fell pregnant, and nine months later Daniel was delivered a sister - and there's no doubt that Mia Karin was a Wimbledon baby.

Although my dad repeatedly told me money would always be available as long as I preserved my health and game, it's difficult to say no when big bucks are on offer. So another regret was all the fuss from the anti-apartheid lobby that surrounded my financially induced decision to play a tournament in Johannesburg. Kim Hughes had recently taken an Australian cricket team to South Africa, while both John Fitzgerald and Wally Masur had both played the Johannesburg event in previous years. But I was the

Wimbledon champion, and that made a difference. The Australian prime minister Bob Hawke went as far as declaring that it was a bad decision for the country's top tennis player to go, and I knew there would be a backlash. There had to be a financial sweetener, and guarantees of $230,000, only slightly less than I picked up for winning Wimbledon, helped ease my concerns.

Anyway I had a few opinions of my own on the situation. Margaret Thatcher made complete sense to me when she claimed that banning everything and everybody from going to South Africa would totally cripple a country that didn't have much industry and was already going broke. Of course apartheid was a terrible thing, and in no way was I supporting anything to do with such a regime. I think my charity work over the years proves that I do care for the underprivileged and oppressed of the world. Furthermore, I did my bit for the black people on that trip. Admittedly I didn't actually go to Soweto because I was told it wasn't safe; but I spent a lot of time talking with the kids and giving out headbands wherever I went. The armed guard on my hotel room door, day and night, was alarming, and the amount of press that greeted my arrival filled me with trepidation; but I thought the tournament was quite relaxed, and as there were plenty of black kids working as ball boys, I wasn't fully aware of the circumstances in the outside world.

Apart from the money on offer, I had other reasons for playing the tournament. Winning one Grand Slam tournament, reaching the final of another, and collecting the title at Nancy still wasn't enough to earn me one of the qualifying spots for the end of the year Masters held at New York's Madison Square Gardens. Basically I hadn't played enough tournaments because I liked my time off to train; also I always felt an unavoidable commitment to representing my country in the Davis Cup, and repeatedly flying home to

Sorry Boris, but I don't find that funny

Australia had left me short on qualifying points. In the late 1980s the Aussie Open could not offer the amount of points it possesses today; so the bottom line was, if I wanted to play the Masters, I had to go to Johannesburg and win.

There were eight places up for grabs in the Masters at that time. Indeed there still are, although the title of the event has been lengthened to the Masters Cup after all kinds of political wrangling during the 1990s when the ATP had their World Championships and the ITF the Grand Slam Cup. Thankfully common sense has prevailed, and so long as the winners of the four Grand Slams don't have really low rankings, they are guaranteed a place in the eight.

Back then I was ranked ninth. Brad Gilbert was immediately above me in eighth position, so my task was pretty clear. Predictably, the two of us reached the final, and I probably produced the comeback performance of my life. Never mind the recovery against Pernfors in the Davis Cup or my Wimbledon wins: that afternoon in Johannesburg was the only time I have ever experienced being truly in the zone.

For a while I thought Gilbert was too good; I was down in the match and really struggling - but then something happened, which I just can't explain. It really did feel spiritual, but for the rest of the match I felt as though somebody or something else was playing it for me. When you are in the zone, my belief is that a higher power has taken control. Perhaps it was God, possibly it was something else, but I went on to win the next eleven games straight, in what seemed like just ten minutes. Gilbert didn't win another game as I took the match and the title. He didn't get through to the Masters, and I did. As far as I was concerned, it was a case of job done, although I still find it impossible to explain the transformation.

I do believe in God. I was brought up a Catholic, and went to

Uncovered

Sunday morning mass every week until I was old enough to say otherwise. Even then I still went occasionally, but grew to rebel against so much of the faith because it didn't make any sense. How many Catholics have cause to feel the same way at some time during their lives? There must be millions. I went back to it when I had children, and in recent years have become more spiritual. Many people were shocked when I first wore an earring twenty years ago, but for the last fifteen a cross has hung from the ring. I also have a tattoo of Christ's crucifixion on my arm, complete with the initials of my four children. Right now I don't feel compelled to go to church every week or stand up and sing; however, the earring and tattoo are symbols of my belief.

The South African business was really causing a lot of grief back home, and nobody was making more noise than the head of Australia's Olympic committee, Kevin Gosper. I have to say that as far as I was concerned, his attitude was pretty blatantly hypocritical. At the time he was in charge of Shell Oil in Australia, and the company was heavily involved in South Africa. Given the opportunity, I raised the anomaly with him, and he just replied that what Shell were doing was purely business. So what was I doing? Excuse me if I've got something wrong here, but isn't playing tennis and winning tournaments my business? Basically he was saying it was fine for *him* to make money in South Africa, but wrong for *me*. He was just making the right noises in the sporting world at the time to safeguard his position in the Olympic movement, but still filling his wallet from his business interests. Isn't that hypocrisy?

Outrage continued back home, with the anti-apartheid movement shaking their fists at anything to do with me. They telephoned Ian Barclay's house to say they were appalled at my decision to play in

176

Left:
Wasn't I cute!

Below:
From right:
Mum holding
Renee, me,
Rosie, Craig and
Ralph at top,
now in heaven.

Above:
Mum, Daniel,
Renee and me.
Are those shorts
back in fashion
yet?

Right:
Not just a tennis
champion. My first
love and still the
best sport to
watch in the world.
Aussie Rules!

Above, top: Playing the doubles final of the Avvenire Cup under 16's in Milan 1981 with Mark Hartnett. Mark also won the singles in our first real venture abroad.
Bottom: With Mark and coach Ian Barclay after the final.

Above: First time on the really big stage. Centre Court winning the US Junior title, beating Guy Forget in September 1982.

Right: Winning the Wimbledon Junior title after a tough match on the old Court No.1.... next the big one!

Bottom: Mark Edmondson, myself, John Fitzgerald and Paul McNamee. A motley crue of personalities gelled together to take the 1983 Davis Cup.

Above: The Duke and Duchess of Kent alongside myself and Paul McNamee who was a big influence on my career. Runners up to McEnroe/Fleming in the 1984 Wimbledon doubles.
Below: Mark Evans and me in the Royal Hotel, Bondi Beach, 1985.

Above: Anne-Britt and Daniel. He started travelling when he was two weeks old.
Below: McNamee, Fraser, myself and McNamara. The Melbourne Mafia, the Davis Cup at Neale Fraser's house after the win in December 1986.

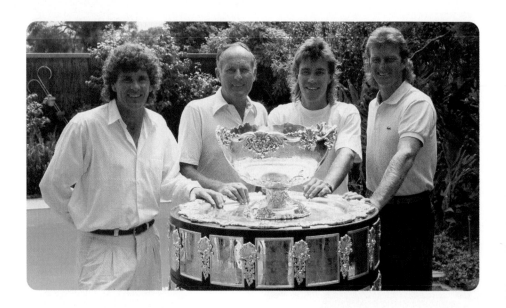

Above: Mats Wilander, one of our many battles. This time I won.
Below, left: Wimbledon 87', moving great.
Below, right: Not surprised I get injured. Flying is dangerous.

Left:
I love this baby!

Below:
The hero's welcome-ish.
City Square in Melbourne. Keys to the city?
My arse.
Didn't open any shops, I tried.

Opposite.
Above: Pumping the fists to the gang - beating Lendl in the 87' Wimbledon final - I'll never get sick of this photo!
Middle: Testing out the roof of the commentators booth. The Cash clan from far left: Jeff Bond (clapping), Ian Barclay (leaning down), Ann Quinn, sister Renee, Dad (in cap), Uncle Brian.
Bottom: Finally made it, hugging Dad with the gang looking on.

Opposite, top: With Barkers and Dad at the Champions Dinner.
Far left: Anne-Britt with Mia, me with Daniel in 89'.
Left: Probably my best shot - a backhand volley.
Above, top: One of the proudest moments in my career - Champions Walk
with all the legends. Steffi Graf in the background.
Above: I'm also very proud to be on this Honours Board at Wimbledon with
these names.

Above:
Beating Mac at the
Albert Hall in the Seniors
Champions Tour final.
There's always action
when Mac and I play.

Above, right:
Emily, the prettiest girl in
the world and always so
supportive.

Right:
Losing to Mac at
Wimbledon in the 1992
Championships.

Above, top: John Dee, the co-founder and driving force behind Planet Ark. One of our big campaigns - recycling greeting cards.
Above: Kylie is a great supporter of Planet Ark. Being a co-founder has its perks!

Above, top:
With Academy partner Gavin Hopper supporting Philippoussis at the
Australian Open in Jan 1999.
Above: Australia v Sweden May 99', World Team Cup. Whilst coaching
Philippoussis I played in the doubles when Rafter was resting, the team won
and I got a trophy!
Left to right: Flip, me, Tony Roche, Sandon Stolle and Pat Rafter.

Above:
The dream team I pieced together. L to r: Brad Langevad, me, Melinda Glenister, Greg Rusedski and Ryan Kendrick.

Left:
Pulling some shapes. Its all about having fun, playing good rock n' roll with my mates

Right:
At home in
Fulham, London
with my princess
Mia and Emily.

Below:
All the boys
together.
I love this photo
very much as it
captures each of
their personalities
so well.
From left: Daniel,
Jett and Shannon

Sorry Boris, but I don't find that funny

South Africa, but they didn't just leave it at that: they also told the Barclays 'we know where you live and we know you have got children.' To me, that was a threat, pure and simple. When the time came around for the Australian Open, they made it clear there would be demonstrations. Tennis Australia's president Brian Tobin, thinking himself a bit of a diplomat, gave them the go-ahead which in my view was not a great way of saying thank you to a player who had twice won the Davis Cup for his country, and had raised the profile of tennis to an all-time high.

Tobin did make certain conditions. They could make as much noise as they wanted and were allowed to carry slogans and abusive banners, but on no account could they interfere with the match. Day one of the Australian Open dawned hot and sunny, and the temperature reached 38C when Thomas Muster and I walked onto the Centre Court at Flinders Park. It was the curtain raiser for the new National Tennis Centre, but all you could hear were protesters shouting and screaming. There were loads outside, and about fifteen of them courtside, doing their very best to make me believe I was a monster who liked to shoot black children for a little rest and recuperation. So when they threw a load of blackened tennis balls onto the court midway through the second set and thereby interrupted the match, it was no surprise to anyone except, apparently, Brian Tobin. No thanks to him when security finally dragged the protesters away, and my dad gave him an earbashing.

I hardly felt like a homecoming Wimbledon champion that afternoon. I may have won in straight sets, but the whole occasion seemed hollow because of all the fuss. Throughout my career I have felt extremely uncomfortable when people show me derision. Call it insecurity if you like, but I always feel as though I need to justify myself, and the feeling was never stronger than when I played the

177

Sydney indoor tournament a couple of months earlier.

For months after winning Wimbledon, I questioned whether I was a legitimate champion or if my victory was just a fluke. So often I sensed that people were thinking Boris Becker would have completed a hat-trick of wins had he survived that shock defeat against Peter Doohan. People kept trying to reassure me, saying I played some wonderful tennis and only dropped one set all fortnight. Maybe it was my natural insecurity resurfacing, but I still wasn't sure and Doohan himself didn't help, repeatedly jesting he wanted a percentage of my prize money for knocking out the runaway favourite. The more I thought about it, the more I wondered if I was good enough to beat Becker. . I tried to play along with the joke, but deep down I believed Doohan was being serious, and the thought just stuck in my head.

So when I faced Boris in the semi-final of the Sydney tournament, I felt the time had come for vindication. Was I a rightful Wimbledon champion, or was I a fraud? The match couldn't have been closer, but finally I won 7-5 in a third set tiebreak. I can't describe the relief I felt: suddenly all the self-doubts had disappeared, and I had justified myself. The match finished extremely late, but there were still a lot of people around when I walked into the press conference. Immediately I declared, Well, that proves I am a worthy Wimbledon champion, and that my winning wasnt just a fluke! I can remember the well travelled Aussie journalist Craig Gabriel and quite a few others looking at me as if they didn't know what on earth I was talking about: I had built the whole thing up in my head.

The fact that I was absolutely crunched by Lendl in the following day's final became irrelevant: I had beaten Becker, and in my own mind this had eliminated a huge area of doubt. I had been extremely envious of Boris for quite a while, but it was hard not to develop an inferiority complex. Not only had he won two Wimbledon titles before his nineteenth birthday, he also adopted the air of somebody totally superior to everyone else. I didn't feel the same about Wilander who also won so much as a teenager, but that was probably because I knew him a little better. Becker was a person who didn't seem to bother about friendships with the other guys. He was extremely arrogant and didn't show any inclination to mix. Before too long he obviously felt he was unequivocally qualified to make critical comments about more mature rivals. I can remember becoming extremely annoyed when he accused me of neglecting my children by taking them on the road with me. Who the hell was he to make a statement like that? I was so tempted to say something back about his gross arrogance. However, it wouldn't have been wise to have got into a war of words with him. Again I heeded my dad's advice of not stooping to that level and waging a childish catfight through the press.

Without doubt Becker was a very weird young man, but when he emerged at Wimbledon, hitting all those big serves and hurling himself into those volleys, there were a lot of jealous people and if I were to be quite honest, I would put myself extremely close to the top of that list. He monopolised the spotlight, and became a great champion at such a young age. Certainly the fame and adulation must have taken its toll on him as a person. I thought the pressure was bad enough in Australia, but what might it have been like in Germany? That sort of thing messes you up for years to come, and I still think Boris is paying the consequences. Initially he wasn't liked at all, but in the later stages of his career he settled down a little bit, becoming more comfortable with himself, and then he was a far nicer, more caring sort of person. There were even times when he could be described as just confident without being arrogant.

Nowadays he is in a really tough situation. I know he loves his children very much, but the break-up of his marriage must have been extremely difficult. I can remember we attended a big social televised event together in London, an Evening with Elton John. After the show there was the obligatory party, and I was having a wonderful time. The guest list was impressive - Sting, the Spice Girls, and so on and so forth and Boris's wife (later ex-) Barbara was enjoying herself, talking to my wife Emily and Queen's drummer Roger Taylor (who, I have to say, is a great bloke). Then all of a sudden Boris became extremely uncomfortable and insisted he wanted to leave - perhaps it was because he wasn't the centre of attention, I don't know. Barbara tried to persuade him to stay a little longer, insisting she was having fun, but Boris then barked at Barbara and she jumped to attention. They left immediately and it looked awful, but I immediately recognised the problem or to be more accurate, recognised *my* problem. When you are a tennis player, you are the most important thing: the boss, the breadwinner, the star. Everyone must revolve around you, and it didn't matter that Boris had almost retired, that was still the way things had to be.

Though I possessed the original player's entourage, with trainers, physiotherapists and psychologists looking after me, Boris used to travel around with twenty or more people at a time. They were all totally subservient to him, and if he said jump, they were expected to ask, how high? I saw fear in Barbara's eyes that night, and her dilemma really points up the fact that a special kind of woman is required to be a successful tennis wife. There are very few well balanced, top tennis players, active or retired. Boris has always been a very generous man with his money, and I would like to think I'm the same; but in many ways we are just compensating for the other things we don't give to those we try to love.

Boris is really having a hard time coming to terms with life as a player on the senior tour. It's still so important for him to win everything, and it's become a matter of pride because he is the youngest and the newest to the scene. Somebody should try to tell him that it honestly doesn't matter, because his playing record is a thing to be admired. But Boris has never really been somebody who listens to the advice of others. He collected every Grand Slam title but the French, and he won Wimbledon three times, reaching the final on another four occasions. Admittedly he has a few tax problems and paternity suits to take care of, but he is an extremely rich man. Yet still he strives to be the very best which, if you think about it, is a necessity for somebody with such arrogance: it's very hard to switch off the brain after programming it the same way for years.

At last year's Royal Albert Hall event he demanded his own locker room, and the fact that nobody else was afforded such treatment didn't seem to matter. Having played the event for several years I just went into the same room I'd always used and started getting ready. In walked Boris, asking what was I doing there, because it was his room. My immediate thought was an old, familiar one: who the hell does this guy think he is? He wasn't exactly chucking me out, but the inference was clear. I asked the officials what was going on, and they informed me Boris had requested his own locker room. I then told the long-standing tournament director John Beddington that this sort of shit didn't happen on the senior tour.

Boris was in earshot and seemed quite shocked, saying I could stay. It didn't matter; I was on my way. But within a day or so, an injury forced him to pull out of the event, and the tournament organisers, along with John McEnroe, were furious. Mac had already been let down by Boris at a big exhibition at the US Open, and he doesn't have the utmost patience. Plus he knows the senior tour needs people like Boris to take over the reins. It remains to be seen whether Boris is up for the task. I hope so. During his main career he was certainly able to capture the big prizes, and he won two Australian Open titles, which gives him another distinct edge over me.

Probably the biggest regret of my entire career was not winning that tournament in my home city. I must admit I thought I was on my way to the title in 1988 when I didn't drop a set on my way to the semi-final. After overcoming both Muster and the anti-apartheid demonstrators, I beat Aussie Carl Limberger. Next the familiar face of Paul McNamee again appeared over the net. Although I knew it was his last tournament, I wasn't going to let up on my crafty mate, and he only managed to win four games. Jonas Svensson faired only marginally better, and another rematch with Michel Schapers resulted in a fifth emphatic straight sets win.

Perhaps it had all been too easy, but a strenuous five-setter against Lendl in the semi-final really took the sting out of my game. Still, I did experience a moment that would have made any Aussie proud during that match: no more than a few hundred metres away from the new National Tennis Centre stands the hallowed Melbourne Cricket Ground, and Australia were playing a one-day international. News of me beating Lendl to reach the final was flashed up on the MCG's giant television screens, and apparently the resultant roar was louder than the fall of any wicket that day. It's amazing how little things make you smile when you remember them.

Maybe Wilander owed me one after the number of times I had

Sorry Boris, but I don't find that funny

beaten him in big tournaments, but the Swedish Koala Bear had the edge on me in the final. The wind was blowing off Port Phillip Bay that day and Mats was one set up when a squally shower sent us back to the locker room. For some reason they didn't close the new sliding roof and when we returned, I felt sufficiently fired up to win the second and third sets. When the rain returned it was much heavier and the roof was finally closed, causing a break of more than half an hour. The delay was enough to switch the momentum of the match again, and this time Mats was on top. Then in the final set I just didn't have sufficient sting in my game - I'd slowed down a fraction, and wasn't getting into the net. And although I hung in there, he finally broke my serve and finished me off 8-6 in the fifth.

Defeat was a huge disappointment, and unquestionably contributed to my refusing to make a speech at the presentations. It was not something I remember with any pride, and I was indisputably guilty of failing to show my appreciation to the crowd who were so supportive. In Australia the verb 'to barrack' means something completely different to the rest of the English-speaking world. When you barrack for somebody Down Under, you are not heckling, but supporting them big time. And those fans barracked just fine for me. Every year when I go back to the now renamed Melbourne Park I think what might have been. In the five more times I played the tournament, I never got further than the fourth round. If I could have won my home major as reigning Wimbledon champion and in the year the new National Tennis Centre was opened, I don't think I would have asked for anything more from my career. It would have been fairytale stuff.

I suppose if I had to mark the beginning of the downturn of my career, it would have been on that blustery day in Melbourne. However, five months on, I enjoyed my best French Open. I made it to the fourth round before losing to Andrei Chesnokov on a day where it drizzled so constantly that small puddles gathered on the clay. Every other player was back in the locker rooms, and conditions were so slow that Chezy repeatedly passed me with ease. Twice I requested the long-standing referee Jacques Dorfman to inspect the court, but to no avail, and he made us play on in the rain. In my opinion Jacques was spending so much time indulging his favourite pastime of looking at nude tennis players in the locker room that it had affected his eyesight. He was to retire soon afterwards - not quick enough for me. In retrospect, the only answer as to why Dorfman made us continue is that Chezy must have a better looking bum than me!

There had been considerably more cause for jubilation a month earlier when I became a father for the second time with the arrival of my beautiful daughter Mia. Unfortunately the pregnancy had added more tension to the already stressful situation of being Wimbledon champ. Anne-Britt found she was expecting on the day I played a seventeen-year-old newcomer called Andre Agassi in my first match after winning Wimbledon. I had more set points in both sets of that match at Stratton Mountain than Andre had hair on his back, and the defeat made me angry beyond belief, as I had set my sights on winning the US Open.

It wasn't to be. I lost in the first round to the Swede Peter Lundgren who in those days used to do everything possible to look like Bjorn Borg. Now, considerably heavier around the waist, he coaches the impressive young Swiss Roger Federer who has the capabilities to become a Wimbledon champion one day. The stress and strain I put on myself when I defended that honour, didn't make my return to the All England Club an enjoyable time.

My form was poor to say the least, and I lost meekly to my old

Sorry Boris, but I don't find that funny

mate Darren Cahill at Queens. The defending champion always begins proceedings on Centre Court, and I was sure that this would be a wonderful sensation; but my experience of the feeling was sadly coloured by the fact I was playing so badly. Things were soured even more by the behaviour of one particular security guard.

My psychiatrist Jeff Bond's first instruction after arriving in London was for me to actually go to Centre Court and do some visualisation for my first match against Todd Woodbridge, another seventeen-year-old who would progress to win a title or two during his career. To stand on the very turf where I had been so convincing twelve months previously would be inspirational - but as I neared the playing surface, the security guard approached. I asked if I could just feel the corner of the court, well away from the actual playing area; but I was told he would have to consult his superior.

Are you serious? I responded with a distinct air of incredulity. I am defending my title here tomorrow. I will be running, sliding, spitting and sweating all over the court. And you have to ask the boss if I can step on the far corner? And no prizes for guessing my reaction when I heard the reply over the guard's walky-talky: Under no circumstances is any player allowed to set foot on the court prior to the championships, came the decree from on high.

Although I was fourth seed, reflecting the highest ever world ranking I achieved during my career, my progress through to the quarter-final to meet Becker was a struggle. My only easy wins came against Woodbridge and John Fitzgerald, but I had little hope against Boris because my already poor form was getting worse. I couldn't return properly and my own serve was inconsistent. Could I just manage to bring everything back together and beat Boris?

No chance. Boris beat me in straight sets, and even had the cheek to play the fool. On one point I ran to a miss-hit drop volley and fell over the net. Making the most of my misfortune, he thought it would be fun to run and plunge over the net as well. He thought it was hilarious, and the crowd seemed to like the joke, but the humour was lost on me. Feeling desperate and almost without hope I resorted to some time-honoured Aussie sledging. Merv Hughes would have been proud of me as I eyeballed Boris before informing him: You're a fucking smart-arse Kraut!

The plan was that it would put him off his game. Needless to say it backfired, and I lost in straight sets. Eager for some good confrontational copy, reporters asked Boris what I had called him. He replied it was too rude to repeat, but the secret was out before too long. Photographers get to hear everything, sitting so close to court, and they must have readily passed the information on to their colleagues. Next morning the press were at my door asking me if I regretted calling Boris what I did. Of course I was in a happy, chatty mood to discuss losing my title to a 'fucking smart-arse Kraut. I said nothing, but I was impressed at the lengths the media would go to. Did I regret it? Not at the time, but I do cringe at the memory now.

Reporters were back door-stepping me several months later, but this time the setting was Anne-Britt's house in Oslo. Our relationship had gone from bad to worse, and was now in the death throws. Everything had gone wrong, the arguments had got worse, and we'd experienced a terrible time in Australia. Even my parents, who thought the world of Anne-Britt, could see we were close to the end of the road. Basically we were two feisty young people who had just had kids too early in life. Though both of us loved Daniel and Mia more than anything, the lack of freedom to live a little had destroyed our romance. Then just as we were sitting there, desperately trying to patch things up, two London-based journalists

Sorry Boris, but I don't find that funny

from Melbourne's *Herald-Sun* parked their car outside the front door.

One was a reporter, the other a photographer, and their orders were to stay put until they saw me. So effectively all four of us were trapped inside the house. The situation might have been a little better if we could have got out for a walk or something, because the atmosphere inside was terrible. I couldn't take Daniel out to play in the snow, I couldn't even stick my head out of the door. Things really blew after five days of that pressure, and we had a huge row. I couldn't take any more, and escaped from the house at the dead of night, checking myself into an airport hotel. Beforehand Ann-Britt's mother had arrived, but I told her I'd had enough, and I meant what I said. She begged me to stay, and reminded me, as if I needed telling, that I had two young children. I responded by telling her that she didn't live with her daughter, that I did, and that I couldn't stand it any more. She got the message: she knew what Anne-Britt could be like.

I have to say, of all the things I have done in life, nothing has been as tough as leaving my kids behind. Daniel was three years old, Mia barely one. Deep down I believed I would see them again, but I knew I would never live with them permanently. They were the two most beautiful, innocent children in the world, and they were being forced to suffer. Just the memory of that evening still tears me up inside, and even to this day, I get so emotional just saying goodbye to them. I see them regularly nowadays, at least once every three months, and Daniel now spends a lot of time down in Australia with me. But it's never truly been the same, and that hurts.

Chapter Ten

WHAT THE HELL HAVE YOU GIVEN TO THIS GUY?

Ever since I've been old enough and sufficiently incensed to look a line judge squarely in the eye and question his parenthood, people have drawn parallels between John McEnroe and I. To my way of thinking, that is the biggest backhanded compliment anybody can pay me. With due deference to other illustrious colleagues such as Laver, Hoad and the rest, the finest player ever to walk onto a tennis court was that curly-haired kid from New York who shouted so loud that people couldn't help but take notice of his talent. I may have been good at the game, but I wouldn't begin to put myself in the same league as Mac.

We were two of the sport's most notorious outlaws. People delighted in criticising our behaviour, calling it a total disgrace and an insult to the heritage of tennis. Many times throughout the preceding pages I've admitted there have been outbursts and actions that I now regret, and I'm sure John feels the same way about some of his tantrums. But people loved to see us play, and even those who repeatedly condemned us could never deny that; even though we are both considerably past our playing best, that still seems to be the case today.

The fact that both of us are of Irish descent might explain our fiery nature, along with a few other similarities. For instance, we both dote on our kids; we love to play music; and sometimes we go flying full speed into projects which, given a little more thought, we might have done better to avoid - the reason being, we're both men of passion who find it difficult to do anything half-heartedly. Another thing John and I have in common is, deep down, we'd have been far happier as team sportsmen than individuals - which would explain our enthusiasm to play Davis Cup for our respective countries. I was reared playing Aussie Rules Footy, and still wonder what might have happened if I'd pulled on the brown and gold of Hawthorn rather than tennis whites. John was a good soccer player as a kid, and liked to get involved in baseball, too. Once he admitted to thinking tennis was such a solitary game - he didn't like being out there on court alone. Then after reaching the Wimbledon semi-final as an eighteen-year-old qualifier, he decided he ought to at least give it a try.

John McEnroe has been a factor in my life for two decades. I've gone on the record as saying I see many facets of his personality, but don't understand many of them. In anybody who's the best at anything, it's a fine line between genius and insanity: John has always walked that line, and periodically he has gone over it. What I am saying is, there have been occasions when I've been convinced that he's stark raving mad. We have laughed at each other; we have almost come to blows. We have done things together that aren't for repeating. Nowadays we still try and go through the motions on the senior tour, and often share the same commentary box during Wimbledon for the BBC. I'd like to think we are friends - but there are still times when I question whether I know him at all.

What the hell have you given to this guy?

Facing Mac for the first time in singles is a daunting experience at any time. Just to add further spice to my earliest confrontation with him, it came on Wimbledon's Centre Court in the 1984 semi-finals. By that stage I was more than pleased with my performance during the tournament, but I was also exhausted. Quite apart from several tough matches in the singles, Paul McNamee and I had gone the five set distance in every doubles match bar one. Adding singles and doubles together, I ended up playing more games than anyone else at Wimbledon that year. Knocking up against Mac, I was immediately put off by the speed of the ball coming off his racket. He needed so little effort, and like so many of the greats, possessed something extra that nobody else had. Though I played reasonably well in the first set and got to a tiebreak, I was never in a position to really mount a serious challenge. There were no histrionics, no tantrums: he was just too damn good.

One of my worst experiences with John came shortly after I won the Wimbledon title. I'd won the contentious South African tournament in Johannesburg, and then in pursuit of dollar bills I immediately winged my way to Palm Beach's Apollo Country Club in Florida. McEnroe, Lendl, Edberg and myself were about to play the tennis equivalent of *Who Wants To Be A Millionaire?* - or, to give this type of event its more common name, a Skins game. Each of us started off with $250,000, and we played a series of first to fifteen tiebreakers. If you served an ace, you received $1,000 from the other guy, while a double fault would cost you a grand. Each time the ball went over the net it was worth $100, so if you won a ten-stroke rally you were a $1,000 better off. If you lost the point, you would be that much poorer. Frankly it was all too complicated for me to work out, and I just strode onto court intent on winning every point.

After day one, I was unbeaten and sitting on something like $600,000, with Lendl second in the money list, Edberg third and Mac a long way last. Next day, completely the opposite happened, and I lost against all three. When it came to playing Mac he was still some way behind and seriously out for revenge. He'd been in an incredibly grumpy mood anyway, but then he always is when things aren't going his way. So no one could have been truly surprised when right in the middle of the tiebreaker, he went absolutely nuts. First a bad call ignited his temper; then he missed a relatively easy shot.

Swinging round, he let fly with enormous pace and swiped a ball straight at the offending line judge. It went so fast the official didn't move, and it must have missed the man's head by no more than half an inch. If it had connected it would have broken the guy's nose for certain, or possibly even blinded him. Everybody around the court was seriously shocked - spectators, officials, and even me, standing on the other side of the net. Frankly I lost my taste for the contest after that, and Mac ended up beating me by something like 15-10. Walking up to the net afterwards, I went to shake his hand but told him in no uncertain terms what an idiot he'd been. He didn't say anything, and just stormed off. Maybe I shouldn't have said what I did, but even to me, who had called numerous line judges a whole variety of names over the years, his behaviour was totally unwarranted.

Having watched John play on the Senior Tour for several years, I've come to the conclusion that he just can't help himself. I, of all people, am not one to point the finger, and this is just an observation. But I'm sure he doesn't mean to do some of the things he does, and is subsequently embarrassed by his actions. He just doesn't possess sufficient self-control. We've all heard his jovial

What the hell have you given to this guy?

claim that he's contractually obligated to lose his temper twice every match because that is what the crowd pays to see. Well, I'm sorry, but that's just an excuse, and Mac would start a fight with anybody in order to win a tennis match. I'm convinced he would even do it with his own mother. He doesn't do it for show. He does it because he works himself into such a rage that he's completely out of control. His will to win is just incredible even now, years after quitting the main tour. Mac's the player on the Senior Tour who needs to win more than any other, and with that sort of overwhelming desire, he does so frequently.

Tennis history has it that there have been players who have physically got hold of Mac in the locker room after a match. Steve Denton was one, Brad Gilbert another. I didn't witness these incidents, I only heard the rumours. However, it would be truly amazing if nobody ever resorted to physical violence with the guy; he may have been a supreme player, but he was also a verbal bully who'd test the patience of anybody.

Thinking back to that Skins tournament, I ended up playing Lendl in the final. It turned out that the event had been organised by Proserv, who just happened to be his management company. I'm not saying they could influence the weather, but it seemed to me the overriding aim was to win their man a million bucks. The court was a Supreme surface laid on clay, and because it had been raining, the balls had become soft and everything was just so slow. In addition we played the final at night, so it was cold, and by the end all the money I'd won was gone; in fact I owed Lendl something like $200,000. As we walked off court he stared at me with those unforgiving dark eyes and made the evening far worse. I must buy you dinner some time, said Mr Shoebreaker, giving an invitation I'd have loved to refuse. Therefore, should I be surprised he never kept to his word?

Another bad run-in with McEnroe came quite recently in a Senior Tour event at California's Newport Beach. I'd beaten him three times in succession, so patently he was intent on retribution. If I was being brutally honest with myself, the last thing I wanted to do was seriously antagonise Mac to the extent he wanted to retire, because I know it's him that keeps the tour alive, and you don't cut off the hand that feeds you. Walking onto court I can even remember thinking that I hoped he'd beat me. I'd convinced myself the important thing was just having a bit of fun and producing some good points. After all, we were on our set fees so I wouldn't earn any more money by winning.

Naturally all those thoughts disappeared when we actually started playing. In fact, Mac regularly manages to annoy me, just in the way he walks out onto the court. I've tried to laugh at him when he strides out there with his hands held high as if he had just won a war, because deep down it really pisses me off because he's attempting a little one-upmanship against somebody he calls a friend. He is trying to show he's the king of the castle, and that's a feeling he loves. Disrespect is another word for it, or am I being overly sensitive? In the match that day, I went a break of serve to the good, and Mac was complaining about every second call - the ball would be a clear six inches out and he'd still have a bitch. Clearly the umpire was petrified of taking any action because he didn't say a word, although Mac was clearly stalling at every opportunity. Then I got another break point and he hit a volley that was so long it was laughable. No call ensued, so I took issue with the umpire, which in turn started the crowd booing. Somewhat forcibly I asked the guy in the chair: If I yell and complain like he does, will you overrule?

What the hell have you given to this guy?

At this, Mac started having a real go back at me, which I thought was totally unwarranted. I was really taken aback, but realised it was important just to bite my tongue. I sat down and tried to rationalise the whole thing, telling myself if he wants to ruin a friendship over something as trivial as this sort of tennis match, then fine, but I'm not willing to play along with the act. It took all the strength I possessed over my emotions to avoid getting into a fight with Mac, and though he ended up winning the match, I could see he wasn't thrilled. There were no words afterwards, just a handshake. Then again he's never apologetic. You can see his feelings by looking into his eyes, and on that day the disappointment he felt over his actions was so evident. There are times he just cannot help it, and I suppose there have been many instances when I've experienced the same sort of thing.

John McEnroe can fall out with anybody, regardless of the respect and affection he might hold for that person. Not too long ago, he was hardly on friendly terms with his younger brother Patrick - a nicer, better mannered guy you'd be unlikely to meet. But here's the bottom line: Mac isn't exactly a fun person to be around when he's got a racket in his hand anywhere near a tennis court. Away from that pressured environment, he can be both hilarious and affable company.

Our mutual love of rock music has pushed us closer together over the years. Both Mac and I were both very much in awe of the way Vitas Gerulaitis would mix with people we had regarded as legends. Then gradually we began moving in those circles ourselves, and the Hard Rock Cafe jams before Wimbledon were the result. We loved to get up and play, and it seemed rock stars enjoyed coming along to watch. On the first night Keith Richards turned up at Mats Wilander's invitation. Pink Floyd's Roger Waters arrived too, and subsequently we had guests such as Ian Gillan from Deep Purple, Bernie Marsden of Whitesnake and the Allman Brothers. Living in London, I had a group of musical mates such as Bill Barclay and the guys from Iron Maiden, who could form the core of a band with the likes of Vitas, Mac, Mats and myself. Todd Witsken played drums, as did Jim Courier, and Carlos Kirmyr was also very talented.

For a couple of years those evenings were so much fun, but unfortunately they started getting bigger and bigger, and then the ATP tried to get in on the act by revving up the publicity. Eventually the tennis players didn't enjoy themselves any more, because as soon as they walked through the door there was a bank of photographers. Bob Green, a former player who then worked for the ATP, took the whole thing over. He fixed up interviews for us during the evening, which weren't part of the original idea at all. We intended the nights as a little private fun, and once Green took control everything became far too public and the jams sadly died.

However, they did spawn something else. I'd long been a huge fan of Deep Purple, and an all-star cast had just re-recorded their classic Smoke On The Water as a special track to raise money for the Armenian Earthquake Appeal. The band's singer Ian Gillan and I hit it off at one of the Hard Rock Cafe gigs, and he in turn introduced me to John Dee, who had produced that remake. We swapped telephone numbers, and not long after, John Dee rang me up to say the Armenian people still needed a lot of help and another record would be a good idea: could John McEnroe and I possibly do something to contribute to this? It sounded great to me, and so was born Full Metal Jacket. Putting together a band, I pulled in a couple of favours from Steve Harris and Nicko McBrain from Iron Maiden, as well as a guitarist mate called Andy Barnett. He was a session musician who played for bands as diverse as FM and Steve Strange's Visage. More importantly, he knew Roger Daltrey of The Who.

Anyone who knows anything about modern music has to acknowledge that Daltrey possesses one of the greatest voices of all time. Before I knew it, he was singing his lungs out for us on a remake of the old Led Zeppelin number Rock N'Roll. I distinctly remember walking into the recording studios, and Daltrey was already rehearsing. Initially I thought somebody was playing a tape over the sound system. Walking through three supposedly soundproof doors, his voice grew louder and louder. It was phenomenal, and Roger himself was having the time of his life, insisting that Led Zepp's Robert Plant based his vocal on Rock N'Roll from a Who track on the album Live At Leeds. I think he's right, too.

As is often the case, everybody recorded their various parts at different times, and I was the only common link on the promotional video. McEnroe's busy schedule meant he could only be in London for about half a day, so I sent him a load of tapes with which to rehearse in New York. Mac telephoned back, in normal style, insisting he already knew Rock N'Roll off by heart as it was one of his all-time favourites.He'd been listening to it for years and wouldn't have a problem playing his guitar part. Yet when he arrived he had absolutely no idea.

From time to time around the world, Mac and I used to smoke the occasional joint together when it didn't interfere with our playing commitments. So when he arrived after the flight from New York I already had one rolled, thinking it would relax him for the recording. Time was pretty tight, so before too long the producer John Dee asked everybody else to leave the studio because they were distracting Mac and it was imperative he recorded his contribution. Andy Barnett and I had been recording all afternoon so we headed off do dinner, thinking Mac would get down to work. But a couple of hours later we telephoned for an update and received a shock: What the hell have you given to this guy McEnroe? was the anguished enquiry.

Apparently Mac couldn't manage to play a single note in tune, though John Dee said he'd be patient and wait for things to calm down a little. But when we phoned back a little while later, things sounded considerably more fraught. Now Mac was trying to play the drums, and was insistent he could do the vocals at least as well as Roger Daltrey. Though Mac can play in tune, anyone who's heard him sing with his group the Johnny Smythe Band would be bound to react with that time-honoured phrase: 'You cannot be serious!'

Mac was like a kid in a sweet shop, and John Dee was getting increasingly concerned because our reserved studio time was rapidly running out. Eventually an SOS was sent out to Andy Barnett and I. My job was to take Mac away, and it didn't matter where; so we went to a nightclub, and hours after smoking the joint he was still really stoned. Andy was deputised to record the part Mac was supposed to play, but there was a problem: the only guitar left in the studio was Mac's left-handed model, and Andy was right-handed.

Now bordering on the frantic, poor John Dee insisted there was one part Mac had managed to record which was tolerable, except for a horrendous bum note right at the end. Andy, playing left-handed, managed to dub over the final note and somehow managed to complete it with a beautiful harmonic sound that smacked of sheer professionalism. Every time the track got played afterwards,

What the hell have you given to this guy?

I always used to compliment Mac on the wonderful last note; and without fail he always nodded his head in a modest but incredibly proud manner as if to say, 'Ah, it was nothing!'. To this day, Mac doesn't know that somebody else had to play it for him because he was so far out of his head.

The Full Metal Jacket record sowed the seeds for my own charity project, Planet Arc. John Dee and I discussed what I could do to help the environmental issues in Australia, and we decided to copy a concept started in England by Paul and Linda McCartney that involved other celebrities. Well known Australians such as Jimmy Barnes and Tommy Emmanuel stepped up to help, as well as the actresses Rachel Ward and Jenny Morris. More recently Kylie Minogue, Nicole Kidman and Pierce Brosnan have done their bit, with Planet Ark continuing to grow.

One other, less savoury memory from that period centres around the infamous British publicist Max Clifford. At the time of Full Metal Jacket he was handling my public relations and got me to do all kinds of crazy things, as Max does. An Australian female journalist had been pressing me for an interview and she rang while Max and I were in a car driving somewhere. He answered the call, lying that I was busy in a recording studio with Mick Jagger and David Bowie.

Clearly the journalist was impressed, and Max realised he could have a little fun. So he began to embellish the story, saying George Formby, who must have been dead for years, was also involved. No suspicion was apparent on the other end of the phone line, so Max decided to really go over the top. He told her the name of the band was Ginger Minge. The whole thing was very hairy, and opening up all the time.

I was cracking up in the back seat when Max ended the phone

conversation, promising he'd try to get me to call her back. To this day we've never had that conversation, and I can only imagine her writing the article and submitting it to her editor. I'm told she's now the sports editor of a leading Australian newspaper that decided to dispense with my regular column. I'd have to say I'm not really surprised, but would just like to point out the conversation she had was with Max Clifford, and in no way instigated by me.

Getting back to John McEnroe, he and I are now able to talk about most things. However, I do feel somewhat uncomfortable writing about these private times, and there are stories we've shared that I'd never divulge; as a friend he should be able to talk to me without the contents making the bookstores. He's told me how Donald Trump is pledging him $1 million if he plays Venus Williams at the billionaire's Atlantic City hotel and casino - but that's common knowledge. On a more serious note, he used to confide in me about the problems he had in striking any kind of common ground with his former father-in-law Ryan O'Neal. Nowadays his ex-wife Tatum is a subject that never gets a mention, although he sees a lot of his sons Sean and Kevin from that ill-fated marriage, and I know that means a lot to him. Despite all his tempestuous ways, he never appears anything other than a picture of marital bliss with his second wife Patty, and when she comes on the road from time to time, we hardly see a glimpse of Mac away from the courts.

Patty used to front a band called Scandal who had a hit record called 'The Warrior' back in the 1980s, and I think Mac felt very comfortable in rock music circles after all the problems he had with the acting fraternity. He's hung out with a number of well known guitarists such as Eddie Van Halen and Mick Jones of Foreigner, and has got to know his real childhood idols, the Rolling Stones, extremely well. I also consider Ronnie Wood and Keith Richards as good mates, and they were involved in another comical episode involving Mac at Wimbledon. Ronnie likes to come and watch a bit of tennis each year on my tickets, occasionally in the company of the snooker player Jimmy White; they might watch a set or two, and then they generally head for the bar. Back in 1999, the year Mac teamed up with Steffi Graf in the mixed doubles, Keith decided to make the trip as well.

For a while it looked as though Mac was on his way to another Wimbledon title at the age of forty. Then Steffi, who'd just won the French Open title amidst those stormy scenes that saw Martina Hingis climb the umpires chair at Roland Garros, decided to pull out of the mixed at the semi-final stage. She claimed she was safeguarding a leg injury, and wanted to concentrate on the singles - which did indeed turn out to be her last major final, although she lost to Lindsay Davenport. Most people understood her reasoning, but not Mac: he was absolutely livid, and when I saw him in the locker rooms, smoke was literally funnelling out of his ears.

Deciding he needed a little cheering up, I came up with an idea: the car hire company Hertz had a corporate hospitality area next to the new Number One court, and they used to slip me some money if I would go in there late in the afternoons and sign a few autographs. They were even happier if I took a few celebrity guests with me. The actor Hugh Grant, who lives near me in Fulham, accompanied me one day with his mother. On this particular occasion I arranged for Ronnie Wood, Keith Richard and the champion snooker player, Ronnie O'Sullivan, to stop by. Thinking it was just the right sort of convivial atmosphere to quell even the fiercest of tempers, I telephoned Mac to join us.

Though Ronnie had been warned off the booze, he and Keith

were drinking at quite a pace. In addition one or other of them seemed to disappear discreetly to the toilets every five minutes, and re-emerge considerably more animated than when they went in. Far be if from me to suggest what they were doing in there, but I think we can all speculate.When Mac arrived, he was clearly still very angry and I can remember the two Rolling Stones saying: We'll have a bit of fun here.

Years earlier at a junior tournament in Melbourne I had kept the boys entertained on my walkman cassette player by playing Derek and Clive tapes recorded by Peter Cook and Dudley Moore. I appreciate they were not to everyone's taste, with more obscenities per sentence than acceptable words. However, I used to think they were hilarious. In their deep, nicotine-stained voices, Ronnie and Keith adopted a similar style to try and lighten up Mac. They didn't exactly ask him what was the worst job he ever had, but they gave him the full benefit of their views on the German race. Mac, born in Weisbaden it has to be added, was soon nodding his head in agreement. Then they started on the frailties of women tennis players, before moving on to fathers being found guilty of tax evasion. All the time they were winking at me, while Mac's newly ignited loathing of the future Mrs Agassi grew increasingly more intense.

Mac just sat there, head now in his hands. He was swearing and cursing with even more regularity than Ronnie or Keith, repeatedly stressing that he was going to win that mixed doubles title. I had to do everything I possibly could to restrain myself from bursting into uncontrolled fits of laughter, and looking across at Ronnie O'Sullivan I could see he was suffering exactly the same predicament. It was an episode to remember, and proved one thing: Steffi Graf may be an extremely nice lady, and one of the all-time

What the hell have you given to this guy?

great female tennis players, but Johnny Mac doesn't like being denied a Wimbledon title when he thinks his name is already on the trophy.

Though I had my differences with Mac, and firmly believe he can be one of the world's most disagreeable human beings on a tennis court, he is still preferable every time to any player guilty of blatant cheating. The three players whom I found it all but impossible to respect in the course of my playing career were Thomas Muster, whose honesty I really could not believe in; Horst Skoff; and Alex Antonitsch, in that order - and I wasn't alone in my assessment.

Skoff was universally disliked; even his two fellow countrymen refused to play Davis Cup with him on the team. He was arrogant and badly behaved on court - there were times when he'd just stand and laugh at his opponent, almost goading him into committing some kind of code violation. Everybody knew how to play Skoff because we'd all readily give tips to rivals on how to beat him. Antonitsch was also extremely arrogant, and not averse to bending the rules.

In my opinion, Musters attitude was all but intolerable. He was just as bad as McEnroe for intimidating officials, and would quite blatantly cheat in the course of a match. He tried to rip me off during one of my comebacks at the tournament in Dubai, but I wasn't going to take any of his antics and walked straight up to the net, telling him in no uncertain terms that any further cheating would result in him having his head severely punched the moment we got back to the locker room. Muster didn't say a word - and neither, to my total surprise, did the umpire. I was convinced I'd get at least a warning, but for once it seemed the official took my side, because he definitely heard every word I said.

Most years Muster used to avoid the grass court season at all costs. Then on one occasion he came to play at Queen's, which might just have had something to do with a friendship he was having with an extremely high profile english woman. A visit that was most notable for the names he called Mark Woodforde out on court. Although I have enormous respect for Woodforde's achievements on the doubles court, I was never any great friend of his - but nobody should be taunted with words like faggot from their opponent when they are trying to play a tennis match. Things like that were part and parcel of Muster's game. Sarah Ferguson was nice enough and I don't know what she saw in him.

One of my unhappiest Davis Cup memories dates back to 1989 when we had to play Austria in the first round. The tie was staged indoors on clay in Vienna just a few days after the Australian Open, and I wasn't in a particularly good mood, having been annihilated 6-4, 6-0, 6-2 by Edberg in only the fourth round. In addition Anne-Britt and I were just about to split up, and I had got myself into even more trouble with my post-match comments. Originally I had intended to miss out on the press conference and take the fine that automatically follows a no-show, but for some reason changed my mind at the last minute. Even so, I wasn't feeling very communicative, and when inevitably somebody asked me what was wrong, I came out with the reply: Oh it's nothing, I've just got my period.

There's no question, I should really have known better after all my past experiences; but not surprisingly, the shit really hit the fan, in big style. Television history was made as they continuously replayed the film clip on every possible news bulletin; women's groups were up in arms, and they dug up all my previous indiscretions: how many times I had sworn, how many times I had been offensive - everything was thrown at me, except the kitchen sink.

I couldn't get out of Australia quick enough, but of all the places to go to, it had to be Austria and a confrontation with my good pals Muster and Skoff. I don't recall ever playing on a court so slow: the under-surface seemed to be a kind of cricket matting with the red clay laid on top, and after a while the clay would get swept away, just leaving the matting that would cause the balls to stop. The lights were so poor it was impossible to pick up any passing shots, so my volleys were cut right down to size. Prior to the draw I asked Neale Fraser not to pick me because I'd no confidence, but Mark Kratzmann and Darren Cahill had been delayed playing doubles in the Australian Open.

Killer should really have played, but he was still jet-lagged, so Skoff chopped me in the opening rubber. Then John Fitzgerald and I lost the doubles in five sets to Muster and Antonitsch, giving the Austrians an unassailable 3-0 lead. To round off the most horrendous of ties, Muster beat me 6-2, 6-0 in the dead rubber. Frase was so upset by the conditions he campaigned for a court standard and light regulations rule to be introduced the following year.

There had to be some form of consolation, and it came in spectacular form. Killer and I had always wanted to play doubles together and the opportunity came that night when we had some fun with a Viennese racket stringer who possessed the world's biggest breasts. The volume was turned up to full on the stereo and the other guys were hammering on the door, desperate to join the party. But we wouldn't let them in - not that we were doing anything, of course.

For some reason Wally Masur wasn't in the team that weekend, but he'd been in Mexico City a year earlier for our first round tie, and became the innocent victim of an episode he will never forget. (Where Skoff and Muster are eminently unpleasant, Wally is unquestionably one of the great guys. He's good and honest, and although he once said he'd never have children because he's too selfish, I'm glad to say he's got four now, and by all accounts still breeding.)

The Mexican tie was staged at quite a plush country club, and though we were playing on clay, our least favoured surface, the altitude favoured our quick serve-and-volley style. Though the surroundings were extremely pleasant, there was quite a long walk from the court to the clubhouse, and the route wound around a swimming pool. I managed to win the tie in a fifth rubber against Francisco Maciel, but Wally didn't have a good time, losing both his singles matches. After the second of those encounters, he wasn't in the happiest frame of mind as he made his way past the swimming pool. At this point a boy dashed up to a somewhat surprised Wally, asking for an autograph. Purely by accident, Wally bumped into the boy and just caught him off balance, sending him tumbling into the swimming pool; but there didn't seem to be any harm done, as the kid was laughing and even pulled his mate in for a wrestle.

Midway through my match that followed, Wally was confronted by all kinds of dramas in the locker room. It appeared that the boy who fell in the pool was the son of the country club's president. Somebody, seeing the image of big dollar signs before their eyes, persuaded the kid to put his arm in a sling; then the police were informed, and Wally was going to be arrested for attempted murder, no less. Suffice to say, the Tennis Australia president Brian Tobin hadn't even turned up. Fortunately a member of the Australian Consulate was on hand to defuse what might have been a

What the hell have you given to this guy?

particularly difficult international incident. When I arrived victorious back in the locker room after dodging the cans and coins being thrown at me, I was confronted by a very relieved but still tearful Tennis Australia official Tony Ryan. Come on mate, it's no big deal. The match wasn't even close! was my immediate reaction, until I was told the full story of Wallys experience.

Wally, a former team-mate so many years before in Ian Barclay's little squad, was one of a trio of my regular doubles partners (the others of course being John Fitzgerald and Paul McNamee). Over the years I played with various other partners, such as Patrick Rafter and even Tim Henman and one partnership I shall never forget was when I teamed up, just once, with John McEnroe.

It was in April 1989, my personal life was a mess after the break-up with Anne-Britt, I'd rotted my stomach by drinking too many Flaming Zamboucas, and I desperately needed a break from tennis. Nevertheless the financial guarantee was a nice big round number, so I headed off to play the tournament in Tokyo. In the first round Mac and I played two Japanese guys, and frankly it was no contest. We were leading 6-0, 4-0and then Mac walked up to me and said we must let the Japanese win a game. He insisted he was superstitious that whenever he won love and love, he suffered a bad loss in the next round. I argued the other way, saying if I didn't try and win every game, there could be bad consequences.

It should be no surprise to learn it was Mac who got his way as he threw the next game, and we eventually ended up comfortable 6-0, 6-2 winners. No problem, you might say: but the very next morning, when leading comfortably in my singles match against Bill Scanlon, I pushed off a bit hard to get into the net on my second serve, and felt a sharp pain in my leg. I fell to the ground, thinking I had hit the back of my leg with my racket, and my immediate reaction was, How the hell did I manage that?; but within a second or two I realised the problem was infinitely more serious.

I'd been suffering the occasional Achilles tendon problem for some time by then, and the physiotherapists always said that when the thing snapped, I'd really know about it. I lay on court almost motionless for several moments as an Aussie trainer called Rob Hannon confirmed my injury; for some reason Pam Shriver also came out on court to console me. Strangely I didn't feel excruciating pain, but the specialists told me I should undergo immediate surgery and that the surgeons in Tokyo were exceptionally good.

Meaning no offence, I informed them they had to be joking, and demanded to be put on the first available flight to Melbourne. My dad met me at Tullamarine Airport. He was anxious on two counts: naturally he was concerned about the ruptured Achilles tendon, but he was also mindful that tax restrictions meant I could only spend six months of every year in Australia, and I was nearing my limit. Consulting his diary, he told me I had twelve days to have the operation and recuperate. With two days to spare I had the stitches removed, a new plaster placed on the ankle, and was wheeled onto a flight for London.

I was still only twenty-three years old, but my life was just about to take another huge change. However, if I am being brutally honest with myself, I was never the same tennis player ever again after tearing the Achilles. Many's the time I wonder what would have happened if Johnny Mac *hadn't* let those Japanese guys win that game.

Chapter Eleven

Love on one leg in the Limelight

Life, as we all know, has its ups and downs. And let me tell you, the bad times were just as desolate for somebody who'd won Wimbledon less than two years previously, as they can be for anyone else. The Pat Cash who hobbled back into a decidedly quiet and empty Fulham house on crutches after the twenty-four-hour long flight back from Australia was wondering what else could go wrong. I had split up with my girlfriend and had no idea when I would see my children again; my playing career seemed to be lying in tatters, with my ankle encased in a plaster cast; and most painfully, I was alone.

Thankfully I soon had company in the shape of Mark Bertalli, an old Melbourne mate who felt the need to put 12,000 miles between him and some problems at home. So the two of us just sat there drinking beers in front of the television for days. Anyone who thinks that globetrotting tennis stars have a glamorous life should picture that scenario and make an immediate reassessment.

With boredom threatening to add insanity to my list of problems, Mark and I decided it was time to break out. So I picked up my

209

crutches, called a taxi, and we headed for the bright lights of London's West End - or, to be more precise, the Wag Club. The men on the door were very welcoming, insisting it promised a great night, and that we were guaranteed to have a good time. Perhaps it should not have really surprised us to find the place totally dead, with no more than four people inside. Realising we'd been duped, and feeling considerably more downcast than when we went in, the two of us left after just one drink. The doormen were extremely apologetic, maintaining they were only doing their job by luring customers into the establishment under false pretences. But they tried to make amends by advising us to try the Limelight Club the following night.

At that stage I was a relative stranger to the London nightclub scene, but surprisingly somebody recognised me when Mark and I arrived at the doors of the converted old church in Shaftsbury Avenue, and we were directed up the stairs to the VIP Lounge. There to greet us was a beautiful woman called Emily Bendit-Davis. You know the saying about every cloud having a silver lining: well, at that precise moment I realised it couldn't have been more true. It was love at first sight. As Emily went to get our drinks, the first thing I said to Mark was, 'I'm going to marry that girl'. And little more than a year later, I was as good as my word.

I'm sure it was an evening decreed by fate - there was even a fellow Hawthorn supporter working behind the bar called Jane Southwell, who has become a great friend. In no time I was totally immersed in conversation with Emily, and it was hard to believe the number of coincidences between her life and mine. We liked the same music and the same movies; she came from Houston where I had spent quite a bit of time; she had just split up from her husband, and I had recently parted from Anne-Britt.

210

Love on one leg in the Limelight

A couple of days later I had stopped at some traffic lights while driving down the Fulham Palace Road, and she crossed the street in front of me. It turned out she lived just a few streets away from me - and romance was off and running. We wanted to see each other all the time, which was just fine by me, because tennis was firmly on the back burner with my leg still in plaster. Suddenly life was fun again, and I was having the time of my life with Emily. Her ex-husband worked in the music business, tour-managing rock bands such as Bon Jovi and the Scorpions, so she had connections and we used to go legging around town in the company of rock stars. It was a constant stream of nightclubs, concerts and parties, and I loved every moment.

Because I was so infatuated by Emily and entranced by the London scene, something else happened around that time: I started to experiment with drugs. All the pressures I had experienced from my tennis career seemed comfortably stored away in boxes for a while, and coming into regular contact with people taking cocaine made me increasingly curious. I had been smoking the occasional joint since I was a teenager, and can even remember baking marijuana cookies with Mark 'Piggy' Zuker, the son of my physio David. As far as I was concerned, that was just a little harmless fun, and in fact I remain firmly convinced - though I have now long since turned my back on any form of drugs - that marijuana is considerably better for you than booze. Those cookies were just little treats for the girlfriends, and never once did we imagine they would get into anything heavier.

Cocaine, however - or coke, charlie, snow or whatever you want to call it - was different altogether, and very much the 'in' thing in this particular social circle. There was no danger of me being drugs-tested at a tournament because I had no idea when I would be able to play again; and I had no intention of it becoming an addiction, because I had seen what that had done to somebody I admired, namely Vitas Gerulaitis. Still, I remained intrigued by the stuff, and as Emily was given some coke from time to time, I decided to try the occasional line. Initially it scared me, probably because I knew that what I was doing was wrong for an international sportsman, but I trusted the people around me. They understood cocaine and what it does for you, and I have to admit I enjoyed the experience.

Ecstasy was another drug that became incredibly fashionable around the clubs at the time, though I have to say I just couldn't stand the music that went with that scene. Besides, since then I have been horrified by some of the tragic stories about youngsters dying after taking an 'E'. Back then, I just thought the stuff gave me an amazing buzz; I suppose it was a subconscious reaction after being totally consumed by tennis for so long. I had seen my obsession with looking after my body destroy so many other things - and for what reason? I was now hobbling around in a plaster cast. There was nothing as depressing as being injured, but now I had the opportunity to break out of my shackles for a while. I was having fun after all the terrible rows with Anne-Britt; basically I was just saying 'let's live a little'.

I have since come to realise that the whole drug thing is another world, a complete fantasy existence. It's escapism, in much the same way that a regular man would go into the pub and have a few pints with his mates. It's an opportunity to temporarily get away from the problems with the wife or work. Did I ever worry about what I was getting into? Initially I'd have to say the answer was yes, but I was so in love with Emily. Gradually I became more relaxed about the whole thing, and realised the human body is very strong. Look at the amount of drugs people can take and still be

Love on one leg in the Limelight

alive; take Keith Richards of the Rolling Stones, for example. I was never going to be that serious - I was only messing around, and sampling this and that.

Sooner or later I realised I would have to get back to some physical work, but I tried not to think about it too much because life with Emily was far too enjoyable. Deep down I knew I was still a tennis player and I was still determined to play, but I'd found a temporary release, which I intended to exploit. But six or seven solid months of partying really did affect my fitness, and I put on weight because I was drinking quite a bit as well. Obviously I couldn't do any running, so the only exercise possible was upper body work in the gym, which made me really big, or swimming, which I hate.

I'd only been out of plaster for a couple of weeks when I put any chance of a comeback into real jeopardy. The Stella Artois tournament, held at Queen's Club in June, is the traditional curtain raiser to Wimbledon, and though I obviously wasn't competing, I got some tickets for the Deep Purple vocalist Ian Gillan. On that particular morning I was having my hair cut in the West End, near Green Park station. I thought I would have plenty of time to get back to Baron's Court; after all, it's only a matter of a few stops on the Piccadilly Line. Unfortunately there was a tube strike, so that particular mode of transport was out of the question, and the traffic was grid-locked. After half an hour I gave up any hope of hailing a taxi or jumping on a bus, and so there was only one option left to me: I couldn't leave a rock god like Ian Gillan waiting at the gates of Queen's, so I started walking.

Some would call the route down Piccadilly to the pedestrian underpasses at Hyde Park Corner, past the Royal Albert Hall and through Knightsbridge and Kensington High Street to Baron's

Court a pleasant stroll, particularly on a warm June day. With an extremely tender ankle and a recuperating Achilles tendon, I would categorise it as torture. I managed to get the tickets to Ian in time, but at some cost: I developed a limp from an improper walking pattern, which I still have to this day.

Eventually I felt obliged to start preparing for a return to my tennis career. Obviously I was still in touch with Ann Quinn, but she was involved in other things in Australia because, even if I had been totally engrossed in my recovery, inevitably it would still take time. Jenny Brown, one of the British Olympic team's top physiotherapists, did a terrific job, and three times a week I visited St George's Hospital in Tooting. In fact I actually made medical history because it is virtually impossible to stretch out a re-sewn Achilles tendon; whether I possessed unnatural flexibility I don't know, but I managed to do it.

I started my comeback gradually, and got back on court in doubles at the beginning of the year, actually winning the title in Sydney with Mark Kratzmann and getting to the Australian Open quarter-finals alongside Stefan Edberg. But singles were far more demanding and require a far greater level of fitness. Finally, just three weeks short of a year after snapping my Achilles tendon on that court in Tokyo, I pencilled in my return at the extremely lucrative Lipton Championships, staged in the beautiful setting of Key Biscayne nestling in the bay off the South Floridian coast. There are few more picturesque places in the world for a tennis tournament. Pelicans swoop into the sea in search of fish just yards from where players crash in the aces and scurry around on the baseline. However, I was in no mood to appreciate the spectacular sunsets over the skyline of Miami: I was far too petrified my career would be halted for good almost as soon as it had managed to get started again. All my months of partying came back to haunt me with horrific effect, because I was drug-tested.

One of the first things I promised to myself when I started experimenting with cocaine was that I wouldn't let it interfere with my tennis. I always believed I had it under control, and never went on anything vaguely approaching a binge. It was just the occasional line here and there, but nothing too regular or serious. In the weeks leading up to the Lipton I didn't really feel fit enough to justify a comeback, and honestly didn't expect to go very far in the tournament. However, I was awarded a wild card and the money on offer was too good to refuse.

Then a fortnight before the tournament began I ran into a well known player who shall remain nameless. He was in possession of some cocaine and felt in a very generous mood, and because my expectations in the forthcoming tournament amounted to not very much at all, I decided to accept his offer of friendship and snort a line or two. Unfortunately the number of lines amounted to rather more than just a couple, and I took considerably more of the drug than I had ever experienced before.

Not surprisingly I lost my opening match in straight sets; and when I was informed I'd been selected for a random drugs test, I was thrown into absolute panic. I had no idea how long cocaine remained traceable in the body, and wasn't even really sure how much I'd taken. But I was convinced the results were going to be positive, and I didn't know what to do, or in whom to confide. I agonised about the consequences. My sponsorship deals had become a little tenuous anyway because of my long injury lay-off, so it would certainly mean the end of those, which involved a considerable amount of money. Then I realised, just who am I kidding here? Never mind the end of my sponsorship deals: this could be the end of my whole career. I was terrified.

Finally I completely freaked out and told Ian Barclay; he seemed to be the only person I could talk to. Though convinced I was about to go down, I didn't dare tell my father. Informing him Anne-Britt was pregnant was a stressful enough experience, but this was a million times worse. I knew he would go absolutely ballistic, and in the event I wasn't far wrong: when Barkers told him, he has apparently never been closer to cardiac arrest. I know my dad didn't understand, because quite frankly I didn't understand myself. So it got you high? It gave you a good time and produced an enjoyable experience? But what is the point of putting at grave risk, something you've worked so hard for since childhood?It was absolutely ridiculous.

Mercifully for me, the test proved negative. Subsequently I found out that cocaine remains in your system for around five days, and I was well clear. Several years later both Mats Wilander and Karol Novacek tested positive, but let's examine the issues. In my opinion the use of performance-enhancing drugs such as steroids should be the prime concern of the drug testers, because that is cheating, whereas someone abusing their body by taking recreational drugs isn't going to worry the other players.

What I do know is that I was taught a lesson I never forgot, and from that day forth I never 'did' any drugs remotely near to a tennis event or to a training period. Admittedly I continued to use cocaine recreationally for several years, but only when I was injured or out of a tournament. Years later I realise that drug abuse is a disease, and one that needs to be treated.

Breathing an enormous sigh of relief, I continued on the comeback trail, and next headed for the far-from-glamorous surroundings of Seoul in Korea. I must admit I'd fostered regrets

Love on one leg in the Limelight

about not travelling there to represent Australia in the Olympics back in 1988. Although I was having some initial problems with my Achilles at the time, I believe I could have ended up with a medal, and it could quite easily have been gold. Paul McNamee eventually convinced me not to go, but I didn't need much persuasion after playing in the exhibition event at the 1984 Los Angeles games. I loved being at the Olympics because it was great to watch the track and field events; but sadly the tennis was a total shambles by comparison. Though things had improved considerably sixteen years later when the Olympic flame was lit in Sydney, the tennis event still remained just another tournament for most of the competitors. Perhaps something will be changed in the format for the next generation to feel differently.

By the time I flew out to Korea, Emily and I were engaged. I had proposed on Valentine's Day, which sounds all romantic but wasn't intentional. In retrospect I should have chosen somewhere considerably more attractive to introduce her to the world tennis tour. And to anyone who has never been to Seoul, take a tip from me: don't bother. Though I arrived with a world ranking of 634, I thought the comeback of a former Wimbledon champion might justify a wild card into the main draw. How wrong I proved to be.

The Koreans wouldn't give out wild cards to anyone other than their own youngsters, so I was forced to play qualifying. My overwhelming recollection was one of being insulted, and my mood was not helped by the standard of the hotel: if it merited two stars then it was overrated, and as everyone in Korea seems to smoke at least sixty cigarettes a day, the room stank. Fearing for my lungs, I headed off to practise - and ran into another old Melbourne mate, Rohan Goetzke, who was coaching a young Dutch teenager called Richard Krajicek.

Uncovered

My self-esteem at the time was pretty low, but Rohan gave me a boost by saying this gangly eighteen-year-old, who had a serve so fast it sometimes flashed past almost invisibly, had modelled his game on mine. Apparently young Krajicek was determined to be a serve-and-volley player, and was honoured to actually hit some balls with me. Not long afterwards he made his breakthrough, and slightly more than six years later became Wimbledon champion.

Back at Hotel Ashtray, Emily was having problems. She tried to use the gymnasium, only to be told it was 'men only' establishment. If the receptionist had been slightly more accurate she would have said it was a special kind of massage parlour. Ignorant of this fact, Emily stormed in anyway, to be confronted with a bunch of largely undressed guys lounging around in chairs. Realising the error of her ways, she made a tactical retreat to our reeking room, opened all the windows and waited for my return.

Fortunately I won a really tight match against Andrew Castle to qualify, and then checked Emily and I out of the tournament hotel and into the Inter-Continental. We were talking about a difference of $250 a night, but the other place was an intolerable health hazard that wasn't good for anything except a little hand relief in the gym. Perhaps it was sheer anger that propelled me all the way through to the final where I faced one of my least favourite opponents, Alex Antonitsch. I ended up losing because I was preoccupied by the Austrian's antics. He would laugh behind your back, make strange noises and pull faces. Although he played a good match, in the end it required a real effort to even shake the man's hand.

Worse was to come, because the tournament organisers then dragged out the Olympic rostrum for the presentation ceremony. In forceful terms I told them there was absolutely no way I'd be climbing onto the silver medallist's step. The two beaten semi-

Love on one leg in the Limelight

finalists had long left town, so the bronze medallist's place would have been left vacant anyway. If they thought I was going to grin up at Antonitsch and gave him a celebratory hug while he appeared king of the castle, they were soon put wise to the matter - and my use of language was not choice.

I was furious. Some people might have considered that being runner-up in the final in the first tournament back after a serious injury, surgery and a long lay-off was a really commendable effort - and given more favourable circumstances I might have done the same. Instead I hated the tournament, I hated the place and I hated the champion. The runner's-up trophy didn't particularly offend me, but the moment I got back into the locker room it suffered the brunt of my anger: I smashed it into a thousand pieces; I crashed it against the wall; I jumped on it, and then kicked what remained into the corner. At that moment Mark Kratzmann walked in, surveyed the damage and said: 'Hey Cashy, you've done a good job on that, mate. Not planning on coming back next year, then?'

No Kratz, I certainly wasn't. What is more, I never intend to return to that godforsaken city if I can find any possible method of avoiding it. However, the following week I savoured my revenge over Antonitsch by winning the tournament in Hong Kong for my first title in more than three years. I also teamed up to win the doubles with Wally Masur. I thought the bad times were at last behind me - but I was about to suffer more anguish.

So much of my game was based on speed around the court, and it just wasn't there any more after the snapped Achilles tendon. After believing I was one of the quickest players around the court, I now felt so slow, and my confidence suffered. Those two tournaments in Asia lulled me into a false sense of security. I knew I wasn't up to the clay court season, but I was looking forward to the grass - and then I lost in the opening round of Queen's to an American college player called Paul Chamberlin (who admittedly had reached the Wimbledon quarter-finals a year previously).

Wimbledon that year saw me win three matches before again losing to Boris Becker. There was no abusive sledging this time, probably because none of the players I beat were particularly notable scalps. First there was a Russian qualifier called Dmitri Polyakov who took me to five sets; next was the Swedish-born, naturalised Australian Johan Anderson; and finally Juan Aguilera, a Spanish baseliner who only played that one grass court tournament during his entire career.

The US Open wasn't much better, although I did produce back-to-back five sets wins over huge Swiss Marc Rosset and Mark Kratzmann. I played well against Michael Chang in Tokyo, which did wonders for the confidence because he was the world's most fleet-footed player by some distance. Then returning to the Davis Cup fold I scored singles' wins over Argentina's Alberto Mancini and Martin Jaite in Australia's 5-0 semi-final win at Sydney. When it came to the final against the United States in St Petersburg a couple of months later, Neale Fraser just saved me for the doubles and opted to go with Richard Fromberg and Darren Cahill in the singles against Andre Agassi and Chang.

Frankly it was a final nobody expected us to win, and the Americans were guilty of gross gamesmanship. They failed to meet the deadline in announcing both their team and the court surface, and got fined $4,000 accordingly. Then they said the court would be European red clay, which we insisted also contravened the Davis Cup regulations. According to the rule book the court used should 'in general use in the host country'. With the exception of the grass courts at Newport, Rhode Island, every competitive tennis surface

Love on one leg in the Limelight

in the United States was cement, carpet or green clay, which is vastly different to the red stuff they imported from Germany.

Not content with that, the Americans next stated the starting times would be 5pm on day one, noon on day two and 1 pm on day three. This meant the players in the second singles rubber could theoretically still be on court at midnight, which wouldn't exactly leave them in good shape to play doubles if selected the next lunchtime.

This wasn't a problem for the Americans, as Rick Leach and Jim Pugh were Wimbledon champions and one of the best doubles teams in the world. Agassi was at the peak of his obnoxious phase at the time, and annoyed us with his cocky pre-match comments; but unfortunately the hosts were just too good. They led 2-0 after the first day, and though Fitzy and I did our best, the Leach/Pugh combination and the acrid smoky aftermath of a giant firework display proved too much. My third and last Davis Cup appearance ended in disappointment.

Just to round off an unsavoury final, Agassi retired injured against Cahill in the dead rubber, although there appeared to be absolutely nothing wrong with him.Killer really got stuck into Agassi in the post-match press conference and accused him of being quite a few things. I wonder if Andre remembers those comments now he employs Killer as his coach.

Every cloud does have a silver lining, however - or in this case the lining was silver tasselled. As it was Ian Barclay's birthday, we managed to sneak two strippers past the security and into the locker room for a post-tie party. We all needed some cheering up, and what gave me the most pleasure was holding the door shut on Brian Tobin and the other Tennis Australia crew as they tried to get in.

I didn't need too long to come to terms with the Davis Cup defeat.

Uncovered

By then I had been a married man for more than four months, Emily and I having got married in the idyllic setting of Ocho Rios near Montego Bay in Jamaica on 22 July 1990. It couldn't have been a smaller ceremony: Dean Barclay was my best man (and, as I repeatedly remind him, only man), and my two children - Daniel (then aged five) and Mia (two years old) - were there, although both were suffering the after-effects of chicken pox. As her bridesmaids Emily had two friends, Josephine Campbell and Rachel Schadt. Nowadays Josephine runs a very successful cafe in Brixton, and is one of the few people to be told the secrets of my sensational pancake recipe. Rachel is married to Tommy Flanagan, the mean-looking, scarred actor who appeared in the film Braveheart.

Emily and I always promised ourselves that we'd return to that heavenly place - and we did, on our second wedding anniversary: but it turned into the most horrific experience of my life. We weren't able to hire the same house, but stayed in the same village near the Dunn's River Falls. Sadly things had deteriorated noticeably in the short time between our visits. There were more tourists, more locals trying to rip them off as well as sell them cocaine and dope, and consequently much more crime. But it was still an exquisite setting, and one evening, with Daniel and Mia tucked up in bed and their English nanny Silvia taking an early night, we decided to look at the stars while sitting beside the pool.

We had been warned to be vigilant, but assumed we'd be safe enough after employing an armed security guard, complete with dog. Walking out into the garden I was greeted by two black guys who were coming through the door. Initially I thought they were a couple of friends we'd met in the local village, and went to greet them. But I pretty quickly changed my mind as each produced a huge carving knife and grabbed hold of Emily and I.

222

Love on one leg in the Limelight

These guys weren't Rastafarians, who just smoke loads of the herb and stay totally relaxed. No - this pair had short-cropped hair, and seemed ruthlessly menacing, as if they'd been taking crack. My assailant was clearly agitated and held the knife to my throat, while the other intruder had his blade pressed over Emily's wrist. They ordered us to give them our money, and ripped the gold chain from around my neck. It had great sentimental value as my mum had had it specially made; but I was more concerned that I might not live long enough ever to see her again.

Emily was obviously petrified, and though I had never been so scared for my life, I tried to appear calm, insisting I'd give them all our money. I started walking upstairs to our bedroom, knowing the children were asleep a floor below. I wasn't sure whether the intruders just wanted cash or really wanted to kill us like thieves might have done in America. What I did know was that I still had a knife held at my throat, and I suddenly accepted the fact I was going to die. It's a weird and peaceful feeling because there is nothing you can do about it; yet suddenly I thought far more clearly.

The panic stopped, and I gave him all the money we had, which amounted to a couple of hundred pounds. Then he grabbed my sports bag and started to ram in t-shirts and tennis shoes before walking out of the bedroom. Momentarily I thought we were going to be safe and as long as everybody lived, things would be all right. Then I was struck by the terrible realisation they were going to rape Emily and the nanny. I could hear them speaking in Patois but didn't have a clue what they were saying. Returning to the hallway I saw the other guy still had Emily by the wrist, while the one with the money had gone into Silvia's room and got on her bed.

Silvia was quite a big, strong girl and she started shouting and swearing at them, saying she hadn't got any money and if they knew what was good for them they should piss off. I admired her bravery, but it seemed to work because the two men were leaving. They ordered us to stay put, cut the telephone lines and then made their exit. I gave Emily a hug but neither of us dared move for something approaching ten minutes.

Eventually I thought it was safe to take stock. As well as the money and tennis gear, a video camera had gone; but mercifully the children were still sound asleep. I woke the housekeeper and cook in their quarters, and they couldn't believe what I told them, asking what had happened to the security guard. The answer was he'd been fast asleep throughout, and his dog seemed half dead. I was so furious I barely got any sleep that night and the next day, with the phone lines fixed, I first called the police and then my travel agent in England. The police wanted a statement but I insisted we were leaving as soon as possible and we'd never be coming back to their terrible country. The travel agent was ordered to get us out of that place and send us anywhere safe. In the end we headed for the Cayman Islands, while the Jamaican authorities requested we play the whole thing down. They knew who I was, and pleaded for no adverse publicity.

I really wasn't bothered about telling the press. I was just glad we were all still alive - but the episode made me reaffirm my belief in God. I wouldn't say I became a born-again Christian, but it pushed me back to religion and opened my eyes to things spiritual. Being confronted with death is an educational experience, although I'm sure not I really appreciated it with a huge knife being held to my jugular vein. However, it was an episode that will live with both Emily and I until our dying days.

Chapter Twelve

HOW COME ALL THIS HAPPENS TO ME?

One word has caused me so much anguish and mental torture. The suffering stretches right back into my childhood and has continued throughout my adult life. The word is both an accusation and an insult. In my opinion it is one of the cruellest things you can call anybody. It became a label unfairly attached to me during my playing career. A cheap shot readily available to my critics and a vicious barb in the hands of loved ones. Sadly both my parents have been guilty and I harbour bad feelings about those occasions to this day. The word is hypochondriac.

My dictionary's definition of hypochondria is 'a chronic or abnormal preoccupation with one's health'. I would have been really pleased never to have suffered a second of pain during my life; unquestionably it would have made me both a better and more successful tennis player, and certainly a far happier one. Never once have I felt an ache or a twinge and thought, oh, good.

I'm not exactly breaking new ground when I say the most important tool of any professional sportsperson is his or her body. You rely on it to succeed; you can often blame it if you fail:

therefore if anything feels wrong, you need to take notice of what it is saying. Pain is a signal to the nervous system that something is wrong. But what course of action should you take if somebody repeatedly calls you a hypochondriac? Should you just ignore the discomfort? That can't be right.

Throughout my entire career I have been forced to block out any negative thoughts. If I was in pain or just plain angry, it was wrong. I couldn't be ill or injured, because if I was, people used to call me a hypochondriac. If I got angry or upset I was accused of having no respect yet any psychologist will tell you that it's natural to express these feelings, and to hold them in would be repressive and counterproductive. Long before I ever picked up a tennis racket, I possessed a furious temper and was repeatedly told off for my tantrums. Then when I started to play tennis and mentioned various things hurting, my mum called me a hypochondriac.

There were definite occasions when Dad used the word as well. It was a different world when he played at the top level of Aussie rules football; for instance, if your leg was broken in only two places rather than three, you'd still get out on the field. I could always hear his criticism reverberating around my head but in fact it was Mum who used that one horrible word more often. The experience made such an impression on me that I'd never say anything like that to any of my children.

Nobody needs to tell me I suffered more than my share of injuries. Had I not been hampered with back and knee problems as well as the ruptured Achilles tendon, I think I could have risen higher than fourth in the world rankings. Whether I would have reached the top spot would have been open to debate, because Ivan Lendl played so many tournaments. And lets face it: I played in an era when tennis was at its greatest. There was Becker, McEnroe,

How come all this happens to me?

Wilander, Noah, Edberg and Mecir, not to mention Lendl or Connors. However, I'm confident I could have got to number two in the world, and also won at least one other Grand Slam title.

The injuries certainly took their toll, not just on my body but on my mind as well. I tried hard not to plunge into the depths of self-pity, yet there were occasions when I wondered why I had been singled out to suffer so much bad luck. As I've mentioned several times, there's a depressive streak that runs through my family, and sometimes I used to get so down-hearted. Even when I was fit, it was almost a case of waiting for the next injury to happen, and so many times I used to wonder, why me?

Many people have accused me of over-training throughout my career, and I suppose there is a grain of truth in that theory.I don't deny that I often preferred being in the gym, or working on specific aspects in practice, to actually playing tournaments. It all dated back to the pressure I felt in the early years when the whole of Australia seemed to expect so much from me. Whereas so many other players viewed gym work as absolute purgatory, I loved those weeks with Ann Quinn, and found everything so interesting: the exercises, the sprint work, the testing of body fat. I was in my element, but being a person with an obsessive personality, I sometimes trained too hard and suffered the consequences.

Then there were other occasions when I just became totally sick and tired of tennis. The worst of those periods led me to commit, in tennis terms, a heinous crime: I threw - or as we say in tennis, tanked - a match in the tournament I revered above all others, Wimbledon. I purposely lost a match at the place of my greatest triumph.

It was 1991, I had been married to Emily for less than a year, and there seemed so many enjoyable things to do other than play tennis.

I'd been suffering niggling little injuries, mostly connected to the Achilles tendon, and hadn't been playing well, which meant I was getting beaten on a too regular basis. My ranking was dropping so much that I was in danger of falling outside the top hundred and at the same time I was convinced that umpires had some personal vendetta against me, because I was repeatedly getting screwed. Once I can remember losing a match in Adelaide and being so angry I went back and completely wrecked everything in the hotel room. It was inexcusable behaviour. All I really wanted to do was go to nightclubs and get blasted. And then everything came to a head at Wimbledon.

I'd beaten Jeff Tarango in the first round, but unfortunately my motivation wasn't nearly as strong against the Frenchman Thierry Champion. We were playing on an outside court, and I knew that in a nearby court, Britain's Nick Brown was doing well against Goran Ivanisevic. Nick was a good friend of mine who'd been working with Ian Barclay just before the Championships, while I'd been more interested in playing some rock n' roll; and I knew the winner of Nick's match would next face either Champion or myself. Sensing their match was over, I asked a ball girl who'd won, and she answered it was Nick.

Quite frankly, the thought of playing a mate, who also happened to be a British guy and consequently would have the entire crowd behind him, was an appalling prospect. I really couldn't be bothered, so at four all in the fifth set against Champion, I tanked: I threw in a couple of double faults, which made it blatantly obvious I wasn't trying. I don't know whether Champion realised this or not, but suddenly he seemed consumed by his own nerves, apparently to such an extent that he couldn't win a match that was being handed to him. He hit two double faults himself as he served

How come all this happens to me?

for the match, and then, with the whole of the court at his mercy, hit the simplest of shots into the net.

What was I to do? I suppose I could have quit, saying I was injured when I wasn't, but that would have been taking things too far. However, I really didn't want to win, and it took forever until Champion finally came out on top 12-10 in the fifth. Amazingly, whoever wrote the *ATP Yearbook* the following year didn't appear to have understood what was going on, and insisted Champion and I played one of the most memorable matches of Wimbledon that year - which says a lot for the exploits of eventual champion Michael Stich. If that writer had only appreciated the truth.

One person who did realise what was going on was John McEnroe. I tried to talk the problem through with him, and he told me he'd experienced the same thing himself. Like me, he had wanted to get away from the game because he couldn't stand playing any more. Again, it was a combination of the pressure and an awareness of more enjoyable pursuits, in his case family, music and perhaps his art. Mac told me how he had planned to take half a year off, but people started offering him huge sums of money to play exhibitions. And he explained how it could become a vicious circle: you play, and hate yourself for not being the player you used to be, so you take time off. Then you get a lucrative offer to contest a nothing match, which seems too good an offer to turn down; but straightaway you are back in the same situation again.

Mac told me to take his advice and have a six-month break. I knew the pitfalls: players who lay down the racket for even a short space of time rarely come back a better player. Yet what choice did I have? I'd committed the unthinkable and tanked a match at Wimbledon. Ian Barclay finally made up my mind for me. That's not the Pat Cash out there that I used to know, he said. If you keep on playing like this, you'll end up hating yourself.

My decision made, I spoke to my dad about sorting something out with Barkers. I'd been paying him US $100,000 a year - a top salary back in the early nineties. Yet he was basically only working part-time, as I didn't want to declare him redundant after all those years. He'd been a magnificent coach, and not just tactically, but in so many other ways. For instance, there was the time in South Africa when I had all my telephone calls diverted into his room, so he had to deal with the press at all hours of the night. Then one year at the US Open, I'd destroyed all my rackets so I had to freight another load over to New York. Barkers was sent to collect them from the darkest, dingiest area of the borough of Queens near JFK Airport; he was forced to sit in a queue while these giant black guys would park their trucks outside and push to the front, shoving all the other slips of paper out of the way. He stayed there four hours and eventually emerged with a huge box from Yonex, only to find no taxis available. So he walked back, with one of the rackets in his hand in case of attack. There was nothing this grey-haired old guy wouldn't do for me.

Barkers was more tolerant with me than he was with his own son, but eventually it became clear we had gone as far as possible. Tactically he was extremely good, but problems arose over my forehand and serve. Everyone else could see there was a problem, but he denied anything was wrong, and my feeling is that he didn't know how to fix it. I have to say, that phase was a disappointment to me. I suppose every player/coach relationship eventually runs its course, although that doesn't make it any less sad when it ends. Barkers knew me inside out and took so much shit; he was always a great supporter, and never harboured any bitterness.

Bjorn Borg used to tell me he always managed to keep his

230

How come all this happens to me?

emotions in check on the court because he knew he could go absolutely nuts at Lennart Bergelin in the privacy of the hotel room afterwards. So the coach used to cop it all, and Borg would swear and scream with no inhibitions, while everyone outside those four wells revered him as the Ice Man. And when he walked back on court the next time he was cool again. Borg and I differed in this, in that all too regularly I let my feelings show on court; but my relationship to Barkers was very similar to Bjorn's with Bergelin.

I told Dad to pay Barkers until he found another job, and as he'd been doing some work with British players, he was soon snapped up by the Lawn Tennis Association. For several years we kept in touch. His son Dean was my best mate, and I was invited for barbeques and parties at the Barclay house in New Malden, Surrey. Then completely out of the blue, Barkers rang to say he urgently needed to speak with me. I asked what was the problem, and he tried to tell me my dad had been ripping me off for years. I still remember his closing words with a sense of shock: 'I need to tell you some things you're not going to like hearing about your father'.

I immediately rang home in Melbourne, asking what had been going on, and if there was anything that had been kept secret, or that was untoward, that I should know about. Dad's reply left me even more astounded: I didn't want to tell you this son, but Ian is suing you.

Dad and I spent two hours on the telephone going through everything, and then he sent me a screed of faxes. Barkers was insisting he was owed money dating back seven or eight years, amounting to more than £30,000. He was claiming expenses for his wife Jackie, and the house he'd bought at the very top of the market before prices had fallen. In addition there was a situation with an insurance company; though at the time, not only did we get a great deal for Barkers, but had helped him pay.

My shock was immense - never in my wildest dreams could I have imagined this to happen. Admittedly Barkers was a great one for exaggerating, but that was something of a family trait, and he had never once lied to me or done anything like this before. I was instructed to meet him in a couple of days, and my Dad, an extremely efficient lawyer, briefed me as if I was going into court.Barkers and I sat down, spread all these sheets of paper over the table, and went through all the points one by one; by the end of the meeting he was in tears. It was so sad to see, and the basic problem was that he owed me money because I'd been paying his house insurance. He'd made all these claims to counter that debt because he'd been hit hard financially, perhaps hadn't been getting the money he deserved from the LTA.

Whoever had advised him on this was stupid, and I felt real sympathy for the man I'd known since I was kid. So I spoke to my dad, and we agreed to forget about the money owed to me. Nevertheless the whole business sadly took its toll: my father has never spoken to Ian since, and my own relationship with my former coach, who was there through all my great triumphs, is very different. I told Dean to stay out of the whole thing, but our friendship was also put under strain. Certainly I'm still friendly with Barkers and Jacky, but things have never really been the same since that time - though it now feels like they had an issue with my dad, and not me. Besides, as far as I am concerned, one bad incident isn't going to spoil all those marvellous memories, and those years of supreme trust. Barkers is a terrific guy who's very popular with the people he works with; on this occasion he was desperate, and in an awkward financial position, and it still makes me feel ill remembering the whole episode.

How come all this happens to me?

Tracking back to my break from tennis, it was an enjoyable time and money wasn't a problem. Emily and I travelled the world, scuba diving on the Barrier Reef, visiting the Grand Canyon, and exploring the Brazilian rainforest. I came to appreciate things away from the tennis court - but like any sabbatical, the break was never going to last forever. I finally made my return at Birmingham, a tournament that was almost instantly forgettable, dying after just one year. Quite frankly so was my performance, although that wasn't altogether surprising.

So many months of inactivity meant that my year-ending ranking had dropped to 113, which wasn't good enough to merit direct entry into the Australian Open. Thankfully somebody at Tennis Australia still respected my sense of duty to the national cause, and awarded me a wild card into the tournament. Hatred alone was a sufficient motivational tool to take me past Horst Skoff in the first round, despite the fact that I was cramping with nerves at the end of my straight sets win. Unfortunately in the second round a determined Emilio Sanchez proved too much over the full five sets.

From then until the British grass court season I played just one singles match, and by the time of Queen's I was considering myself as very much a part-time player. That one match was a trip to Tokyo to save my racket contract with Yonex. The small print stipulated I had to play every three months or the deal would be cancelled, and as far as the match was concerned, things didn't look good because I wasn't ranked high enough to get directly into the event.

Not knowing if playing qualifying was good enough to satisfy the Japanese company's demands and save a $US 500,000 a year contract, I decided it was worth gambling on taking the trip to Tokyo. For the first time in I don't know how many years, shortly after I arrived I had a lucky break: as I was heading out for the qualies, the ATP rep stopped me and said I'd got in the main draw. Amazingly two players had pulled out, and three more had forgotten to get the correct visas.

Undeterred, Yonex finally found an excuse to cancel the contract. It was when I appeared on a British television programme hosted by Bruce Forsyth, and the veteran pop singer and tennis aficionado Sir Cliff Richard and I had to play a few points using a sofa, complete with a reclining Brucie, as a net. For effect I had to use an old beaten-up racket the BBC had found somewhere deep in their wardrobe department; I've no idea who were the manufacturers of this relic, but it most certainly wasn't a Yonex. In playing out this little scene, the company told me I'd infringed my contract; but after numerous legal talks and a trip to Japan, my dad secured a substantial amount in compensation. As Mr Forsyth might say: Good game, good game!

By the time I got to Queen's, I was wondering exactly where tennis figured in my list of priorities. However, that didn't prevent me from taking issue with one British reporter who asked me what exactly I would put down as my occupation if I had to fill in a new passport form. I'd like to think I proved my point by winning three matches to reach the Stella Artois quarter-final, before going to Wimbledon and staging my last great battle on the regular tour with John McEnroe.

It was the year Andre Agassi took the title, and the tournament was not exactly viewed as a vintage occasion by those who judge that kind of thing. Nevertheless, although they may not have rated the whole fortnight, they loved my Centre Court five-setter with Mac - somebody even called it the greatest early-round match at the All England Club. Sadly for me, Mac won in five - and even after all those years, he still felt the need to intimidate a lame umpire into overlooking a three-minute stalling break in the middle of the third set tiebreak.

Soon after this was that horrific holiday to Jamaica, but I was to lament more than just the loss of some money and my gold chain, because the robber didn't just take a few T-shirts and tennis shoes, he also took some orthotic inner soles, specially made to my individual specifications to provide precise support for my feet. Ask most tennis players, and they'll tell you their orthotics are priceless. It was impossible to get another pair made in time for my next event, the Huggy Bear Classic, a serious pro-am event on Long Island, and I suffered the consequences - my right knee became so painful, I couldn't play the US Open. Two weeks later I tried to contest a challenger event in Monterrey in Mexico, but the harm was done: I'd suffered cartilage damage and a stress fracture to my right patella, the small triangular bone that protects the kneecap. I wouldn't hit another competitive tennis ball for fifteen months.

During that time I frequently dissolved into a flood of frustrated tears; and I can remember another occasion when I literally tried to tear my hair out. The pain was immense, and I started visiting a physiotherapist in Sydney called Jenny McConnell who's another specialist I'd have no hesitation in putting into the category of wonder woman. Most weeks I would fly up from Melbourne so she could massage and stretch out my kneecaps. I also underwent experimental treatment, whereby local anaesthetic and salin were injected into the tight strips of ligament that hold the kneecap in place. After surgery had basically shaved all the cartilage right down to the bone, I was in such agony I couldn't even walk up the stairs or bend down to play with Daniel and Mia when they came to stay.

Uncovered

After a while I could do some swimming to keep fit, and soon Emily and I set off on our travels again. Maybe absence was making the heart grow fonder, but by now I'd come to the conclusion that I missed tennis and would do whatever it took to return to the best possible level of fitness (I will immediately qualify that statement: I'd do anything *legal* that would help me to get back).

When I was at home in Melbourne, Ann Quinn and I used to work out at a gym in the suburb of Nunuwading. It was like a factory in a tin shack and used to get swelteringly hot in the summer, but I went there to get on a sweat and not worry about appearances. Body builders used to come in straight from the construction site, and one guy took me to one side and gave me a recommendation. He told me there was an anabolic steroid available that could be in and out of the system in one day. It would give me the capability to work harder than I'd ever done before, but be totally undetectable after just twenty-four hours; so if I were drug-tested a day later I would be clean. I'm sure he was talking about nandrolone, but I wasn't tempted in the least because as far as I was concerned, the use of illegal performance-enhancing drugs was cheating, and to me that's one of the worst crimes in the book.

One legal suggestion made to me around that time was the use of insulin. We talked to several doctors about the benefits of injections, and during one training period over the Christmas period I took home a load of vials made up by the body builder, stuffing them in a little plastic bag at the back of the refrigerator. My mum spotted them almost immediately and, not surprisingly, was suspicious. Naturally she was concerned about the legality of these drugs, and stubbornly insisted they weren't good for me. I tried to tell her there wasn't a problem - but injecting the stuff into my butt every day became a really tedious chore, and frankly I couldn't see that the insulin was making any marked difference, either.

Another experiment was much more beneficial. I'd been one of the first guys to use amino acids in the late 1980s, and an American company called Metametrix used me as one of the guinea pigs. I used to mix up these powders that glowed in the dark and tasted disgusting, but they guaranteed better recovery and the ability to work harder. The amino acids helped me recover from the ruptured Achilles tendon and also promoted muscle growth. When I started training, the circumference of my legs would expand unbelievably, as if somebody were pumping air into them. I was only taking what was recommended, but it was the same with my shoulders and chest. Basically we're talking about a man-made steroid, but more importantly, they were legal.

When Petr Korda was busted for allegedly taking nandrolone during Wimbledon, he got no sympathy from me. Sure, I thought he was a nice guy, and I'd even played doubles with him; but ask yourself the question, how does a player who has whinged about injuries all his career suddenly become fit enough to win the Australian Open at the age of thirty? There is no doubt Petr was good enough, but he now has a shadow of doubt over his results. He insisted he was misled but always refused to name the doctor. When I made my feelings known on the subject, Korda became furious. But after a while sensible guys like Todd Martin, Jonas Bjorkman, Jim Courier and Pat Rafter said their piece, too.

Since then, several other guys have been found guilty of taking nandrolone, such as the two Argentines, Juan Ignacio Chela and Guillermo Coria. And I'm sure there were many Spanish and South American clay court players who used the stuff before testing became stricter. Call me suspicious if you like, but I also wonder why my old friend Thomas Muster disappeared so abruptly from the tour when drugs started to become an issue.

Here was a guy who underwent a complete knee reconstruction and subsequent rehabilitation after being horribly injured in a road accident. Only a matter of months later he was winning tournaments on clay, which is the most demanding surface. Many people had their theories about Muster, though I'm just pleased it was Boris Becker, rather than me, who voiced them publicly and took the fine. Muster was too clever to take something illegal during tournaments, but what about training weeks? I remain vehemently against the use of illegal performance-enhancing drugs, but I wasn't going to say too much at the time; now and again I was still out partying, smoking the occasional joint or taking the odd line of cocaine, and although my experience in Key Biscayne taught me never to take anything when I was playing, I didn't want to start beating the drum about drug-testing.

I also turned down some of the simplest things that were perfectly legal and might have been really helpful to me. Something as basic as cod liver oil would undoubtedly have helped the connective tissue involved in the discs in the back and knee joints; every test decreed it would help, and perhaps some of my injuries could have been prevented. The reason for my stubborn refusal was simple: I didn't want to take something called a fatty acid. I'd become so fanatical and paranoid about my diet that the word fatty almost equated to poison.

Perhaps I wouldn't have been sidelined for Wimbledon in 1993 - and that was the time I really started missing tennis. Just seeing somebody like Todd Woodbridge get close to the world's top twenty was impetus enough for me to get back on court; after all, I was still only twenty-eight years old. Todd was a reasonable

How come all this happens to me?

enough singles player, and nobody can take anything away from his magnificent achievements on a doubles court; but I thought, if he can do it, I've still got to have a chance.

Being sidelined from tennis I involved myself with other things, such as investing money into a speedboat project with a former RAF pilot called James Wakeford - who ironically had started dating Anne-Britt. There was also a multimedia light show production I'd formulated and designed to enhance tennis matches. Basically it was a forerunner of all the big displays we see at places such as the US Open today. Sadly, the clumsy hand of a certain Bob Green once more made sure it was well and truly ruined by the ATP Tour. I understand Green is now a successful restaurateur in Jacksonville, Florida, and that the ATP's chief executive Mark Miles is one of his financial backers. I wonder if Bob is let loose in the kitchen?

Under the coaching guidance of my old buddy Rocky Loccisano, I began practising again. He'd been working at a club in Germany, but came over to London to help get me in shape. Naturally the instructions of Jenny McConnell and Ann Quinn were also being followed to the letter. By September I was relatively pain free, which was fortuitous. The business ventures and my travelling with Emily meant we had started eating into the savings built up over the years; financially it was therefore time to get back to work, particularly as the list of cancelled endorsement contracts was building up.

Without any exaggeration, I'd say I was keener to play than at any time since I'd won Wimbledon six and a half years earlier, and my comeback was planned for the year-opening tournament in Adelaide. Having become something of an expert on the subject, I knew there were three distinct phases to a comeback. The first is getting over the injury, the second is getting back onto court, and the third is recapturing your game. Initially two out of three would be fine for me, just as long as my body held up. Therefore playing three sets against the emergent and highly talented Russian teenager Yevgeny Kafelnikov was fine. I lost, after taking the first set, and I could hardly walk the next morning, but that didn't matter. Just playing well in my first comeback match was the important thing, and at least I had a world ranking again: number 1,183!

In those days there was no such thing as injury protection rankings like there are today. It didn't matter what you had previously achieved in your career, if you'd been unable to play for more than a year then you were a nobody. You could ask for wild cards, but there was no guarantee you'd get them. With my ranking absolutely shot to pieces I started writing letters and appealing to anyone who'd listen. I really had begun to wonder about the ATP. Several years earlier they wouldn't even have had a tour if top players like Mats Wilander and myself hadn't been willing to break away from the MIPTC. I can remember sitting down with Weller Evans and telling him he could count on my full support. Six years later he was moaning about giving me wild cards into qualifying.

Thankfully the Australian tournament directors still saw the benefits of involving me in their events. So Sydney's Barry Masters and Ron Read were as charitable as Adelaide's Ron Green. I couldn't say the same about my opponent at Sydney's famous old White City, the distinctly sullen Czech Daniel Vacek; he was another who often stirred my suspicion about the use of certain drugs. Seeing him for the first time in well over a year I extended my hand in a welcoming gesture. He simply looked at my outstretched arm and grunted: I'm not shaking your hand.

How come all this happens to me?

Vacek made it perfectly clear he had no respect for me or my game, and treated me with contempt from start to finish. To make matters worse, I slammed the door of the courtside fridge on my hand - but the real concern was the pain coming from my back. It grew increasingly worse, but I would rather have died out there than handed the match to this most objectionable of opponents.

I again went down in three sets. However, that was the least of my problems: by now it wasn't only the back, but a burning pain shooting down my legs, and before long my shins had gone numb and there was no reflex in one knee. Rapid action was necessary, and next morning Jenny McConnell got me booked into hospital for a scan. It transpired that the problem was in exactly the place in my spine that had been injected by chymopapain all those years previously. At the time the specialists had told me the back would be good for ten years; as it turned out, it held for eight. Now the disc had bulged and was pressing on my sciatic nerve. The only option was surgery, and my reaction was quite unequivocal: no worries, but just stop this infernal pain.

I distinctly remember being helped out of the car by Jenny and shuffling back into my Sydney hotel room, where everybody was staring at me: Emily, Rocky, my parents and the ever-supportive Ann Quinn, and they were all crying.It was like I'd been given six months to live. Obviously Jenny had telephoned the news, and they all felt so sorry for me, knowing the hard work I'd put in for a year and a quarter - all the pain, rehabilitation, swimming, running and gym work, not to mention time on the practice court, and after just two matches it was all over. At best I would be sidelined for another eight months, at worst I'd never play again, and I'm sure that was the fear of at least a couple of people in that room. Not me, however: with so much sadness around I had to be positive; plus I'd

241

rediscovered my enthusiasm, and nothing would stop me from playing again.

We flew back to Melbourne that night, and just walking to the car caused excruciating pain. Emily was helping me, but I couldn't help but stop for a few minutes in the hope the agony would cease. After getting home, I wanted the operation done straightaway, but my chosen neuro-surgeon Peter Dohrman was away on vacation. I couldn't wait too long because I was almost immobile, my muscles were getting weaker by the day and I found it impossible to walk up stairs.

Immediately Dohrman returned, he fitted me in into to his surgical list straightaway and basically drilled a hole through the bone and scraped out the disc touching the nerve. From then on my orders for convalescence were simple: I could either stand up or lie down, but the only time I could sit was to answer the call of nature in the dunny. Emily and I rented a flat in Melbourne and basically I'd lie down all day, watching the cricket. Occasionally I'd go for walks, but I could only eat my meals off an ironing board, and was constantly wondering how to spend the rest of my time. We were planning on trying for a child, which was certainly one possibility!

Several weeks later I was sunbathing out on the flat's balcony when Emily returned home with a huge smile on her face. She was holding out this thing I couldn't see properly because of the sun. It was a pregnancy test - and more importantly, it was positive. Although I was thinking in terms of one rather than two, the twins were on the way; and then the irony of the situation hit me: eight years earlier I was laid up with a bad back and Anne-Britt came over to be with me. She was taking the Pill, but the time difference between Europe and Australia was sufficient for her to get pregnant. Now here I was in a similar condition, and the Cash

How come all this happens to me?

sperm had done their work again. Just goes to show, you can keep a good man down, but you can't keep him out. I also came upon the recipe for boys: have a bad back if you want one; have a really bad back for two.Does that mean have a chronically bad back if you want triplets? I hope I never find out!

With Emily getting bigger by the week, I was once more on the comeback trail, though this time it was a slow one. I was walking about five miles a day around Melbourne, and those who know the place will tell you there are far less pleasant cities in which to stroll. Soon I took up Pilates work with the Australian ballet company, and a former dancer, Andrew Baxter, put me through the basics, which was quite an eye-opener. Eventually the time came to head back to London, where I continued the work under the guidance of Jenny Mills of the Royal Ballet Company three times a week. The work had its perks, and watching prima ballerina Darcy Bussell go through her routine was certainly one of them. Again I was fortunate to have top advisers to make sure my back was recovering in the right way. One was Jenny Mills, and another was Mark Bender, a New Zealander who trained under Jenny McConnell in Australia and is now the British Davis Cup physiotherapist.

On 10 September 1994, Master Jett Thomas Cash was rapidly followed into this world by his brother Shannon Louis. Shannon comes from my Irish heritage, Louis is after Emily's father; Jett is the James Dean character from the film *Giant,* and Thomas my grandfather. Physically they are not identical, and they possess extremely different traits and personalities; but they are brilliant boys, and they have changed our lives enormously. Yet within a month of their birth I was off on my tennis travels once more, at the age of twenty-nine determined to prove the game of my youth was not just a thing of memories.

If Sydney's White City was a venue steeped in tennis history, the same cannot be said for places such as Brest, Aachen, Nantes, Cologne and a town called Rogaska situated deep in the Republic of Slovenia. This time there were no sentimental wild cards into the big events, and somebody ranked outside the world's top thousand was where he belonged: down on the Challenger circuit. My best showing came in Rogaska when I reached the quarter-finals and picked up the grand sum of $730 for my efforts. Just enough to keep the twins in nappies.

Yet the back held up to the rigours of playing nine matches in six weeks, and that was good enough for me. Early the next year I returned to the main tour, though I hardly gave Pete Sampras too much cause for concern. Yet for reasons that should be (or will soon become) glaringly apparent, three wins gave me particular pleasure. In Dubai I beat Thomas Muster, and then I went to Copenhagen and got the better of both Daniel Vacek and a twenty-one-year-old lefthander who was then still listed as Canadian: Greg Rusedski. Results were not brilliant, but the word from Wimbledon was that their 1987 champion figured prominently in their plans for wild card distribution. That alone was reason enough to keep going.

Given my dislike of things Austrian, I probably should have known that an invitation to play the grass court event in Annenheim would present problems - particularly as the tournament director was my old enemy Alex Antonitsch, who strangely had extended me the hospitality of a wild card. Going for something no more taxing than a morning jog, I tore half of my instep right off the bone. Needless to say it hurt considerably, but I couldn't possibly let Alex down, so I went through the motions against Mark Petchey that afternoon, losing predictably in straight sets.

Back in London, both Jenny McConnell and Doug Stewart, the

person who does my orthotics as well as working as a consultant to the top sports shoe companies, examined the injury. They agreed it would heal with rest and the correct taping. I played Queens a week later and lost the first round to Petr Korda; but Wimbledon was paramount in my mind. I had indeed been awarded a wild card, and was determined to take my place in the draw. After playing an excellent match with David Wheaton at Hurlingham I felt considerably more confident; but then I managed to aggravate the injury again the following day.

Two days before the start of Wimbledon I didn't know what to do. I couldn't possibly pull out after being shown such generosity and respect. Hearing I'd been drawn against the Belgian giant Dick Norman, I went to see the tournament's official doctor, Peter Tudor Miles. I'd known him for years, and he'd always been both friendly and helpful over trivial matters like summer colds. Telling him I'd torn the plantar fascia muscle, I asked if it was possible to have a pain-killing injection before my match.

At the time, it wasn't that common a request in tennis, although footballers were being given pain-killing injections all the time. I'd often wondered if I'd had one in my shoulder before the 1987 Australian Open final against Edberg whether I would have won the title - but that was history. All I wanted to do at the time was get through my match against Norman. I'd been told the 6ft 8in left-hander had a big serve and not much else. Basically I was just asking for a local anaesthetic in my foot, but Tudor Miles said he didn't believe in pain-killing injections, and in all his time at Wimbledon he had only ever administered one, to somebody about to play a final.

Tudor Miles agreed to at least examine my foot, and subsequently delivered a look of complete scorn. Talking to me like I was a child, he insisted I hadn't suffered a torn plantar fascia but had simply bruised the heel. Added to that, he insisted the injection wouldn't last the whole match. This convinced me of his ineptitude. He was disagreeing with the diagnosis of two of the world's best physiotherapists and a foot specialist. What I was hoping for was a knowledgeable sporting doctor, the kind I had always dealt with, rather than a friendly conservative and staid English physician. This was the biggest tennis tournament in the world, and yet they employed a doctor who was still back in the days of Florence Nightingale.

Wondering what to do next, I telephoned Mark Bender who suggested we contact a doctor called Nick Webborne. He was an extremely knowledgeable sports physician who'd done a lot of work with Paralympic Games representatives. After explaining my injury I experienced no problems in getting Webborne to agree to the injection, and arranged for him to receive a locker room pass. Taking him into a spare treatment room no more than a quarter of an hour before I was due on Court Three, he administered the jab.

Despite the fact I've had a million needles pushed into me for acupuncture and blood tests, I still don't like them. Consequently I was feeling decidedly funky when I started the match against Norman. Then at five all I pushed off into a serve, and felt the muscle in my instep tear again. It didn't hurt because the foot was both numb and taped, but I couldn't move properly. I looked up to my coach Rocky in the box, sadly shaking my head. After losing the first set in a tiebreaker, I decided there was no point in continuing. Convinced I had played my last ever match at Wimbledon, I was extremely depressed and went straight home to bed. When I awoke the next morning my foot was still partially numb, sixteen hours after the injection - making Tudor Miles assertion that the anaesthetic wouldn't even last the match absolutely farcical.

Webborne later introduced himself to Tudor Miles, and promptly received a disparaging letter saying only one doctor was allowed at the All England Club. My thoughts on the matter were that they should get somebody who knew what he was talking about, particularly as a scan I had later that week proved I did indeed have a torn plantar fascia rather than just a bruised heel. But at least this story has a happy ending, because although Tudor Miles is still the Championship's head doctor, Webborne now also works in the second locker room.

As for me, I could jog again after two weeks, but was right to pull out because I would never have been fit enough to play another match against Stefan Edberg two days later. And I did get one more outing at Wimbledon two years later, when I qualified a decade after winning the title; only to lose in the first round to Byron Black.

Fate had delivered one last painful blow ten months previously when I'd also qualified for the 1996 US Open. I'd won through to face the Russian Andrei Olhovskiy, but towards the end of my last qualifying match, I jerked my back while trying to change direction for a ball spinning off the net cord. The next day I was almost totally immobile but determined not to default. I thought I'd injured the troublesome disc again, but luckily had only torn the ligaments that attach the back muscles to the pelvis. I lost 6-3, 6-1, 6-1 to Olhovskiy, and really shouldn't have been out there.

For the only time in my career I left the court in tears, and can remember looking into the faces of both Emily and Australia's top tennis writer Leo Schlink. They were two people who both understood my pain. Throughout my life there have been hundreds of others who didn't, and who called me a hypochondriac. On the evidence of the preceding pages, you can make your own choice on the matter.

Chapter Thirteen

WHEN YOU GET TO THE BOTTOM

Rock music fans the world over have chilling cause to remember 22 November 1997: it was the day Michael Hutchence, vocalist with the band INXS, was found hanged in his Sydney hotel room. And tennis followers might nearly have had something to mourn as well later the same day: feeling that my own life had plummeted to such depths that there seemed little reason to carry on, I seriously considered following Michael's example by committing suicide.

This wasn't just a bad day turned worse by the horrendous news of a friend's death; it was a feeling of being submerged by all the pressures that had been building up throughout my life. And it wasn't the first time I'd considered taking such drastic action, as bouts of depression had recurred throughout my life. In fact there's a history of this problem in my family, because my stepbrother Ralph took his own life, as did a young female cousin, Gabriel. She was the daughter of my dad's sister, and a regular Sunday playmate of mine at the weekly family get-togethers when I was really young. The pressures of teenage life eventually got too much for her, and she decided to end it all.

I knew how she must have felt. The events of the preceding few months had worsened my state of mind to an extreme low. It wasn't just the tennis, the injuries and the hassles: Anne-Britt and I couldn't come to terms on anything, and because of this I was finding it increasingly difficult to have access to Daniel and Mia. Any parent who is separated or divorced will know this sort of pain: there is nothing worse than being denied the opportunity to see your children. My particular situation was complicated by the fact that they lived in one country and I was forced to skip between many others.

I first heard the terrible news about Michael while watching CNN in a depressing Frankfurt hotel room, and my initial reaction was that his death was such a tragedy. Then gradually over the next hour or so, my own thoughts unravelled, and I can remember looking at the window, working out the long drop to the ground and thinking: should I give it a go?

I'd become reasonably well acquainted with Hutchence over the years. INXS was the biggest band to come out of Australia, and I'd known some of the other guys since the beginning. Michael and I would catch up for dinner in assorted venues around the world, and he would always be extremely friendly. After a while we also used to hang out in the clubs. He seemed a very switched-on guy, but possessed strong emotional qualities as well. I used to think he had a presence about him, reminiscent of everything I'd read about the legendary Doors singer, Jim Morrison.

Jon Farris, one of the other guys in INXS, did warn me about Michael being rather kinky. He was wild, and into sexual experimentation. I recall one night in Los Angeles when Emily and I were having dinner with Michael and his then partner, the super model Helena Christiansen. Maybe I was getting the wrong vibes,

When you get to the bottom

but it seemed to me that Michael's trail of conversation was leading up to a suggestion of us swapping partners. I just laughed it off, and rapidly moved on to something completely different.

To my way of thinking, Michael was somebody who had everything I really wanted from life. He was a millionaire, one of the world's great rock stars, and was adored by women all over the place. Recently he'd fallen in love with Paula Yates and they'd had a baby daughter. If somebody possessing all that can feel life's not worth living, then what chance did I have? I thought my existence at the time was the pits, though later on I learned my depression was partially drug-related. All too often a crashing low follows getting high, and my melancholy had driven me to go out and party more regularly. It's a vicious circle: you feel down, and think going out will help pick you up; then when the effect has worn off, you feel even lower. In addition I was getting pressure from my father to go out and work because he was dealing with the bills - my fortune was being eaten away, and you can't live the high life if you're not earning. My self-esteem had nose-dived; I'd been on medication, and was seeing a psychotherapist.

Things weren't going well at home with Emily, either, because I'd taken my frustrations out on her, repeatedly shouting my displeasure as if she were an umpire. To compound the problem, both the twins were sick. Every time I rang home she was crying, and eventually the boys had to go to hospital. I knew I should be back with them, but I couldn't make that step. I felt sad, lonely, and forced to be in a place I didn't want to be. There's no denying I was in a terrible state, all but convinced that the easiest option would be to kill myself.

What was I doing in Frankfurt, you might ask? It is indeed a good question. Basically I'd been forced off the main ATP Tour against my will to play with the seniors. That circuit was supposed to be for the over thirty-fives, and I was still only thirty-two, so I felt insulted and manipulated.Though my results hadn't exactly been stunning over the previous couple of years, I knew that injury free, I could still be competitive. I'd written to more than thirty tournament directors, pointing out my past record and basically begging to get into their tournaments. In return I received four wild cards, two of which came when I really shouldn't have been playing because I was suffering from 'flu. Needless to say I took them anyway because my ranking was so low; most of the time I couldn't even get into the qualifying rounds.

Not even my compatriots would help. A supposed long-time friend, Colin Stubs, refused to give me a wild card into Adelaide, claiming his hands were tied by Tennis Australia. Then the late Barry Masters in Sydney also refused; I've got him on video film saying he thought Richard Fromberg was a better draw for the spectators. I tried to point out that I'd won Wimbledon along with two Davis Cups for his country, but Masters replied: Oh, Richard got to the final here two years ago and his ranking has dropped so he needs the wild card.

What about me, for Christ's sake? My ranking was down outside the 1,000 mark. Then my long-time friend Paul McNamee explained that if I wanted to receive a wild card entry into the Australian Open, I had to prove my fitness at the Sydney qualies. Unfortunately I lost in the final round. Then, after winning my way through qualifying at the Australian Open, I started to run a high temperature and was feeling dreadful, and by the time I actually got out on court to play Javier Frana, I was just too sick. The following week in Philadelphia I got a wild card, but I was still really ill, and lost in the first round.

When you get to the bottom

I remember asking Weller Evans, the ATP Tour employee who always dressed as a player, perhaps so fans would think he was important, why I couldn't get a wild card into Key Biscayne (which was then curiously called the Lipton Players Championships). He replied it was always customary to go straight down the ranking list for wild cards, and also to help the youngsters from Nick Bollettieri's academy, because the tournament director had done a deal. I pointed out that Magnus Larsson had been awarded a wild card, and Evans countered that it was an exception. I asked whether a former Wimbledon champion might be considered for another exception, and he ended the conversation by saying rules were rules.

Six months previously John McEnroe had declared that the last remaining two great bastions of Communism were North Korea and the ATP Tour. How the hell could they treat a former Grand Slam winner like that? I ran around getting tremendous support from all the former winners of major titles, such as Sampras, Agassi, Edberg, Courier, Chang and Stich. They were all adamant that former Grand Slam champions should be allowed wild cards - but the ATP weren't interested in what the top players said.

It was a horrendous time, and totally degrading for a former Wimbledon champion. I requested a wild card into the Milan event, run by Sergio Palmieri, who was supposed to be my agent with IMG. He refused, which perfectly illustrated his commitment to actually managing my playing affairs. However, he is a man who always seems to have an alternative agenda, and in this case it was improving the standard of the Senior Tour; so with the air of somebody who'd done me the ultimate I favour, he said he'd get me into some Senior events. To me, that seemed an insult. However, I needed the money, and wasn't really in a position to say no.

Hence my arrival in that terrible dark, dingy Frankfurt hotel, with the most uncomfortable pillows ever made. At the tennis the crowds were typically German, by which I mean unfriendly; the atmosphere had been exactly the same a few weeks earlier as I made my last ever appearance on the regular tour in Stuttgart, suffering a 6-2, 6-0 humiliation from Andrei Medvedev.Now here I was on the geriatric circuit. Would my luck ever change?

Like so many who consider suicide, I decided against the option, not because I was ultimately not brave enough to end my life - at that moment, looking at that window, it would all have been so easy but because several hours of serious introspection made me realise that an act of such selfishness, regardless of the torment I was experiencing, would make things so painful for those loved ones who'd be left behind. I had four children and a wife to consider, besides my parents, brother and sister. Taking my own life would have been such a simple personal release, but a cause of immense suffering and anguish for those who needed me.

Tennis was another thing altogether. I felt defiled by both the ATP and the Senior Tour. I'd had a huge row with one of their public relations staff called Benito Perez Barbadillo, who had just laughed at me when I enquired why I wasn't included in the yearbook's collection of former champions. The guy just asked, what was my problem? I might have replied, how about not being afforded any respect by a mere minion? To him it may have been something really petty, but if he disregards achievement so lightly then he shouldn't be working in a sport where success counts for everything. Even now, after numerous complaints to various people, I'm still not in that book.

In addition, I'd been cheated out of $30,000 a few months previously by a Dutch tournament director who had signed up

When you get to the bottom

Henri Leconte, Peter McNamara, Guillermo Vilas and myself to play an exhibition, and had then paid us only peanuts. I also found myself being owed $60,000 by promoters of the official ATP senior tour events held in Sydney and Melbourne. Even though 10,000 people turned up to watch McEnroe and Borg play in Melbourne. The promoter Wayne Reid filed for bankruptcy the next day. Both the ATP and IMG denied responsibility but I ended up the only player not to be paid. Consequently I felt no obligation to fulfil any commitments so, regardless of being scheduled to play Bjorn Borg in the following day's final, I caught the last available flight out of Frankfurt to London.

I wrote a note telling the organisers exactly where they could stick their tournament. My knee was hurting and I was going home. Feeling the need for some immediate consultation I went to see my therapist the following morning. On some occasions these people tell you want you need to hear; on others they come out with something that infuriates you. This was a case of the latter, as he told me to catch the first plane back to Frankfurt, alleging that it would save both my money and my arse; besides, good work like a final shouldn't be just tossed away. My response was quite simple and to the point, basically that no way was I playing for people like that.

Perhaps the therapist was right. After all, they are paid to think clearly when other minds are cloudy and muddled. Yet at the end of the consultation he realised I was *not* going to head back there, and so advised me that the most sensible plan would be to take six months out. I needed to clear my head and sort out the issues that were causing such torment. Exactly six months later I got an offer to coach Mark Philippoussis, but that was still a long way off.

In the meantime I soon found out that running away to hide in search of some peace was not a viable option. I still had to earn money, though more and more barriers were being erected. Two days before the start of the Honda Challenge, I received a fax informing me that Sergio Palmieri and his IMG cohort Patrick Proisy had cancelled my contract with Peter Worth, who owned the Royal Albert Hall event. Not only was I effectively banned from playing in London; my money from Frankfurt was also being withheld, although I'd fulfilled all but one of my commitments. Admittedly the absence of one finalist was a tricky obstacle to overcome, but the IMG people were supposed to be on my side. How silly of me to think I'd get some support from my management.

So many disappointing things had happened to my life. Even somebody I thought merited implicit trust caused me to reconsider my assessment. Exactly a decade earlier Charlie Fancutt, Paul McNamee and myself were sitting in Melbourne when we came up with an idea. Mixed doubles was an entertaining but distinctly under-used form of tennis. We decided there would be a market for an international competition that involved both male and female players from leading countries first playing singles and then joining together in mixed doubles. Harry Hopman, the legendary Australian Davis Cup captain, had died a few years previously and people were wondering how best to honour his name. All three of us had spent a considerable amount of time at Harry's tennis camp in Florida. We were also extremely fond of his widow Lucy, and decided this competition would be highly appropriate as a lasting tribute.

Paul McNamee had recently retired. He always wanted to be a Labour politician and was an extremely intelligent man, having completed the first year of a law degree before quitting college to jump on the tennis circuit. In due course, he'd become my mentor and closest tennis friend. After I won Wimbledon, he even co-produced and featured in a video, tracing its way back through my career before celebrating the victory. Plans for the new competition began to take shape. Macca and Charlie would market the tournament while I would play for the first three years to get it up and running. The three of us would split the profits accordingly.

We even managed to entice Hana Mandlikova to play, after she had taken Australian citizenship by virtue of a short-lived marriage. Ironically the unlikely pair of Aussies lost to Czechoslovakia in the final; but otherwise the tournament was a great success. Crowds were good, and the city of Perth was an excellent host. After I snapped my Achilles tendon, Wally Masur stepped in as a substitute and everything was going great - until Macca informed me the rules had been changed.

My initial question was to ask why I, as a partner, hadn't been consulted in this extremely important decision, but it was quickly glossed over. Macca said that he and Charlie had agreed that it was better for the tournament if the players involved were the highest ranked from the various countries, otherwise it could just be construed as an exhibition. If for some reason the top players weren't available, substitutes could legitimately be brought in. In all honesty, I struggled to disagree with such logic.

Coincidentally, my ranking had dropped behind players like Wally, Todd Woodbridge and Mark Woodforde. I had therefore played two years out of the agreed three, but was then effectively frozen out for the good of the tournament. To a certain extent I understood, but was still upset that Charlie and Macca had changed the rules without consulting their third partner - namely, me. It had been like a family tournament, since McNamee's best man was

Fancutt; my sister worked at the tournament, along with Macca's wife; Macca was my son Daniel's godfather; and Mrs Hopman attended without fail. It was all so cosy, like happy families. Furthermore, as far as I was concerned, I'd also made an investment with my services, so would continue to be part of the earnings. Particularly as the television ratings were growing, Channel 7 had signed a deal and sponsors were queuing up to be involved. How wrong I proved to be.

By then I was based in London, and when you're away from home you lose track of what's happening. My Dad studied all the legalities and insisted I had a case for suing. But try as I might, I couldn't bring myself to take to court somebody who'd been as close to me as Macca. I was so infuriated because supposed mates had screwed me - but then again, if they do things like that, they can't really be mates any more. The whole thing broke my will, and in the end I came to the conclusion that if they were that desperate, they could have the tournament. I wiped my hands clean of the whole business.

Several years later Macca also forced Charlie out by skilful negotiation. Charlie then told me that Macca had informed him that I didn't want to be involved any more, and was prepared to move on. He said he had copies of all Macca's notes, was prepared to sue, and asked if I wanted to join him. I told him to go ahead himself if he wanted, but to count me out because it was more important to remain friends with my son's godfather than to bicker over money. Eventually I did receive a payment of $30,000 when Macca sold the tournament to the International Tennis Federation. I don't know what he pocketed, but my guess is something close to $1 million.

The lesson I learnt was that Macca, like any successful businessman, looks after number one. Eventually my father acted

When you get to the bottom

as an independent legal mediator between Macca and Charlie, as they settled their financial differences out of court. I never wanted to know the deal, and Dad didn't tell me. People who know more about business than I do, maintain that the quality Macca showed throughout was blind ambition.Now he is heavily involved with Tennis Australia, and currently tournament director of the Australian Open, where he is doing a great job. Many tip him to succeed Geoff Pollard as the next president, but I think he's too good for such a role. I just view him as somebody who used to be one of my closest mates, and a great partner with the girls around the wild bars of Melbourne run by our good friend Stewy 'The Night Club King' Harrison. In the end I lost my two closest friends in tennis, Ian Barclay and Paul McNamee. I don't hold any grudges, but it's all such a shame.

In the end you become cynical and wary of whom you befriend, though if you think about things like that too much, you become a little mixed up inside; certainly by the time I was heading for Tuscon, Arizona and a rehabilitation clinic called Cottonwood, I was more scrambled than a gross of eggs. By this time, more than a year had passed since that horrible afternoon in the Frankfurt hotel. I'd been on the road with Philippoussis and without taking too much advantage of the life. First I was partying too much, which manifested itself in several evenings coming to a close without me knowing too much of what was happening. When you are presented with staying in your hotel room and looking at four walls or going out to party, the choice isn't a hard one to make. The problems come when those couple of drinks start to multiply, and one thing leads to the next. Secondly, I was enjoying the pleasures of life on the road without the stress of actually being a player; so when I got back with the family it was hard to slot into home life again. I'll leave you to work out the consequences.

Emily was the first to enter the establishment. At the time I didn't really understand what rehab actually meant, thinking it was a place for people who shoot up heroin, get totally reliant on cocaine, or become alcoholics. She wasn't any of those things, but was suffering from acute depression. After so much initial happiness, she and I had some real problems with our relationship. Our carefree life of nightclubs and jetting around the world had changed with the arrival of our twin boys. In addition I wasn't making big money any more, and she didn't like some of the friendships I'd developed, though most were innocent.

Initially she'd spent a couple of days in The Priory at Roehampton, and that seemed to work. Her therapist insisted Cottonwood would be a natural follow-on, so off she went to address her problems, leaving me in charge of the boys. I wasn't totally happy with the situation, as I was travelling with Philippoussis and still contractually obliged to play the London Seniors tournament after being banned the previous year.

Before long my displeasure had turned to anger. Emily didn't telephone once in three weeks while she was sorting herself out. Extremely reluctantly, I was due to head for Arizona to take part in something they call family week. Cottonwood's plan was to talk in a controlled environment about why things had been going wrong, and to try to heal the problems. My intention was to rip into Emily for her negligence, and I was expecting an enormous confrontation. Once again my selfishness was the overpowering emotion - but the week was a real education. Very quickly I was made to realise that *I* was pretty messed up as well. No sooner had I gone home than I decided to turn straight around and check myself in for therapy.

My life had really become a mess. Things went in a pattern: I

When you get to the bottom

wouldn't do well in a tournament, so after losing I'd go out to a nightclub. There I'd get really wasted on booze, and usually a few lines of cocaine. I'd get home around 4am and antagonise Emily. Then when the time came to play the role of Dad with the twins I'd be feeling hung over and depressed, as you do after taking drugs. Browns, situated just off Holborn, was the club I frequented most in London, and all kinds of famous people like George Michael, Elle McPherson, Mick Hucknell and numerous footballers used to turn up. Some were doing drugs, others weren't. Then there were the special nights in other clubs, run by a friend of mine called Janette Caliva. I remember one night with Elle McPherson, Paula Yates and Michael Hutchence. My mate James Wakeford went to the toilet and took forever. When he got back, I enquired about the delay and he said Paula and Michael had gone in before him and locked the door. Apparently their over-enthusiastic tongue wrestling almost brought the walls down.

The supermodel Naomi Campbell had apparently been in Cottonwood a few months before me. Once I was there I confronted everything, in meetings concerned with alcohol, narcotics, gambling and even an addiction to sex. I couldn't really relate to any, but saw some parallels in some. I listened to other people's stories and tried to work myself out. It was a very healthy place with a basic community, and I shared a room with four other men. Naturally everything is dry: no booze or drugs, and there's very strict security. However, they used to let me out at 6am every morning for a run; apparently I was the only person ever allowed out like that, but they knew I'd come back because I was so keen to get better.

When you go into therapy you're told it's like peeling an onion: you keep taking off more and more layers, and it gets increasingly painful on the eyes until you're right down to core issues. Inevitably I found that many of mine were related to playing tennis, and all the stress I suffered when I was repeatedly criticised as a youngster. I actually required trauma therapy for the Davis Cup final I played when I was just eighteen. Going back even further there were childhood issues, such the absence of physical affection from my parents, being called a hypochondriac, and trouble with teachers. They'd been festering and poisoning me since I was a young teenager but hadn't been able to deal with them because I was always in the spotlight.

Some days I thought I was doing really well, others were horrendous; and the whole process cost an absolute fortune. When you come out of those places you're considerably more bruised than when you go in. Then the following six months were probably the unhappiest of my life; I didn't smile once because they had taken away all my fun: the drinking, the girls, the late nights, the cocaine and therefore my carefree attitude. I continued to attend therapy meetings in London - and there I met with somebody who has become a true friend.

Everyone calls him Johnny Too Bad, although his real name is Elichaoff; he once played the drums with King Crimson and Peter Gabriel. I found him to be a terrific guy, a real diamond as they say in London. He introduced me to a company called Damco who have basically reinvented the AC electric motor that's used in dishwashers, lawn mowers and even little things like shavers and hair dryers. They now use considerably less power and consequently last more than three times as long. The old motors used to burn out, but the new ones won't. Not only have they been tested out at the university in Hong Kong, but the college have also invested heavily in further development. Johnny convinced me that

When you get to the bottom

it would be a worthwhile investment, so I put in £20,000, with an agreement to receive a similar amount in shares if I did some promotion for the company. Fortunately the share value has spiralled.

Another great friend is Brad Cooper, a successful Sydney businessman whom I can forgive for being vice-president of Hawthorn's fierce Aussie rules rivals Collingwood. In times I've needed help, he's given financial and more importantly emotional support. Recently Brad's friendship has given me plenty to smile about - although there wasn't any happiness in the months after Cottonwood. I distinctly remember sitting at home in the following June and being amazed at my reaction of actually laughing at a comedy programme on the television. It had been so long since Id laughed at all; I'd just been a crying, blubbering mess for all that time.

In retrospect, the whole process certainly saved my life. It was a last ditch resort to try and heal something from an existence that had just gone sour. A lot of professional athletes go off the rails a little when they retire: some put on weight, some start drinking, a lot leave their wives. Stefan Edberg is content to sit in front of his computer all day long and make even more money on the stockmarket. I don't know if he's the lucky one or not; he was always extremely frugal with his cash when he was playing.

I do know I was very fortunate because I'd been suicidal more than a couple of times and it was getting dangerous. In all honesty, I can say I would have jumped out of that window or off a bridge somewhere; though what worried me was that I wouldn't have done the job properly. I was petrified of ending up handicapped and needing somebody to feed and wash me for the rest of my life.

Suicide is now something I can joke about in the company of

263

somebody who has become a great influence in my life. Throughout my troubled times I'd been reading several self-help books by authors such as Dr Wayne Dyer and Mary Anne Williamson. Then my brother Daniel introduced me to the work of a Malaysian called Dr Yong Lim, who is basically a reiki healer. He can harness the energy in the universe, and channels it through his hands to heal people. In addition, Yong is a clairvoyant who sees things such as auras and spirits. I wouldn't say he is a Christian or a Buddhist; he's non-religious, but very spiritual. Most of all I'd say he appealed to my sense of curiosity.

Yong lived in Melbourne for part of the year, and held open house once a week to try and heal people's illnesses. He immediately recognised that I was prone to bouts of depression that bordered on the suicidal; apparently this was immediately visible from an indentation at the bottom of my throat, and the fact that it was hairy made it even worse. As you will immediately understand, a lot of what he told me seemed extremely weird, but gradually he made me far more aware of much higher powers, such as God.

Emily really wasn't keen on Yong. So many of the things he taught were in conflict with her beliefs and caused a considerable amount of friction between the pair of us. She insisted his intentions weren't as nice as he claimed - in fact she thought he was full of shit, and likened my belief in his powers to the way the Beatles got sucked in by the Maharishi all those years earlier. I can understand her point of view because some of the things he taught were so far into left field. Try this one for size: Yong insists there is no right or wrong, as an all-loving God wouldn't judge us; therefore he believes someone like Adolf Hitler isn't in hell. As I understand it, Hitler believed implicitly that the horrendous things being carried out on his orders were right. Such belief appeased him.

When you get to the bottom

Of course I'm not surprised a lot of people view that particular theory with great scepticism, not to say revulsion. However, I'm prepared to listen to most of the things Yong teaches. Why? The answer would have to be, my experiences have forced me to doubt so many traditional values. Though I was brought up a Roman Catholic, I'm now convinced so much of the faith is based upon guilt. Some of the teachings are fantastic, but the rules are bad. Many years ago, when I was still a teenager, I went to church in Florida around Easter. Just a couple of days earlier I'd been with my pals from Iron Maiden who looked rough and wild, but were really down-to-earth, family guys with the right values. The priest in that Floridian church started delivering his sermon on the City of God and the City of Sin, and insisted that guys with long hair who played 'geetars' would all go to the City of Sin. But these were my friends he was talking about, and I knew more about them than him; and I suddenly realised that many of the men who stand before the alter really spout a great deal that is untrue and plain ignorant. Fortunately I have a fantastic priest back home in Melbourne who has christened three of my four children.

When I speak about Yong I always refer to him as the craziest or strangest man I've ever met.My knowledge has grown so much since I met him, and though I wouldn't say he's calmed me, I now can be more patient with other people. He's convinced me that there's no such thing as right or wrong. Many of the things he showed me caused discomfort on my behalf. I wasn't happy with matters like voodoo and the dark side, but he also taught me so many alternative health therapies.

Not long after Cottonwood, I went to Malaysia for one of Jong's master courses to learn reiki healing, but I also became involved in something many people would find really scary: I began to

265

communicate with the spirits of dead people. Previously that sort of thing had me completely freaked out, but with Yong and his assistants in attendance, I was willing to give it a try. Or was I? When the person who wanted to make contact with his dead father started moaning and screaming on the verge of a fit, I wasn't so sure. A group of us were sitting around with our hands all placed on top of a table that suddenly started tipping because the spirit was communicating. The man, sitting ten feet away, had meanwhile gone into a trance.

I know what the cynics amongst you are saying: yes, we've all played at seances and moving glasses on weaji boards. But this was not a set-up, and Yong quickly arrived to assess the situation. He made the other four of us stand up, but keep our hands on the table. Now the next few sentences will be unbelievable to many, and like a scene from the *Exorcist* to others, but the table tipped onto two legs and, wobbling from side to side, walked the ten feet to the guy. I was neither scared nor amused, but Yong assured us everything was fine, and that the man's father just wanted to communicate: the spirit had entered the room, and there was energy apparent that was moving the table. Yong told the man his father had arrived, and they should dance together. Though we still had our hands on the table so as not to break the energy, both the man and the table were dancing together.Then he bowed as if praying, and stayed there fully five minutes before falling back and awakening from his trance. He had no recollection of the dancing, and didn't remember too much at all, but had an idea his father had been in the room.

This sparked a curiosity in me to learn whether any of my dead relatives wanted to contact me. Yong insists spirits are everywhere, and that most of them love to communicate if you are willing to put in the effort. I've since made contact with both my stepbrother

When you get to the bottom

Ralph and young cousin Gabriel, who both took their own lives. With Ralph the communication wasn't too strong, which might have had something to do with either his reluctance or my inexperience. Sometimes people close their eyes and get visions, but the only thing that came into my mind was a car. Ralph did used to love cars, but maybe I was putting the thought into my head.

When I was a child I used to spend a lot of time with Gabriel. She was a teenager who became depressed and took too many sleeping pills. When I made contact with her, she spelt a message she wanted passed on to her family: it said 'I am in heaven'. Passing the message on to her mother and sister was an extremely emotional experience, and at the time I didn't know whether I was doing the right thing. However, I'd promised Gabriel. So I told my Aunt Mary and cousin Elizabeth that what I was about to say might sound really weird, particularly as I didn't know whether they believed in this sort of happening or not. The first thing they asked was, could it have been a trick? I assured them it could not, and I think the message gave them some form of relief.

Several years earlier I'd got to know Princess Diana quite well. I'd heard she was quite a fan of mine after watching me win the Wimbledon final, and I met her for the first time when Boris Becker and I played an exhibition match for charity at the David Lloyd Club near Heathrow Airport. I suppose I talked to her for twice as long as everybody else. After that we bumped into each other quite regularly at film premieres and other occasions. She played tennis, was very interested in the sport, and always seemed to know what I'd been doing and which sort of injury I'd been struggling with. I last met her at the Harbour Club in London about three months before she died. We played mixed doubles against the club professional and a lady called Mandy Sargeant who runs the tennis there. After a few games Princess Diana stopped to take a drink of water. She asked if I had anything to drink, and I replied that I hadn't. She asked if I wanted any of hers. Thinking I couldn't possibly take such a liberty I refused, but she replied: 'Why not? I haven't got any germs'. Ny reply was as crisp as one of my best volleys: 'Yeah, but I have!'

Princess Diana had done a lot of work with somebody I knew called Eileen Whitaker, a naturopath and numerologist. Eileen often used to give Diana particular herbs for her health, and she also convinced me to have my name changed by deed poll. Apparently every letter in your name has a number, and if you add them up, the signals can be good or bad. With a final k at the end of Patrick, things didn't look too healthy, so I changed my name to Patric. I think it has made a difference.

Eileen often used to talk to me about Princess Diana, and I know Yong had some involvement with her. So did an American motivational guru called Anthony Robins, who specialises in neuro-linguistic programming. He's done some work with my psychologist Jeff Bond in the field of positive thought and affirmation. One day I was having a conversation with Princess Diana along with Mandy Sargeant and my wife Emily. We were talking about things Di could and couldn't do, and she admitted that much as she wanted to, she couldn't talk to Anthony Robins because he was termed a guru, and before too long it would be all over the newspapers and magazines.

With that, she picked up a newspaper and started reading about herself. I could see immediately that she was upset about the article, and thought, if ever there was a person who shouldn't read newspapers, it was her. I'd seen the same problem with John McEnroe in that Adelaide breakfast room, and had got so confused myself: all these people who didn't even know me had presumed to write about what kind of person I had turned out to be.

At that moment I felt really sorry for Princess Diana. I'd heard she liked to manipulate the press and was obsessed by what people thought of her. The whole thing must have become so painful for her, so when she died, I almost thought it was a release for her. Regardless of knowing her quite well, I wasn't too upset. She was really a prisoner of her own fame and had become terribly tortured. You could argue she was just finding happiness again in her relationship with Dodi El Fayed - but would she ever have been left sufficiently alone to be truly happy?

Chapter Fourteen

THE FLIP SIDE

After being forced into retirement against my will, I decided to keep well away from tennis. I felt repelled by everyone and everything to do with the sport, and needed something totally different into which to channel my energies. In addition I also needed to earn some money. Now my house in Fulham is close to the fictitious home of that marvellous television character Arthur Daley, and I got into a little bit of business of which the cigar-puffing old geezer in the camel overcoat and trilby hat would have been really proud.

Nothing underhand, you understand; on the face of it, everything was totally legitimate and above board. But the man who'd won Wimbledon and jetted around the world as one of tennis' most recognisable stars was selling baseball caps depicting the flags of various nations before the soccer World Cup. A friend called Peter Bauer at the time ran the company Global Caps, and had the official license for the 1998 World Cup in France. He suggested I sold the caps in England, and it seemed like a good idea.

Soon a shipment of 10,500 of them arrived in the warehouse of Her Majesty's Customs and Excise at Heathrow Airport. Unfortunately they didn't come with bar-code labels, so rounding up ten mates, I set off down the M4 motorway for a few days hard graft. Basically we had to open up all the boxes, take the caps out of their plastic wrappers, snap on the labels, and then repackage them. It was boring but good fun, and as far as actually being in the warehouse was concerned, extremely illegal.

The customs officers said we shouldn't have been in there at all, and on no account were we to go into one particular section of the warehouse. Maybe there were guns in there or something equally dodgy. Still, nobody saw anything as we kicked footballs about as occasional light relief and, as Arthur would have said, it was a nice little earner.

Baseball caps weren't a lasting career option, however, and before too long I was being coerced into much more familiar territory. Undoubtedly the story sounds familiar, but picture an Australian tennis player with unquestioned talent and sufficient potential to win Wimbledon who had lost his way. Pressures from home were becoming too much to bear, and he was wondering whether all the heartache was worthwhile.

By all accounts Mark Philippoussis was on the verge of a nervous breakdown when I received a telephone call asking for help. He'd refused to play in a Davis Cup tie that Australia subsequently lost at home to Zimbabwe. Then to make matters worse, he extremely unwisely allowed the Victorian premier Jeff Kennett to fly him by helicopter to watch the tie upstate in Bendigo.

Turning your back on the Australian Davis Cup cause was unheard of, and not surprisingly everybody was ragging on Philippoussis. The stick was also flying from an all-too-familiar source to me: John Newcombe, who was now the Aussie Davis Cup captain. Mark Woodforde also took some pot shots, and Pat Rafter dumped Philippoussis as a doubles partner. Predictably his form didn't just drop, it crashed, and by the time he arrived at Queen's to defend his Stella Artois title in June, the guy was a mess.

I'd known Gavin Hopper, Philippoussis' coach and fitness trainer, for years, and he'd long been asking me to lend a helping hand to a fellow Melbourne boy. I wasn't at all keen, because back then I was still trying to play on the main tour. As you may recall, I'd never been particularly predisposed to passing on my secrets to potential opponents. But now the situation had changed, and listening to what Philippoussis said when he lost to the Spanish clay-court baseliner Jordi Burillo at Queen's, I could see he needed guidance. He was calling his year pathetic, and admitted he was very confused because he'd been making himself look bad. The first flight back to his home in Florida was beckoning and he was questioning the worth of even playing Wimbledon.

The signs of depression were there for all to see. The well-known saying used in therapy immediately sprang to mind, namely, to start any form of recovery you must first hit rock bottom. To my mind Philippoussis had hit those depths, so I returned Gavin's phone call and was told the blindingly obvious: the kid needed help with his confidence, the insecurity stemming from problems in his game. I mentioned spotting a couple of things that might help, so we all sat down at a house in Wimbledon; and I was immediately impressed by the way he wanted to listen.

I told him he needed to work hard on concentration, and that he was just cruising into the net for the volley when he should really have been charging. I pointed out the Jimmy Connors practice ethic of every single ball really counting, and advised him not to read newspapers because being publicly slated by everyone doesn't exactly ease the mind. Moving onto the practice court, we worked so hard his legs grew sore - but all of a sudden he was getting those volleys. In combination with the rest of the Philippoussis game - that awesome serve, and ground shots hit harder than anyone - the guy certainly had a chance.

The media love labels, and somewhere along the line Philippoussis was given with the nickname Scud because he hits the ball with the velocity of a deadly missile. He hates it, and much prefers to be simply called Flip, which suited me. And the more I worked with him, the better I realised he could be, to the extent where I considered he possessed more talent in his little finger than Mark Woodforde had in the whole of his body. I'm also convinced he was a better player than Pat Rafter. There's no comparison between the capabilities of their serves, and nobody hits either backhands or forehands from the rear of the court like Flip. Admittedly Pat volleyed better, judged on athleticism, and was a tougher character; but breaking down all the elements, I would just give it to Flip.

However, he did have one overriding handicap in the battle: his father Nick. There's no doubt Flip was always heavily influenced by his dad, who in some ways would handle any situation with something verging on paranoia. In a Greek family, the son is viewed as a god, and though Flip has a lovely sister, everything was about the boy. I came onto the scene just as Flip's parents were divorcing, and Nick was also in the midst of a battle against cancer, which thankfully he appears to have won. For his son, an extremely shy young man aged just twenty-one years old, it was undoubtedly a very tough time, and I tried to offer support.

My mind did repeatedly travel back to the first time I'd ever seen Mark four or five years earlier. Allan Stone, then working as the Victorian state coach in Melbourne, asked me if I could hit some balls with this extremely big powerful kid. I was very impressed

When you get to the bottom

when several balls went flying past my racket, but somewhat put off by this person screaming, arguing and repeatedly walking onto the court. Several months later I played doubles against Flip and another Aussie called Jamie Morgan. Nick was dismayed by his son's performance, and hit Flip over the head before hurling a chair down a flight of stairs.

Initially I didn't have a problem with Nick. He was progressing well in his fight against illness, and became involved in a relationship with another woman. Everything seemed fine, and he seemed content to have somebody like me helping his son. Within just a matter of weeks, Flip had regained sufficient confidence to reach the Wimbledon quarter-final, beating seventh-seeded Yevgeny Kafelnikov before losing to eventual champion Pete Sampras. More importantly he was practising and playing like it really mattered. His attitude was back, and he was diving around the practice court like his life depended on the outcome.

Flip was pleased, and made it plain he wanted to work with me. However, there was just one problem: the agent who would work out any deal between us was none other than Tom Ross, that same fool who so nearly got his head ripped from his shoulders for that idiotic display in the Kooyong locker room more than eleven years earlier. Talking to Ross wasn't easy, but he affirmed that Flip wanted me on board through Wimbledon and the US Open.

By then I had grown to like the kid, so I was prepared to put aside all my pre-conceived ideas about his agent, and just concentrate on helping Flip realise his potential. I was still wary, however, and didn't want to get ripped off financially, though I realised I was in a weak bargaining position having no previous coaching experience. But I also wanted an easy get-out if things became intolerable with Nick Philippoussis or Ross. So I agreed on a fee of

$US2,000 a week; it wasn't great, but if things didn't work out, there wouldn't be a problem.

Though results leading up to the US Open weren't earth-shattering, I knew things were moving in the right direction. After ending British hopes by eliminating Tim Henman, everything came truly came together with a magnificent win over Thomas Johansson, who would progress to be crowned the surprise Australian Open champion earlier this year. Flip produced the best tennis I ever saw him play to beat the Swede on Arthur Ashe Stadium that night. He was thrilled, and so were Gavin and I, as we could see great things emerging on the horizon. Some of the clean winners were stunning to watch as the match progressed and the time grew later and later. So when we eventually arrived back in Manhattan victorious but hungry, we struggled to find somewhere to eat in the city that maintains it never sleeps.

An old New York buddy called Jean-Marc Rousseau suggested we could get a bite at his Midtown establishment, called the Lava Lounge. Nothing could have been more perfect for Flip. With so much adrenalin still flowing, sleep was not an option, and by the time we arrived, a string of pretty girls were walking through the door. We stuck him away in a corner table, but before long he'd developed an appetite for something a little more succulent than a bowl of pasta: next door to the Lava Lounge was a strip club, and Flip just loves that sort of place.

Suddenly he seemed like a little boy, begging for his reward for that evenings good deed. I lost count of the number of times he said please, and eventually agreed - but made him promise it would only be for half an hour, and for just a couple of lap dances. I went in first, and before long everybody had gathered, except for Flip. Trying to track him down I headed back to the door to find the

When you get to the bottom

familiar 6ft 4in figure arguing with the doorman about his age because he'd forgotten his ID! Thinking it was a blessing in disguise, I told his buddy Tony Ivans to strong-arm him into a taxi and get him back to the hotel. He was insistent of returning straightaway, paying little apparent heed to my parting words: Flip, you can win the US Open, so don't fuck up. You played the match of your life tonight, and there's Carlos Moya in two days time. We can go to all the strip joints you want after the tournament, but this is your big chance.

Strip clubs aren't really my choice for a good night out, and within half an hour I was also back in the hotel. I rang his room to check he was safely between the sheets, and told him there was nothing to worry about; the strippers weren't that pretty anyway. Two days later he got his reward, after another great showing against Moya; and he was through to an all-Australian final against the defending champion Rafter, who'd given him the flick as a doubles partner. It was an afternoon memorable for one thing - and that wasn't the tennis.

Ask me one person I would never expect to be on the other end of the line when the telephone rings in my room, and I'd probably answer John Newcombe. However, Flip's return to form had stirred the imagination of the Australian Davis Cup captain, who just months earlier had been firing off words like traitor. Newcombe wanted Flip to return to the Aussie team, and for the first time in something approaching twenty years, I agreed with the man. I didn't want my past bitterness to interfere with Flip's career, and firmly believed playing Davis Cup could only be a good thing.

Imagine my total astonishment, therefore, when I took my seat for the final and looked across at the Rafter entourage, there to see Australia's Davis Cup coach and Newcombe's lifelong sidekick

Tony Roche blatantly sitting right in the middle. At the time Pat was insistent he was happier to travel without a coach, maintaining it eliminated numerous logistical problems. Yet there was Rochey, blatantly indicating exactly where the loyalties of the official Australian camp lay. Here we were, trying to get Flip back into the Davis Cup fold, and in return they showed favouritism that couldn't have been more ostentatious.

Flip spotted Rochey immediately, and so did his father. I don't know how much it really affected his performance that afternoon, but there was a lot of jealousy out there on that court. The pair were just about talking again, but friendship was still a long way off. And when they started playing, it became only too clear that Flip had been physically taxed by his wins over Johansson and Moya, while Pat's performance underlined the fact he'd been to this stage before.

Even so, to my surprise Flip wasn't doing anything we planned - for instance he was serve and volleying on his second serves as well as his first. He could damage anyone from the back of the court, but he was undoubtedly scared of Pat getting into the net. You can't argue with Flip's thinking: Pats were the best volleys in the world, and would frighten anyone. I remember Pam Shriver sidling up to do a mid-match interview for television and asking me about Flip's tactics. I tried to disguise my dismay saying: He's doing whatever he wants on court. It's whatever Mark thinks is best.

In the end, it was virtually a one-way traffic, with Flip going down in 6-0 in the fourth and concluding set. Knowing the television cameras were focused on us, I just wanted to get out of there as quickly as possible. But Nick Philippoussis had other ideas, and was furiously flipping the bird to Roche. The TV producer could not have believed his luck as Nick shouted, made gestures, and was generally as abusive as humanly possible from a distance of fifty yards. Come on, I said, philosophically accepting the fact that Rafter was just too good on the day. Let's be good losers. Just because Rochey has done the wrong thing, it doesn't mean that we should as well.

Roche is a quiet, friendly man who was an excellent player and deserves numerous accolades for putting up with all the hours of boredom that must have been involved with being Ivan Lendl's coach for so many years. More recently he has come to be regarded simply as Newcombe's puppet. Rochey will do whatever Newcombe tells him, although he should really have been Davis Cup captain himself. Unfortunately he didn't have the courage to take the job because apparently he doesn't like making speeches. As for Newcombe, he only cares about one thing, and that's making himself look good.

In the locker room after the match Flip didn't concern himself with the relative merits of Newcombe and Roche: he was livid with both. Fuck 'em, he stormed. I'm never playing for them again. They never talk to either you guys or me about my form, and never watch my matches. All they care about is Pat, and Rochey even parks himself right in the middle of his box.

Even now I find Roche's behaviour hard to comprehend. Afterwards I asked him why he sat up there, saying he and Newcombe had shot their chances of getting Flip to play Davis Cup straight through the foot. Rochey just shrugged and said he had to do it for Pat, as they had previously worked together, but that didn't make any sense to me.

Later that evening I felt the time was right to start building bridges, so I suggested Flip might just drop by the Rafter party for a short while. Initially he was totally against the idea, but I told him to trust me because it was the right thing to do. I knew that all the jealousy and bitterness was chewing him up inside, and such resentment would always give Pat the upper hand in future contests. In the end Flip agreed, and fortunately Newcombe or Roche weren't anywhere to be seen. Pat's brothers Steve and Jeff seemed surprised to see us, and we only stayed for one beer, a shake of the hand and a brief chat - but it worked.

To be honest, I can't remember much more about the evening. It was one of those occasions when the booze numbed the memory, but something good emerged. Flip even made his Davis Cup return alongside Pat in Zimbabwe in the following April, and I'd like to think I played a part in his decision. Suddenly after so many years of being an outlaw, I'd become quite the diplomat!

My coaching couldn't have been too bad, either. After the disappointment of a fourth round exit to eventual runner-up Thomas Enqvist at the Australian Open, Flip went on to win titles at San Jose and Indian Wells. Before long he'd peaked at his highest ever ranking of eight, and things appeared to be going great - until, almost a year since first hooking up, we arrived on the London grass of Queen's Club.

Personally, I wasn't going through the happiest phase of my life, and Flip had to play Lleyton Hewitt, who by then was really showing that he was destined to be one of tennis's next big stars. To my utter dismay, Flip produced the most lackadaisical performance, as if he just couldn't be bothered. With no regard for privacy, I launched into an angry locker room diatribe afterwards: You are not putting in the effort, I seethed, as he tried in vain to mumble a reply. You've more talent than all these guys, and you are letting down both yourself and your family. If you want to fire tomorrow, that's fine, but you are wimping out. You're gutless.

Nick took me aside afterwards, and insisted the blame should be

When you get to the bottom

laid on Gavin, for not firing Flip up for lesser matches. The argument was ridiculous, and I told him so; besides, the problem was familiar to me: it was the old Aussie hang-up of playing a fellow countryman, and all the inherent pressures. Hewitt was the next big threat, and Flip tried to adopt his apathetic Greek mentality.

We never did find out exactly how well he responded to the lambasting, because fate then took a hold at Wimbledon. Cruising past a quartet of opponents, including Woodforde and Rusedski, he walked out to confront Sampras in the quarter-final. A few days earlier I aggravated my old knee injury, and surgery was required. Once again history repeated itself, as my surgeon John Browett was about to go on holiday. He had one spot available on his operating schedule, and that was the day before the Sampras match. After checking myself out of the hospital early to be with Flip before he went on court, I was still feeling groggy from the anaesthetic as I stumbled into the locker room. Straightaway I was greeted by the omnipresent sound of Brad Gilbert's voice: Now that's a bad omen, he mocked.

Yet how right BG turned out to be. Flip played like he was on fire to take the first set against Sampras, and many were already prophesying he was on his way to the title. I'm not so sure. Even if he'd beaten the eventual champion, there was still Agassi, Rafter and Henman left in the tournament. However, any such thinking soon turned out to be hypothetical.

Falling awkwardly after hitting a backhand passing shot down the line, Flip heard an ominous click in his left knee. Thinking nothing much of it, he went to jump forward onto another service return, when the left knee gave way. Sensibly he decided to quit straightaway. I limped back to the locker room, only to see Flip in tears on the massage table. This disappointment was all too familiar, and I felt so sad for him that tears were soon rolling down my cheeks as well. Investigations showed he'd suffered semi-serious miniscus damage that required immediate surgery. Meanwhile Sampras was insisting he'd dodged a bullet, before progressing to his sixth Wimbledon title in seven years.

Seriously defective vision meant Flip was also long overdue for laser surgery to correct the problem; God knows how he even saw the ball with eyesight that poor. As I was contracted to work twenty weeks a year with Flip, I arrived at his Florida home at Long Boat Key only to find he'd already travelled to New York for treatment. It's fair to say Flip had an impulsive personality. The laser corrected his eyesight, and everything would have been fine had he been careful and kept using the antibiotic drops.

Just a few days after the operation, before his first match in Indianapolis, Flip decided to play a fun game of basketball. Again bad luck struck, as he bent back a finger of his racket hand, which ruled out a couple of days preparation. Far from learning our lesson, we headed to New York's Chelsea Piers to do more fitness work before a hopeful return at the US Open. Flip was dominating another friendly basketball match with some locals when he got shoved in the act of shooting. Losing his balance, he landed on an opponent's foot and twisted his ankle.

Letting sense prevail, any thoughts of a return to Flushing Meadows were canned, and he finally got back on court in mid-October. By this time I'd spotted the first warning signs that on the business side, things weren't quite as straightforward as they seemed.

Father and son Philippoussis had moved their business from Advantage to IMG. Gavin Forbes, one of Mark McCormack's good

When you get to the bottom

guys, had negotiated a far better deal with me, and assuming I'd be travelling, we were now talking $US6,000 a week. Normally I would invoice Flip through his agent, and even though he hadn't played the US Open, I'd been employed to see him through the tournament, and had spent time in New York for the preparations. Back came the reply that payment was being withheld because he hadn't played.

I let the matter slide because I had a bad knee after my operation during Wimbledon, and wouldn't be around much until the New Year. Money wasn't a huge issue anyway, because Flip had given me an extremely generous $40,000 bonus after reaching the US Open final. However, averaged out, this really only served to pay me the fee I would have charged under normal circumstances.

Flip's spending is legendary. He was a young man who loved his toys, most of them being extremely expensive items with names such as Ferrari, Lamborghini or Harley Davidson. At one stage he owned five different properties, and must have had in excess of $US5 million lying idle in houses and cars he didn't use. For a while he loved riding motorbikes around, although he didn't have a licence. When we practised at Nick Bollettieri's place in Florida, Gavin and I used to have to drive in a car right behind Flip's bike just in case the police pulled him over or he got in trouble.

I remember walking into the house on Long Boat Key near Sarasota during one of Flip's injury layoffs, and he was screaming to know the whereabouts of his new motorcycle. Nick, playing the fatherly role, insisted it was being kept under wraps until his son started playing again. Flip then produced the sort of tantrum I wouldn't have expected from either of my young twin sons: he screamed he wanted it and what's more, he wanted it *now*, and he wouldn't stop shouting until the bike was presented to him. Nick simply turned and ran, while I stood there open-mouthed in amazement.

Next day the motorbike was given to him, and the episode gave me a distinct insight into Flip's personality. When you know that shouting and screaming will eventually get you what you want, it's extremely hard to knuckle down and put in a concerted period of hard work. Similarly it also made life even more complicated for Flip out there in matches, because when things started going wrong, Daddy couldn't come to his aid. He's a nice kid, but is prone to laziness because he's always been so used to getting his own way. Consequently he struggles to really commit himself to working hard for much more than a week or two.

However, there was nothing wrong with his effort during three memorable days in Nice when he won Australia the Davis Cup for the first time since I'd overcome Mickael Pernfors thirteen years previously. Playing on a slow indoor court of red clay, Flip became the hero as he first beat Sebastien Grosjean in straight sets, then overcame both the patriotic crowd and Cedric Pioline's experience to clinch the cup. It gave John Newcombe his finest triumph as Davis Cup captain - but what gratitude did he show to the person who had worked hard persuading Flip to actually play?Nobody need take too long in working out the answer.

Newcombe knew he was in trouble weeks before the final because his favourite player Rafter had shoulder problems and wouldn't be fit. At that stage Flip really didn't want to play, but I kept insisting it was something he should do, not only because it would make him a better player by toughening him up to pressure situations, but also, coming to the aid of his country in its hour of need would make his situation back home in Australia a lot easier. Newcombe had been telephoning me for updates on Flip's fitness

When you get to the bottom

even before the semi-final over Russia in Brisbane. I just gave him the facts and kept out of the issues, because I didn't want Newcombe to think any of our past differences were affecting Flip.

I didn't particularly want to help Newcombe on his way to experiencing the glory of winning the Davis Cup; I just wanted Flip to become a better player. Plus the timing was good, because after a frustrating second half of the year he was fit, fresh and eager. Sitting at home in London I waited for each day's post in the hope an invite to the final would drop through the letter box. Could I say I was totally surprised when nothing arrived, although all the other coaches - Gavin, Darren Cahill and even Nick Philippoussis - were asked along for the ride? Even though I was only two hours away, neither Newcombe or Tennis Australia could bring themselves to invite me.

The matter was still much on my mind six weeks later when I was invited onto a current affairs programme in Australia, just before the Open. I wanted to speak out against Newcombe, knowing that Flip still despised him, regardless of all the back-slapping in Nice. So I asked the question: How is a player supposed to give 100 per cent effort when he's playing for somebody he knows doesn't like him? I said we were talking about somebody who always supports the other guy, and wasn't really interested in healing rifts.

Once again I'd shown the way to starting a big fuss, and this time even the Victorian premier Jeff Kennett got involved, saying I repeatedly opened my mouth when I shouldn't. Now Kennett is infamous for having one of the biggest mouths of all time, and in addition his loyalties have long been stuck firmly in Newcombe's camp. I just laughed at the accusation, responding that I remembered an old story about the pot calling the kettle something? In retrospect I felt bad because I didn't want to get dragged back

285

into that sort of thing, and feared for the harm it might do Flip. Entering the locker room with the intention of apologising, I was greeted by an amused Philippoussis who said he thought the whole thing was funny. And he added that he was thankful for the fact the flak wasn't aimed at him for a change.

After playing in the opening round of Australia's defence, Flip again pulled out of the team, thereby incurring the wrath of the normally amiable Rafter. Pat seemed to think it was his own team, and told Flip he couldn't just pick and choose when to play. Flip replied he'd just won the cup, and basically I think Pat was jealous. He'd done all the hard work for years, and then saw Flip come in to become the hero.

If Rafter was jealous of Philippoussis over that matter, you could probably say there were thousands more who might be jealous concerning something else. Indeed, it produced one of the trickiest problems I've encountered as a coach: basically, how do you tell a fit, eligible young man that it's probably not a good idea to spend the night with Anna Kournikova?

By the time everyone turned up at Melbourne Park for the first Australian Open of the new millennium, Anna and Flip had been enjoying a fling for a while. The Russian ice hockey player Sergei Federov seemed to have been languishing on the rocks, and Flip was most certainly in pole position. Anna and he were photographed having a little peck in the tournament car park, but things definitely went a lot further than that. During the tournament Gavin and I had to physically keep him away from her room, saying it was 'probably not a good idea to visit Anna tonight because there's a big match tomorrow'. As somebody who was forced to drag his tongue off the floor every time she was in the vicinity, believe me it was a tough thing to say: she's a stunningly beautiful girl with a gorgeous face and figure and not surprisingly, she knows it as well. Flip's problem was she ordered him to telephone her three or four times every day, just to tell her how attractive she was. But after a while it became too much effort; after all, he was used to girls ringing him.

Anna just grew so demanding that Flip became really fed up with it. Besides, the Russian was still on the scene, and Flip came to the conclusion that she wasn't worth all the bother. He's a great lover of nightlife, and there was no shortage of beautiful young things more than happy to take Anna's place. Deep down I'm sure he also knew the relationship wouldn't go very far.

Gavin Hopper and I had considerably less attractive issues that required action. And the problem of Nick Philippoussis interfering was also returning. In my absence he'd become increasingly influential at practice sessions, with father and son forever talking in Greek, both before and after matches; and Gavin noted that Flip appeared under more pressure when his dad was around. In the light of this, I first said my piece at the big Paris indoor tournament at Bercy before the Davis Cup final.

Taking Nick to one side and attempting to be as diplomatic as possible, I told him we were all in danger of putting too much information into Flip's head. All we needed to do was concentrate on the basics, and technically his son's game was fine; Gavin and I were just trying to fine-tune a couple of things, but nothing too much was wrong. Nick was in total agreement, insisting his Marco was a good boy, and all he was doing was trying to instil a little added confidence. Fine, we all wanted the best for Flip - and then no more than a minute after walking on court to hit a couple of balls, I saw Nick jabbering away in Greek and motioning how he wanted his son to follow through after a hitting a backhand. I looked at Gavin, he grimaced back at me, and we both just turned away.

After three relatively easy matches at the Open, Flip was drawn to play Andre Agassi in the last sixteen. There couldn't have been a bigger match, and just as I started to warm him up with a few simple ground shots, Nick started giving me orders: don't hit the ball too far away from him; don't hit it too hard; don't play too many winners; make him feel good. I couldn't believe what I was hearing. I'd played a million matches, and warmed other players up for probably as many. With the notable exception of the Davis Cup final, I'd prepared Flip for all his big matches over the last eighteen months; then all of a sudden here is a guy ordering me around who's never played a tennis match in his life. Of course I wasn't going to destroy him before he faced the best player in the world, even if I could.

Shaking my head on that practice court, I realised it was all becoming too much. Glancing down the other end I could see that Gavin, too, was getting to the end of his tether with the man's meddling. There were specifics we wanted to work on before Flip played Agassi, but it became increasingly difficult.

Though Flip played very well, Agassi was just on fire that fortnight. The match was a ripper, and many remember it for a lone trumpeter high up in the stand playing the National Anthem in a patriotic attempt to motivate Australia's Davis Cup hero. It didn't work, but Flip could leave the court with his head held high, and afterwards I told him there was no disgrace in losing a match of that quality.

Flip then told me he was heading off for a few days break before flying to Switzerland for the Davis Cup. I said fine, wished him good luck, and then said I wanted him to put in 20 per cent extra

When you get to the bottom

effort both on and off the court during the upcoming months. If he did that, I assured him he'd win a Grand Slam title because he was getting so close. Little did I know that that would be the last conversation I'd ever have with Mark Philippoussis as his coach.

Flip and his dad had left town by the time I sat down to speak to Tom Ross a few days later. The Philippoussis business had been swiftly returned to Advantage, and Ross has been reappointed his agent.Assuming I was still in a job, I wanted to talk about the upcoming year - but Ross started dodging the issues. He said things had become confusing. Mark hadn't received any prize money at the US Open, but had still had to pay both Gavin and I, which amounted to a considerable amount of money. I insisted it was a fact of life, and pointed out that my deal had dropped from $US6,000 to $5,000 a week, plus the standard 10 per cent of winnings. Ross came back and said the plan was to offer me a base fee retainer of $50,000 for the year. I ended the conversation saying the offer wasn't acceptable.

Two months later I'd heard no more, though Flip had again been sidelined with a reoccurrence of knee problems. The *Herald-Sun*'s Leo Schlink telephoned to ask my whereabouts, and I told him Flip's people hadn't got back to me after offering less than half of what I'd been paid the previous year. When Flip made his comeback at Indian Wells, he was embarrassed by Leo's questioning about me, and pleaded total ignorance of what was going on.

Gavin telephoned to enquire about the situation, and I replied that Ross was only offering me $50,000 a year, when I could earn $20,000 just by playing a few days in a senior tour tournament. He confirmed Flip had no idea of what had been offered, but I pointed out that he was the person employing me, and should talk to his agents now and again. Next I sent an email to Ross, saying I must have a final offer by 1 April, or negotiations were off. No reply was ever forthcoming.

I've never asked Flip the reasons, although Gavin and I regularly speculate. Gavin thinks Nick became jealous because I got some positive publicity when his son was doing well. Although that's partially true, I've never been one for publicly patting myself on the back, and shied away from a lot of interviews. I always preferred to give credit to the player.

By the time of the French Open, Boris Becker was helping Flip, together with his former coach Mike DePalmer. Later that same year Gavin's contract was also cancelled because he was supposed to work exclusively with Philippoussis and he'd been coaching somebody else. So who was Gavin's other player? His nine-year-old daughter Jade. He's still owed in excess of $30,000, but cannot get it out of Advantage. And it's unlikely he ever will, because Flip has now taken his business to IMG yet again.

In retrospect it was the right time for me to go because Nick Philippoussis was becoming a pest, and Flip wasn't putting in the required effort. I was also worried about the state of his knees, and haven't been too surprised at the problems he's suffered since. Now he is having synthetic cartilages injected every few months, and that's not something to suggest a long career. I know he's talked about rededicating himself, and seeing the error of his indolent ways, but I fear it's too late. If he ever wants any advice I'll be only too happy to help - but he must keep his dad out of the way.

I'm not surprised he's still refusing to play Davis Cup, even though John Fitzgerald is now the Australian captain. Several years ago Flip was playing a tournament in the Czech town of Ostrava, the birthplace of Ivan Lendl. As you might imagine from the personality of its most famous son, the place isn't exactly a barrel-load of laughs. After losing a match, Flip went out and got a little drunk, and next morning insisted he didn't feel well enough to fulfil an obligation at a coaching clinic.Consequently he was fined a hefty $US20,000 by a committee that included Guy Forget and Fitzy.

Naturally, Flip was livid and wanted retribution. I told him the best way to hit back against Forget was to channel his anger into the upcoming Davis Cup final. As for Fitzy, I told him not to worry, because there'd be another time. To my way of thinking, Fitzy is a great guy and one of my best mates; but he does have his fingers in so many pies, such as Tennis Australia, the ATP board and Channel 7 television. I also knew he didn't like Nick Philippoussis, and was wary of Flip. When I heard Fitzy was being appointed Davis Cup captain, I knew there would be trouble with Philippoussis.

If somebody asked me to give Flip one piece of advice it would be to take charge of his own life, once and for all. For too long he's allowed other people to take care of it for him, be it his father or his agents. There have been times when he didn't either know or care which tournaments he'd be playing, and left it up to Gavin and myself. He was more concerned about the next nightclub or lap-dancing joint.

To a certain extent I respect his 'Enjoy it while it lasts' approach because for me, sometimes it was too far the other way. But now he has got to change his attitude, and not just for a couple of weeks but for good. When I hear him talk about rededicating himself to tennis after wasting too many years, I do believe him; but it's got to be for as long as his career lasts. How long that will be I don't know, and as I have said already, reports of him requiring synthetic cartilages injected into his knees every few months doesn't suggest a longevity.

But for Mark Philippoussis to end his career without a Grand Slam title to his name would be a tragedy, because there have been few more talented players to emerge in the last ten years. In my opinion he was infinitely more gifted than Lleyton Hewitt, but woefully lacked the same commitment and determination.Flip's not a kid anymore; he's got eighteen months or possibly two years left to prove himself. And that's if he's lucky.

Chapter Fifteen

Values of Ingratitude

Answer me this one question: is there anyone who hasn't done something they regret? Not repeatedly, maybe just once. And even more specifically, was that one mistake something that always threatened to cause problems, but you chose to ignore your own gut instinct, not to mention numerous warnings from others? Of course I've done many things in my time that I unquestionably wish I hadn't; indeed, the preceding pages present something of a catalogue. However, nothing causes me quite such angry remorse as the six months during which a certain Greg Rusedski became a dominant character in my life.

Nobody could say I wasn't tipped off about Rusedski when he started to make overtures concerning my services. His reputation with coaches had become notorious around the ATP Tour. Nobody he employed was guaranteed a gold watch for long service - but that suited most of his cast-offs: by the time the axe fell, they'd already had more than enough. For most people the case of Brian Teacher, who guided him to a US Open final and a spot in the world's top five players, comes most immediately to mind. Teacher, who might just have been entitled to a bonus after helping his man into the big money, was in fact rewarded with the sack.

Another sobering fact was the number of fellow players who refused even to practise with Rusedski. Even Australia's Scotty Draper, one of the nicest guys on the tour who had suffered the utmost tragedy when his young wife died, required lengthy persuasion before he would walk out onto a practice court with his fellow left-hander. And Sven Groeneveld, the Dutchman who was told his coaching services would no longer be required just months after acting as Rusedski's best man though he has subsequently been re-employed - told me to be extremely careful. Heeding the advice of nobody, I galloped in to make one of the biggest gaffes of my life.

My experiences with Mark Philippoussis had partly soured me to the life of coaching a top-flight player. Linking up with Gavin Hopper, my only true ally in the Philippoussis camp, we were in the process of establishing a tennis academy at Hope Island near Sanctuary Cove, about fifty miles south of Brisbane on Queensland's Gold Coast. In addition, I'd come to terms with playing on the Senior Tour, and had even grown to enjoy the competitive element after running into a certain Brad Langevad.

I'd built myself a completely new game after the former Australian player Kim Warwick had introduced me to this slightly strange character who used to play a bit of doubles on the circuit. If you had to categorise Brad, he's a bio-mechanist, though I'd prefer to call him a genius, and maybe something of a mad scientist. Kim recommended him when I was recovering from my back surgery. At the time I thought I knew everything there was to know about both my game and rehabilitation, but how wrong I was proven to be.

Brad worked with videotapes, recording my matches and practice over a period of time. He painstakingly analysed every facet of my movement, identifying which muscles were actually doing what, and pointing out the problems that caused stress and strain on the body. He then sat me down to try and explain. My immediate reaction was of course: If I've got such a shitty game, then how on earth did I win Wimbledon?

If I'd have listened a little more, maybe I could have continued playing on the main ATP Tour for several years. As it was, I thought I knew better; and you already know the rest of the story.The day I lost to Byron Black in my last ever Wimbledon was so frustrating. After winning through the qualifying rounds, I knew I was the better player, but realised I needed somebody who could totally revamp my game. My first thought was Tarik Benhabiles, a long-distant junior opponent who now coaches Andy Roddick. Next I recalled that weird guy Brad whom I knew lived near London after marrying an English girl.

It transpired that Brad had discreetly watched my performances in the qualifying round at Roehampton, and knew exactly what to do with my game.In the months that followed, I grew to respect increasingly Brad's point of view; he completely changed my service action, giving me more power than I imagined possible without exerting such stress on my back. However, these revolutionary measures were not enough to convince sufficient tournament directors to get me back on the ATP Tour. Nevertheless I was a convert to the Langevad methods, and more than willing to use them wherever possible.

Fate decreed that Brad and I would have the perfect patient. Initial contact with Rusedski came when a friend of mine called Don McPherson bumped into him at Heathrow Airport. Greg had just split with Groeneveld after a disastrous injury-plagued Wimbledon and Davis Cup that saw Britain lose to Ecuador on

Wimbledon's Number One court. Don is involved in Formula One, but is one of those people who simply has contacts. He got in touch with Rusedski's then agents, SFX Management, to alert them to my availability. A few weeks later Groeneveld approached me at the US Open where I was commentating for television, saying he'd recommend my services to Greg, with the rider that I should be extremely wary.

Foolishly discounting all the bad things I'd heard from numerous sources, I thought Greg's undoubted professionalism would make him a great person with whom to work. He'd had some good results, and his dedication to the task meant he was always prepared to work hard, which came like a breath of fresh air after a supremely talented but ultimately lazy player like Flip. I knew Rusedski's game reasonably well after commentating on his matches and occasionally practising with him over the years. A succession of injuries had hampered him, but that was hardly surprising: he appeared to put enormous strain on his body, and didn't move too well. I, of course, knew just the person who could help: the afore-mentioned Mr Langevad.

Fran Ridler, who then handled most of Greg's business with SFX, telephoned a while later to say he wanted a chat. At that early stage we only spoke on the phone, and didn't mention dates, although I made it clear from the outset that my priority was the Cash/Hopper Academy. Within days friends were emailing me to express their surprise at the news I was coaching Rusedski, and I wondered where their information was coming from because I hadn't breathed a word.

Eventually I went to Greg's house in Battersea for a meeting with him and his wife Lucy, who from the outset I found very switched on and sensible. Previously I'd only played practice sets with Greg,

Values of ingratitude

which I usually won, and when it came to towelling down afterwards we hadn't talked too much. Within minutes I came to realise Greg is a strange conversationalist: his sentences are very staccato, and it's almost as though he's got the whole thing rehearsed. He told me how bad his body had made the last year, and admitted to having a stress fracture in his back. With no emotion, and almost as if he'd made the admission a million times, he said that if his ranking didn't improve he was considering making an insurance claim, taking the money and retiring from the game. As somebody who could specialise on the small print of insurance policies regarding sporting injuries, the thought immediately struck me that he would have been lodging a false claim. He'd had the stress fracture for years, and had long needed to wear a corset on court.

I had an open mind as to whether to work with Greg or not. However, I indicated there were things in his game that needed addressing, and told him how I sympathised with his back problems because I'd been through similar agonies. I made a list of suggestions, naming people such as Brad, my physiotherapist Mark Bender, and finally Marchar Reid, an Aussie based in Spain who trained with Ann Quinn and became an exercise physiologist. Marchar would lay down a fitness programme, while Mark would study the scans taken of Greg's back, and Brad would fully analyse his game. Some time later Ryan Kendrick also got involved; he was another physical specialist who worked at the Super Sports Centre run by the legendary Australian middle distance runner Ron Clarke near the academy. He was very well trained in ultra-sound and other modern techniques, as well as being an excellent masseur, and he would be another useful addition to the line-up. Basically I was formulating what subsequently became known as Team Rusedski.

Uncovered

My role? I suppose you would call it head coach.

Right from the outset I said, with Greg's agreement, that these were the people I wanted him to see. I told him I'd talk to Brad and get back to him with a price on what Brad required as an initial fee for all the basic analysis work. In fairness to Greg, he asked straightaway how much I wanted to be paid, and I told him not to worry about me so long as he was happy. Initially things were on trust, but I was adamant in my assurances to him that my input would save his career. I didn't tell Greg that Brad and I had watched him working at Queen's with Groeneveld. We realised Sven was telling him to do all the wrong things, like bend his knees and jump up. We knew it wouldn't last very long, and Greg's fitness was suffering.

Things started off slowly; we booked Greg for some Pilates sessions to see how his muscles worked. He and I used to hit tennis balls in the mornings with Brad in attendance before I took on the likes of McEnroe, Leconte and Co in the Honda Challenge senior tournament at the Royal Albert Hall.

All along I was thinking of taking Greg down to the Cash/Hopper Academy in Queensland to work over the Christmas and New Year period, thinking it would generate perfect publicity. Then an extremely concerned Mark Bender telephoned to say he'd studied the scans, and his deductions made chilling reading: Unless Greg changes right now, he's in such bad shape that he won't last more than six months, said Mark. He's got an old stress fracture in his back and another in his neck. If he keeps going it won't just be a matter of not playing tennis again; I'm not sure whether he'll be able even to walk.

Immediately we eased up on the back work because all the injury problems he'd had with his spine, his legs, his foot and even his toe

Values of ingratitude

over the years were linked in part to his world record-breaking serve. All the stress had been down one side and his natural balance had been affected. Greg was clearly carrying some excess weight and had an enlarged left breast, almost like a pubescent girl. Quite frankly, with the way Greg served, I was surprised his head didn't come off, but he listened to everything Mark and I told him. My overriding impression was he seemed to trust us, and I told the other guys we should feel the same about him: I was sure he'd reward us properly if we did a good job.

All Greg demanded was that we abide by two distinct rules. The first was that his father Tom, who lives in Canada, was not to be involved: we were not to telephone him or make contact in any way; if he tried to speak to us or even email us, we were to say nothing. After all the hassle I'd suffered from Nick Philippoussis, that was quite frankly music to my ears. Secondly, Greg was insistent on no publicity concerning his injuries, because he was still planning to make the insurance claim if things didn't work out.

Sticking to our plan, everyone headed down to Australia before Christmas. I got Greg and Lucy comfortably installed at a five-star hotel in Surfers' Paradise, and he even sorted out a Jaguar car through his endorsement deal. Everything was going great, we arranged massages, made a complete overhaul of his diet, and when I headed back home to Melbourne for the holidays, he continued working with Brad at the Cash/Hopper Academy.

Greg's improvement over those few weeks was simply phenomenal. He thrived in the environment and revelled in the work. None of us, in our most optimistic moments, expected him to change his game so quickly. We modified the service action and opened his stance on both fore- and backhand. We worked hard on his stiffness on the volley, and even changed his movement on

299

returns. All this was designed with the specific intention of giving him a top game again, which would exert far less pressure on the lower back.

Throughout his career Greg's work ethic has never been questioned. Still, for somebody aged twenty-seven who'd been on the tour more than eight years, the transformation was simply miraculous, and by the beginning of the New Year he was ready to play.

As luck would have it, Greg's first appearance under the guidance of Team Rusedski came in Auckland against the player who had unquestionably caused him more mental anguish than any other: his British Davis Cup team-mate Tim Henman. Once more I'm not exactly breaking the Official Secrets Act when I say the pair did not get along - in fact to be accurate, one might say that Greg was totally paranoid about Tim. It isn't unusual for there to be jealousy between two players of the same country who are unquestionably rivals. It happened to a lesser extent between Mark Philippoussis and Pat Rafter in Australia, but the conflicts between Henman and Rusedski go far deeper.

Tim is the golden boy of tennis in the United Kingdom, and for one blatantly simple reason: he is British. Greg knows that only too well, and has been forced to face up to the fact almost as long as he's played under the British flag after defecting from Canada. But it doesn't become any easier for him, and he's consumed by envy. A lot of the resentment is based on pure finance. It seems obvious to me that Greg came to Britain for one reason, and that was money. Sure, he was dating an English girl, but that didn't require a change of nationality. Andre Agassi didn't become German overnight after falling for Steffi Graf, and although she lives most of the time in the United States, I don't think she's considered changing her

Values of ingratitude

nationality. Because I have an American mother, I could have played for the United States, but the thought never once entered my head. I'm Australian in the same way that Greg's Canadian; he simply became convinced there were far richer pickings to be had if he were wrapped in red, white and blue rather than the maple leaf.

Greg has won enough big cheques during his career never to have to worry about money again, but even the world's wealthiest men want to get richer. When Greg became British he thought he'd have the pick of the best endorsements on offer. Negotiations for the switch of nationalities had been going on for some years - but Greg hadn't bargained for a really top flight, home-grown player bursting through at just the time of his arrival: namely Tim Henman.

The result was, that all the best deals went to Henman, and some of Rusedski's were cheap by comparison. There are times he doesn't feel part of the British scene, and believes he's never been given proper credit for what he's achieved, either by the public or the press. To be perfectly honest, he's got a point. Greg has been to the final of a Grand Slam, something Tim has yet to manage. He has also won a Masters Series event, beating Pete Sampras at Bercy in Paris four years ago. Tim's best effort at a similar level was reaching the final in Cincinnati. For good measure you can also point out Greg winning the Grand Slam Cup, giving him the biggest cheque available in tennis at the time.

At Wimbledon there's no question Tim has registered the better performances, reaching the semi-final three times in the last four years. Away from there it's a borderline case as to whose results were better, and they jousted in the rankings until Greg started to suffer his injuries. But his jealousy of Tim manifested itself in him saying some really childish things about his rival.

Over the years Greg and Tim have had a few blazing rows. I'm told the first big disagreement came way back, when one wanted to play the World Team Cup in Dusseldorf and the other didn't. Then the most recent occurred at the British tournament at Brighton, just before my arrival in Greg's camp.Allegedly Greg had pocketed a hefty guarantee to play. Then to everyone's disappointment, not least the tournament director John Feaver, he lost meekly in the first round. Admittedly Greg was wracked by physical problems at the time, as proved by Mark Bender's subsequent examinations of his scans. However he managed to play on in the doubles. When one of the singles semi-finalists was forced to default injured before playing his match, Greg received the not exactly excessive request to play an exhibition to appease the paying customers.

As was his prerogative, Greg refused, and Tim, when questioned on the subject, criticised the decision, saying players had an obligation to the fans. Angry telephone conversations ensued between two of the plushest suites in Brighton's seafront Metropole Hotel, with Greg forcibly telling Tim to keep his nose out of other people's business. Consequently, it soon became one of my regular tasks to listen to long diatribes about Greg's festering resentment of his Davis Cup colleague.

My first meeting with Greg came the week after the tournament in Brighton. I was amazed as Greg flew into a frightening paranoiac rage, accusing Tim of being everything from a spoilt brat to an outright arsehole. He even got stuck into Tim's wife, calling her all kinds of names. I couldn't believe what I was hearing, and refused to get involved because I like Tim. One of my lifelong principles is not to say anything negative about people who've given me no cause. In my opinion Tim is one of the most talented players in the current game, and certainly good enough to win Wimbledon.

Some time back I was accused of saying Tim was too middle

class and not hungry enough. Who am I, with an almost identical background, to make such suggestions? Tim's father is a lawyer with his own practice, so was mine, and both sets of parents have tennis courts in their back gardens. I was misquoted on that occasion, but stand by what I said about Tim at this year's Australian Open. If he gauges down his serve like he did against Jonas Bjorkman, the top players are going to jump all over him. If he plays his natural game on grass and believes in himself a little more, he's a potential champion.

I attributed Greg's behaviour in that meeting to still being upset about recent events. However, constant abusive rants about Tim or his long-time coach David Felgate were commonplace over the next few months. Whenever their names were mentioned, Greg just vented his anger. One of the most embarrassing instances came in the Key Biscayne locker room when Greg's abusive jibes were audible to everyone only moments after Tim had walked by. I just hoped the other players didn't think the outburst was influenced by me.

If Greg resented Tim, then his feelings for Felgate were close to hatred. I'd known David for years from his playing days, and couldn't see anything wrong with the guy. However, there was distinct history between him and Greg. When Greg switched from Canada to Britain, he was an IMG client and David's wife Jan, the agent involved. Apparently she worked extremely hard to sort out so many things - but within a matter of months, Greg had moved his business to the rival concern of Proserv, which evolved into SFX Management. David, who spent more time in the various pressrooms of the tennis circuit than most journalists, never allowed his resentment of the episode to cloud his appraisal of Greg's best performances. An extremely interesting scenario now exists: Greg has returned to IMG and David has hung up his coaching tracksuit to become an agent with the company. Many await the results with interest.

Going back to Memorial Drive in Adelaide, the result of that match was a straight sets win for Henman. So Greg, wanting more match practice, made a last minute decision to play the following week's event in Auckland. Other commitments meant I couldn't make the trip but he played well enough to reach the semi-final. On his return, just a day before the beginning of the Australian Open, we sat down to talk. From day one Greg always referred to Brad as Bradley and before long he was chattering on in his rehearsed way about Bradley this and Bradley that. Basically he said things had worked out extremely well between the two of them and he wanted to continue the relationship. Then, looking forward to the Australian Open, he said: Can I pay Bradley instead of you?

This did come as something of a shock, because I'd budgeted to make some money out of the coaching relationship before I'd flown down to Australia. Of course there was my television commentary work, but working with Greg was supposed to be a very handy earner. Throughout that tournament I was still in his corner for all his matches, although nobody was too sure of my title; maybe it was head coach, perhaps chief adviser. Basically there was the Team Rusedski that I had created: Brad on hand to make sure of the technique, and he had also involved his assistant Melinda Glenister, and I was out there every day with Greg as well as repeatedly analysing the tapes with Brad, organising practice courts, talking tactics, planning schedules and even doing interviews on his behalf.

To illustrate the benefits of all our work, Greg beat the world's top-ranked player Gustavo Kuerten in the second round. His five sets win was a totally extraordinary effort. Just a month previously we were wondering how much longer he'd be able to walk properly, and when he arrived on the Gold Coast he was struggling to beat youngsters who played on the third-tier satellite level. Now he had proved himself too good for the Aussie Open's top seed, who had won the Masters Cup in Lisbon just weeks earlier.

Eventually Greg lost in the last sixteen to the small, bespectacled Frenchman Arnaud Clement, who went on to reach the final. But it was still a notable effort. All along the basic plan was to get through the Australian Open and see how everything worked. Although I spent very little social time with Greg, as I commentated most evenings, I assumed he acknowledged the benefits of all the planning and work I'd put in. At the end of the tournament, we had another meeting. I told him I was heading back to see Emily and the twins before playing some Senior Tour events. I recommended he looked after Brad, taking him and Ryan Kendrick on the road, and we'd all hook up again at the big American tournaments in Indian Wells and Key Biscayne.

Up until then I'd not really concerned myself about getting paid, although my Dad kept insisting I should strike a formal deal with Greg. I just wanted the Cash/Hopper Academy to work, and Greg was a perfect flag waver, mentioning it in all his interviews. Call it co-dependency if you like, but so long as Brad and Ryan were properly treated, I remained convinced Greg would present me with a healthy bonus once he won something.

Such a victory didn't take long in coming. Three tournaments later he beat both Lleyton Hewitt and Andre Agassi to win the title in San Jose. In addition to the triumph over Kuerten in Melbourne and another excellent win against Marat Safin on a Milanese indoor carpet, he'd beaten four number ones in the space of six weeks. During the whole time, I'd been talking to Greg on a weekly basis, while keeping in constant touch with Brad.

Senior tournaments kept me busy until Key Biscayne, and everything seemed fine. I put in some practice hours with Greg, and he seemed in good shape. By now the messages from my dad about at least securing a percentage deal on prize money were becoming too regular to ignore. I knew the time was fast approaching for a showdown. However, my attentions were to be diverted by the arrival of a couple of unexpected guests: Tom and Helen Rusedski. Remembering Greg's implicit orders that his father wasn't to be told anything, I was immediately very wary of Tom's presence. My initial impression of him was that of a belligerent man who was also something of a know-all. I could immediately understand why Greg wanted him kept at arm's length.

Every once in a while even the best tennis players have the misfortune to come face to face with an opponent who plays so far above himself, that even he can't believe his good fortune. That was most certainly the case as the normally solid but unspectacular German David Prinosil caught fire to such an extent he scorched Greg in straight sets. Nevertheless there were clearly things wrong with Greg's game. He was tentative, not hitting his serve correctly and just pushing the ball around. Throughout the entire match Greg's father was swearing and cursing while his mother sat by impassively. I occasionally mentioned Prinosil was just too good, but Tom countered it was all bullshit and our game-plan unmitigated crap.

Not wanting to be drawn into a confrontation with somebody I'd been ordered to ignore, I bit my lip. Then as I walked towards the locker room after the match to talk with Greg, his father forcibly intercepted me. Greg's wife Lucy stood by as Tom tore into me. This is all shit, he stormed. Greg's got to move his feet. It's all in his feet. I've done all the drills with him. You guys are doing the wrong fucking drills with him. I don't know what kind of bullshit you guys are telling him.

Greg's mother Helen then began to join in with similar sentiments, and I could hardly get a word into the conversation. When Tom began to really insult me, Lucy had to step in, ordering both Rusedskis to calm down. She was terrific, standing up for me as well as all the work Brad had done. But I was totally gobsmacked. Here I was suffering all this abuse from a man whose son hadn't even paid me a single cent.I walked into the locker room totally shell-shocked. I hadn't asked for that sort of treatment, and certainly didn't appreciate it. Suddenly here I was back in another parental nightmare that was just as bad, if not worse than the one I'd experienced with Nick Philippoussis.

Afterwards the Rusedskis went their way, and I went another with Brad and Melinda. We were staying in a different, considerably cheaper hotel to Greg, but that is one of his ways. Frankly, I didn't mind so long as the sheets were clean and the shower worked. I was considerably more concerned to find out that Brad was tantamount to broke, as Greg had only been paying him the same minimal amount as during that initial trial period in London. Brad, being an introverted character, didn't want to upset Greg by mentioning money. In addition, Greg has repeatedly mentioned he was barely breaking even after having to pay both Brad and Ryan.

As Greg wasn't even paying Melinda, he was effectively getting the services of Brad, her and I for just £200 a day. Out of that Brad had to buy new video cameras and computer equipment. Admittedly Greg did pay his expenses, and even agreed to cover Melinda's accommodation, a measly $20 a night in a hostel. As for me, all I received was still a big round zero. So as far as I was concerned, the time had finally come for action. Greg, however, would have been happy to let it go on forever, as the deal was a great one for him.

Promising I'd take up the matter with Greg, I wanted to get Brad's wage increased, sort out my own deal for the lead-up to Wimbledon, and ensure a bonus if he won anything. I even went to see his SFX agent Ken Myerson, explaining I wanted to talk money when Greg was free after the tournament. He assured me there were no worries, and admitted Greg had a notoriously bad reputation with coaches and had repeatedly done the wrong thing in the past.

I'd done nothing wrong. It is standard practice not to discuss money during a tournament, but by this stage Greg had long since been eliminated. Yet a day or so later he telephoned in high dudgeon, accusing me of talking money with Myerson behind his back. Earlier in the tournament I'd been introduced to Greg's new public relations specialist Sharon Park, and she immediately became his closest adviser. She was even sitting alongside Greg and Lucy after I was summoned to their hotel suite for the long overdue meeting. There's no doubt it was one of the most awkward, uncomfortable and nerve-wracking experiences I'd ever endured.

Clearly there was an air of antagonism as I started proceedings by recommending an increase in Brad's wage. Greg responded by asking what Brad was doing with his money, which I thought was basically none of Greg's business, and told him so. He then insisted he'd never once asked for Melinda's services; but I said, like it or not, she was here and doing a good job.

I think it's a very reasonable question to ask about Bradley's money, snapped Greg. After all, he didn't have a career before me.

Struggling to comprehend the ingratitude, I pointed out that Brad was the best in the world at his job, and had done superbly well. To me, it was abundantly clear that the guy had helped save Greg's career, and the matter didn't warrant an argument. Not in Greg's opinion, however, and whilst he insisted Brad was receiving his worth, he also admitted he'd never paid any coach more than $3,000 a week. I've got news for you, Greg, I said. A decent coach nowadays is paid between at least between $5K and $6K a week.

Greg claimed he'd never heard anything so preposterous and insisted he'd never pay such amounts. I told him I was paying Ian Barclay more than that over a decade earlier. Then I decided to change the subject a little. By the way, Greg, you've not paid me even a cent, yet.

He barked back that he'd offered to pay me, which I admitted was true. However, we'd agreed to see how things went first, and now here I was sitting down trying to discuss the matter. With that he pulled out a sheet of paper and insisted: This is our contract. This is our deal.

It was in fact the basic agreement when he first started to benefit from our advice. By now I was shaking with rage and pointed out the wording 'through the Australian Open', before reminding him that we were by that time in April. I always went by this, and nobody contacted me about it, he jabbered.

Again I tried to point out that this was the very reason for our meeting, but I was getting angrier by the second. So I blew. I realised this guy had absolutely no appreciation for what we'd all done for him. He also had no idea what words like goodwill and friendship meant. The arguments were ridiculous, and I realised it was a futile attempt to get anyone an increase. Listen, you are being fucking tight, I yelled. You've got a bad reputation for being mean, and despite all the things I've done, you've never even bought me dinner.

At this Greg really got annoyed and started shouting, before Sharon butted in to point out he'd paid for Melinda's accommodation; that colossal account stretching to $20 a day in a hostel. The conversation flew around for more than two hours without really getting anywhere, but the subject kept getting back to Brad. I kept saying my prime concern was getting an increase in his money and paying him a set figure when he was at home.

I don't want to pay him when he's not working on the road, said Greg. I'm paying him now for being on the road. Isn't that why I pay him, as compensation for not being at home? I don't intend paying him for being at home. I'm not going to pay him just to live.

Greg seemed oblivious to the fact that Brad still had to pay his telephone bills and put petrol in his car. He just couldn't, or wouldn't, accept what Brad and the rest of us had done for him. In the end I got up to leave and made one last attempt. At the end of the day, it's up to you Greg, I said. I told you what to do back in November, and you accepted it regarding physiotherapy, diets and so on. You have to make the decision on what to do about money. What I humbly recommend is that you look after Brad, and give us maybe 10 per cent of your big wins. Then you pay me for what I do leading up to Wimbledon, on the grass courts and at the Queen's tournament.

Then I also told him that I would, of course, be fulfilling my commentating duties for the BBC. Immediately he wanted to know how much and whether I'd be in the players' box for all his matches; to which I replied that hopefully I would, but there was the possibility of missing the odd match. Again we argued back and forth, and trying to calm things down I said: I'll be there as much as I can. If I don't practise with you very much one week, then don't pay me. If I work a lot with you on another week, you pay

Values of ingratitude

accordingly.

Immediately he fired back with the question of how much. I told him as much as he liked, but explained what I received from Philippoussis, pointing out the bonus after the US Open.All along he kept moaning about not even breaking even for the year after having to pay the likes of Brad, Ryan and Melinda. Admittedly he wasn't as marketable as Henman, but he's still got plenty of endorsements, and just a couple of years earlier he'd won the Grand Slam Cup worth $1 million.

Finally walking to the door I said he could pay me whatever he wanted. When he asked how much for seemingly the millionth time, I replied whatever he felt was right. I don't quite know why, but leaving the suite I thought I'd got somewhere. I was confident Greg would increase Brad's wage and give me a percentage of his prize money as well as something like £2,000 a week for the work during the grass court season.

Next day Greg and Lucy headed back home to London while Emily and the twins linked up with me in Miami before setting off for an Easter holiday in Mexico. Before leaving I sent Sharon Park an email, stressing my confidence and saying: I do feel strongly that if Greg has good results in big tournaments, we will all benefit from it financially. There's been good will from Brad, Melinda and myself so far and a huge amount of effort, determination and talent on Greg's part, which it's hard for 99.9% of the population to understand. I would hate to change a winning formula and disrupt the good feelings in the team. However there is also a fine line between good will, getting your money's worth and taking advantage of somebody's generosity. I feel that line has started to be crossed though I'm sure unintentionally. Sometimes things need to be reassessed technically, physically or financially and quickly addressed. Sometimes it's easier to see from the outside and that's where I'm sitting...well, on the border, actually.

For some reason I'd lulled myself into a false sense of security, but as is so often the case, a realisation of the truth hit me in the early hours of the morning. The Mexican hotel room clock was showing a little after 5am when I sat bolt upright in bed and declared: I know exactly what Greg is going to do. He's going to get Brad in a corner, have Sharon Park there for support, and cut me out altogether.

Call it a premonition if you like, but suddenly I knew exactly what was going on. I tried to telephone Brad, but he wasn't at home so I left messages ordering him not to agree to sign anything until he'd spoken to me. Then I called Melinda, her mother, in fact anybody who may know where Brad could be found. Eventually he returned my call and answered my worst suspicions. Yeah, I've signed something, but I can't tell you what, he said. Greg had his lawyers and management people there, and made me promise not to say a thing, but I can tell you this much: I've got a good deal.

Brad did let slip that he repeatedly asked about me and Greg told him not to worry. He told Greg that he would give me a cut of his percentage but I questioned a percent of what percentage? Then he admitted he'd signed a confidentiality clause and couldn't say anymore. Brad, do you know what you've done? I stormed. You've cut me out of everything. I've never even been paid a cent by this guy and regardless of everything I've arranged, he won't pay because I'm not there anymore. We fixed up this person's game, I fixed his career and now you've all cut me out completely.

I quickly realised that with Brad giving me a cut of his percentage, Greg would assume he wouldn't have to pay me at all. At that moment, I can honestly say I've never felt so angry in my

Values of ingratitude

life. Emily, deciding I needed space, quickly took the boys down to the swimming pool as I continued this heated conversation. Brad kept insisting Greg wouldn't act in that way, but I knew better. My worst suspicions about Brad had come true. There's not a malicious bone in his body but he really is an absent minded professor and doesn't think about money. A few hours later my telephone rang and it was Rusedski.

Pat, it's Greg. Can you talk? said the familiar staccato voice down the line. I've organised something with Bradley and we've come to an agreement. I will only be using him. I don't need you for Wimbledon or anything else. I just need one coach and that's the way it will be. OK?

Yeah, beauty Greg. Just fine. No worries. Good luck. But for the next two days the whole thing wound me up so much. I was fuming, and got back on the telephone: Greg, you call me up after all the work I've done and tell me you don't want me. You've made no offer to pay me any money in terms of a percentage of anything else. I've fixed your career. I've saved it and should have a percentage of your earnings for the rest of your life. Instead you've completely screwed me.

He responded that such an idea was ridiculous, and I agreed. Of course it's ridiculous Greg, but I've got a valid point. I deserve some money for what I did. I don't want a fee, but if you ever win anything I want a percentage, and the average for a coach is 10 per cent. I know you're not going to give me a percentage for the rest of your career, but you've missed the point. If I hadn't put you in contact with all these people, you would be retired in two months. Now you are set to play for several more years.

Seeing I was getting nowhere, I recommended we just leave it to the lawyers to talk the situation through. Oh, you're going to sue me then, are you? came his reply. You've got no grounds. You've got no chance.

I never had any intention of suing, but I kept repeating he couldn't treat people in this way, brushing them off after all the effort they've made. Think about it, I implored. There's a point to what I'm saying. Everybody knows what I've done for you. I've resurrected your career and you've never even thanked me. Not by inviting me out to dinner, paying my hotel room or putting your hand in your pocket. There's never been anything like that. Just because you fire me, it doesn't mean I don't deserve a bonus.

After hanging up, I talked to my manager Duncan March who recommended I speak to a lawyer; but I wasn't interested in ending up in court. First it would depress me; secondly it would ruin Greg's chances of doing well at Wimbledon, and that in turn could wreck Brad's earning power. You repeatedly hear of ex-mistresses suing their wealthy boyfriends, and I didn't want to be like that. I have a firm belief in the goodness of all human beings, and I still held onto the belief that Greg would see reason and send some money my way.

Eventually the press got hold of the story, when Malcolm Folley of the *Mail on Sunday* telephoned to say I hadn't been around and asked what was happening with Greg. I replied that I was no longer working with him and couldn't think why except for the fact he didn't want to pay me. Bang, that was it. The whole business was out in the open and wildfire about to spread.

Then Sharon Park produced a press release on Greg's behalf. It read: Pat Cash and I agreed to work together on a three month training programme. Although I had requested a contract, he adamantly refused and emphasised to both myself and the media that he didn't want to be paid. He made it clear he would not be an

Values of ingratitude

integral part of the team, and wanted to use the association as an opportunity to promote his Australian tennis academy. I find it totally unreasonable that he has demanded 10 per cent of all my future prize money. I did offer to pay him for the time he spent with me, but he refused.

A long time before, my dad taught me never to stoop to other people's level. I refused to get drawn into a public war of words, but immediately sent another email to Sharon Park. In the light of all that has happened, I make no excuse for reproducing it in full:

Dear Sharon,

It has come to my attention that you and Greg have released a statement to the press, divulging private conversations he and I have had. I can only presume this comes in retaliation to some quotes of mine that appeared in the press. Even though I have not seen the article with my quotes, I will remind you that neither you, me or any other person has any control over what the media say or write. If you or Greg thought that nothing about our working relationship would ever be mentioned in the media then you have been very naive. You can't stop me or anybody else from talking to them.

Your press release mentioned a three-month agreement between myself and Greg, which I have never seen, also an agreement of me asking for 10 per cent of Greg's prize money for the rest of his career, which I have also never seen. Clearly these were unofficial and very private conversations between Greg and myself, that you and he have released in an official press statement. I do not want to start a childish tit-for-tat argument through the media. Greg may enjoy doing this, as he has in the past with Tim Henman, but I do not.

I am a very private person, and for me this is a great invasion of privacy, which I don't appreciate one bit. I learned many years ago that if private conversations are revealed in the press, it becomes a no-win situation. I did not intend revealing private conversations and negotiations between Greg and myself to the media, but clearly you do. I did not want to divulge the details of conversations I had with the physiotherapists and Greg about the stress fractures in his back or his plans about his plans of receiving a pay-off from the insurance company. Or even the verbal abuse I received outside the Key Biscayne locker room from both his mother and father, to name a couple. These were private conversations and though the latter was conducted in a public situation, I've respected the fact it did not involve other parties.

I'm sure the press would be much more interested in Greg's situation than mine, and I'm sure they would save it for a Wimbledon release. I will do my best to respect our difference of opinion. Just because we disagree over things, does not mean we need to start a war. I hope you agree with this point, and if not, then that is your opinion also.

Yours truly,

Pat

And that effectively is the end of the story. The email was dated 18 April 2001, and Greg had first formally contacted me early the preceding November. Greg insisted during that time I only worked with him a total of seventeen days. I don't know how he came to that figure, but I think that anyone who knows me, or indeed has read this book, will appreciate my obsessive nature. I've never been able to do anything half-heartedly: it's either all, or nothing.

What Greg failed to realise is that so much work went into forming his support team, with countless telephone calls, emails and faxes, and the whole thing only became possible thanks to my years of experience in overcoming various physical problems.

From start to finish the whole episode lasted a mere six months. Yet it will take me many years to wash the bitter taste from my mouth. In more jovial moments I still joke I never did take Greg to court, but neither did I receive even a penny in payment from him. Last year he reached Wimbledon's last sixteen, where he lost to eventual champion Goran Ivanisevic; and his year-ending ranking was thirty-two as compared to sixty-nine when he walked onto Memorial Drive's Rebound Ace surface for that first match at Adelaide. In annual prize money alone he totalled $459,021 in 2001, and I've no idea what proportion of that he paid to Brad. What I do know is their working relationship also ended in November, before Greg reappointed Sven Groeneveld as his coach.

I'm also clear in my opinion of Greg Rusedski as a human being.

Chapter Sixteen

So what comes next?

There's something about the Australian temperament that makes us folk from Down Under so easy going. Maybe it's the isolation of our country and the knowledge that nobody is really going to bother us all the way down there. As you no doubt appreciate, I have never exactly conformed to what is conceived as stereotypical, and my rebellious streak might have been encouraged by the fact that I started travelling abroad at such an early age. However, I can now look at the whole Greg Rusedski experience and smile; and believe it or not, Brad Langevaad and I often get together and joke about those times. The fact that I can now view the entire episode philosophically is for one good reason: I unequivocally admit that it was my fault entirely.

The reason I got so annoyed was because I was so mad at myself. I'd been warned repeatedly about Greg, but I was convinced I could appeal to the human side of his nature. I have a great belief in humanity, and have always thought that if you treat people correctly, then they in turn will do right by you. But there was barely a person who knew both Greg and I who didn't say something like, 'So you're working with Rusedski then? Just be careful. I didn't want to get my Dad involved in formulating contracts, because I thought Greg would respond to somebody helping him as a mate. I just couldn't believe he'd fail to recognise the value of the work and time I had put in. Now, more than a year on, I realise that was my glaring error.

Greg has obviously always found it difficult to communicate, and this is perhaps because of the way he was brought up - and that's very sad. Having been through therapy myself, and understanding more clearly now the traumas of my childhood, and also experiencing the intense atmosphere of the Philippoussis household, Gregs outlook makes more sense: I'm sure he's been taught never to trust anybody, and consequently he has no friends. I am sure a psychologist would have helped him. So often he was tense and up tight because of the difficulties he found in communicating, and in his refusal to trust anything or anybody; he would go so far as to lock himself away and not talk to anybody. Thank goodness he has found a wonderful wife and companion in Lucy, because he could well have ended up an extremely lonely man.

With regard to his coaches, Greg is still the loser in the long run. Aspects Brad and I were about to work on would have made him a much better player, yet he was just not prepared to pay a few thousand pounds, which I honestly believe could have taken him all the way. Indeed, over the years he has had a whole host of coaches, some of whom were the best at their trade: for instance, Tony Pickard, who took Stefan Edberg to six Grand Slam titles. Just a few days before Wimbledon Greg disappeared, and didn't bother to tell Pickard that he was jetting off to Turkey for some special treatment on his injured ankle. And before that Brian Teacher, who did a wonderful job in harnessing his charge's game. Greg had slumped to 81st position on the world rankings when he took Teach on board, and less than a year later he was up to fourth spot and a finalist at the US Open. And what did he do next? That's right, he fired Teach.

However, this whole episode I am now ready to store away in a file marked 'PAST'. As far as my own life is concerned, all bingeing and bad living are well and truly consigned to history, and there are so many reasons to be optimistic. I now understand myself so much better, yet if I consider my life as a long dark tunnel, only now am I coming out at the other end. Naturally my entire tennis career was based around winning - but is that because I was frightened to lose? Defeat equated with embarrassment, and ever since I can remember, the thought of being shamed was something to be avoided at all costs. There have been a couple of times when I seriously wanted to die, and that was basically because I was so ashamed. In various attempts to avoid or mask that feeling I resorted to partying after being totally obsessive about my fitness. The whole object of the exercise was to combat my one big underlying problem: feeling bad about myself. Believe me, shame is a horrendously powerful emotion.

Therapy was an enlightening experience. Those who have been through a similar experience will understand - and I also know that those who haven't, will struggle to do so; and I appreciate you may well be saying: 'What the hell is wrong with this guy? He's won Wimbledon. He's been a famous tennis star. He's rich. He's got a stunning wife and four beautiful children. He's had everything in his life.' Others will know exactly what I'm talking about.

Dr Lim Yong has been a great help. I only see him a few times a year if I'm lucky, but he's always there for support, giving sound advice over the telephone. Being hot tempered and a perfectionist, I want things to go right, and if they don't, I get frustrated; but Yong is a voice of reason. I think I found him at just the right time, although he might have been helpful a little earlier. Yet everything happens for a reason. Perhaps I would have shoved him away as a crank when I was younger because I found listening pretty difficult then. As the saying goes: when the pupil is ready, the teacher shall be there.

One thing I now appreciate is that I'm happy to be me. Unfortunately some people I've met along the way are also happy to be me. I think I'd better explain. Not long after winning Wimbledon I befriended a guy known as Johnny Talbot. He was a fun-loving young Aussie who maintained he'd been an actor, written songs with John Cougar Mellancamp and even trained with Olympic athletes. Over the course of time I discovered that this twenty-two-year-old was the greatest impostor I'd ever met.

Initially I became wary after falling for that old line of lending him some money for his mother's operation. Friends had been warning me for six months, until finally I had a telephone call from the manager of the complex where I owned an apartment in Port Douglas, North Queensland, and once and for all learned his true colours. Johnny had first conned his way into getting the door key, and had then enjoyed ten days of high living, running up a tab of more than a few thousand bucks for food and drink!

Promptly kicking him out of my life, I warned him that any further hassle and he might expect to be paying a similar sum in hospital bills. Then a couple of years later somebody in New York rang to tell me his chequebook had been stolen, and his account was several thousand dollars light, courtesy of somebody called John Thomson. It transpired this New Yorker's sister had kicked her boyfriend (Thomson a.k.a. Johnny Talbot) out of her house when she went on vacation, but he had broken back in immediately she departed. He stole the chequebook, cashed the money - and left my telephone number as a contact before vanishing.

Talbot was conning his way around the world, insisting he was my fitness trainer. So my advisers contacted Interpol and reported him for fraud, which forced him to lie low for another couple of years. Yet if we thought that was the end of the matter, another surprise was in store.

Billy Barclay is one of my best and oldest friends in the music business. At the time he was managing a tour for another Fair Dinkum Aussie, Jason Donovan. One evening I called Billy's office, requesting a couple of tickets for Emily and myself. Yeah, I know it wasn't exactly my kind of music, but Jason is a good mate.

Why Mr. Cash, your six back stage passes are already waiting for you at the will call window, came the reply.

After explaining no knowledge of any previous request, both Billy's team and I were curious to find out who'd been scoring tickets in my name. The answer came when the impostor arrived at the will call window with four children and an attractive female companion. He was immediately lured into an inner sanctum on the pretext of some pre-show hospitality before a 6ft 4in, 220lb security guard locked the door.

I just wanted to keep you here until the real Pat Cash arrives, countered Billy when his orders were questioned. You see, Pat is one of my best mates, and he's coming to the show tonight. He doesn't like people falsely using his name, and we don't like being cheated on back stage passes.

You've probably already guessed the guy was none other than Johnny Talbot, and he immediately broke down in tears, and started wailing about his sordid past. He begged to be released, insisting with good cause that on my arrival, I'd kill him. But showing no mercy, Billy ordered the security guard to handcuff Talbot to a heating pipe. Then they discussed their options, which included roughing up the fraudster, sending for the police, or leaving him alone with me for thirty minutes. Typically Emily and I were late for the show, and Billy, being busy and needing the office, grew weary of the howling and blubbering. So lamentably they let him go, watching the person who masqueraded as Talbot/Thomson/Cash and doubtless several other names, break the world 100m record as he dashed away and left his lady and kids to fend for themselves.

Thankfully Talbot has yet to appear at the gates of the Cash/Hopper Tennis Academy - but maybe it's only a matter of time, and he should be warned that I'm ready. The Hope Island project is going too well for anybody to wreck it, but I'll remain vigilant. And so will Gavin Hopper, and he's not a person that it's wise to cross.

I've known Gavin for more than fifteen years, from the time he used to coach Mark Kratzmann. We share the same beliefs on fitness, and he's worked with some top players, such as Amanda Coetzer, Monica Seles and MaliVai Washington. We formulated our ideas of putting something together during our time with Philippoussis, and now things are moving forward. We can boast sixteen courts with surfaces of cement, clay, grass and Rebound Ace, and have recently finished building the gymnasium. In addition there are another eleven courts across the road at the Sanctuary Cove Resort, so there's no danger of overcrowding. Negotiations are also in progress to expand with similar centres in Florida, Japan and Hawaii.

Just recently I've had to face up to an exceptionally tough personal task at the Academy. It's hard enough seeing any

So what comes next?

youngster agonising with the pressures of proving themselves at the game, but you can multiply the anguish about a thousand times when that kid is your own. My eldest son Daniel is like me in many ways. He's now sixteen years old, and doesn't like others telling him what to do. He's a bright kid who's extremely switched on, and he'd set his heart on becoming a tennis player.

From my experiences with Nick Philippoussis and Tom Rusedski, I was only too aware of the pitfalls you encounter when you force your kids towards a tennis court. In some ways I regret I didn't get him involved in the game a little earlier, but it wasn't easy for him as he lived most of the time with his mother in Norway. When he came to visit me, time was precious and I just wanted to spend it simply being his dad.

When I had my first tournament win on the Senior Tour in the Austrian town of Portschach, Daniel came along for the ride. Usually I made it clear that I took no commitments during the time Daniel and Mia came to stay, but this was an exception. There were loads of kids playing on the outside courts, and Daniel, then aged twelve, wanted to join them. Unfortunately he didn't have a racket, so he borrowed one of mine weighing 390g. That's heavy for anyone, let alone a kid of that age.

Daniel played for five hours every day and became hooked. Late in 2001 he enrolled as a pupil at the Cash/Hopper Academy, determined to be a serve-and-volley player like his old man. However, there was no disguising the fact that he definitely possessed the Cash temperament, and from the outset that was very worrying. He was a perfectionist on court, even worse than me, and ripped his heart out every time he played. I was afraid he was losing the plot, and as his father, it was horrible for me to stand and watch. I recognised so many of the signs from my own adolescence, and

325

was determined he wasn't going to suffer the same mental agonies. It's tough enough when a sixteen-year-old is struggling to succeed at a sport, but the pressures are infinitely tougher when that kid's father has been a champion himself. The muttering was completely understandable at every tournament Daniel played: See that youngster there? He's Pat Cash's son!

No decision about a child should be taken alone when there are two parents involved. So I telephoned Anne-Britt in Oslo and explained the situation. Understandably she was in complete agreement, and we decided the best decision was to stop Daniel from playing tennis until he was able to understand that sport is something to be enjoyed. The message may take a lifetime to sink in, but if we hadn't taken those measures, Daniel's life might have been very short. We both love him too much to let him go through that pain. Sadly too many other tennis parents have adopted a different point of view, and consequently there are a lot of mentally wrecked kids out there.

Fortunately Daniel's sister Mia doesn't like playing tennis at all; however, she excels at handball, and throws the thing like a bullet. I must admit there have been times I've thought, 'What if she could serve like that. Think of the damage she could do in the women's game!' Then I come to my senses and just appreciate the fact that Mia is an incredibly wise and stunningly beautiful girl with the strong will of both her mother and father.

As for the twins, it's too early to tell, but Jett is certainly a fighter and is progressing well at Tae Kwon Do, and won a bronze medal in the United Kingdom championships for his age and belt. Shannon meanwhile has inherited Emily's artistic nature, singing and acting with the best.

My children will always be the most precious thing in my life,

So what comes next?

and the days I cherish the most are when all four of them are with me. If I have one overriding regret it's that I've spent too long separated from all of them at some stage, and it's time I can never recapture. My dream for a family future is that we can all be together for much of the time, enjoying the beautiful Queensland weather; but time will tell.

There are still many other things to occupy my attention. My charities GOAL and Planet Ark are still vitally important to me, I still get up on stage to play guitar with my rock band The Wild Colonial Boys, and there are the not-so-hair-brained inventions as well. A few years ago I developed a thing called The Intonet. Now the computer technology wizards needn't start telephoning their lawyers, because I'm literally talking Into Net: it's a kind of guttering that runs along the bottom of a tennis net and returns the balls to the serving end. Some day one of the schemes will make me millions. Hopefully that day will dawn soon, as still being able to play competitively means I'm a credit to modern physiotherapy. I don't know how long the knees will hold out, allowing me to be competitive on the Senior Tour. In fact I regularly worry how long the Senior Tour will hold out.

The financial aftermath of 11 September has had a marked effect on the amount of money people are prepared to risk, and there is currently only one senior event scheduled for the United States. In my more optimistic moods I believe things will improve, so long as John Patrick McEnroe continues to do his stuff and the younger guys step up, like Boris Becker and possibly Stefan Edberg. I'll be there as long as I'm physically able, and I'm sure my body will let me down before the Senior Tour folds.

Once I overcame the resentment of being prematurely put out to graze with the oldies on the Senior Tour, my feelings on the circuit were very similar to those I experienced when I started playing golf. I used to smash or throw my clubs because I couldn't do a damn thing and hated it. One day after breaking half a bagful of clubs I told myself: 'That's it. Either relax about this thing or quit.'

Senior tennis is much the same. For the first couple of years I took things really seriously and was determined to win. I was a young guy who felt he could still be competitive on the main tour, and could not face the humiliation of losing to opponents older than myself. Much the same, in fact, as what Boris Becker is experiencing now. Then I convinced myself to chill out and enjoy the tournaments for what they are: an opportunity to make some money, keep fit, experience the competitive element but also entertain the paying customers. Some days I will not play as well as I did to win Wimbledon but that doesn't matter as long as I give 100 per cent.

Television commentary is work that particularly stimulates me. To my mind, the guys who were the best thinkers on the court turn into the best commentators, people like John Lloyd, John Fitzgerald and of course Johnny Mac. I've no doubt the very worst would be players like Mark Philippoussis, but we are all cut out for different things. Andre Agassi would be excellent if he ever felt the desire, and of course Brad Gilbert would be a great analyst because I'm sure he even talks under water.

My theory in the booth is just to keep things simple, not to show off too much, and talk as if I'm watching a match at home with a few mates. People want insight, to be told about something happening in the match of which otherwise they might be unaware. It's one of those instances when you've actually had to be out there in circumstances similar to what the players are experiencing to truly understand. I've tried to adopt the same idea with this book -

So what comes next?

and if you've got this far, I can't be doing too badly!

I work with Channel 7 in Australia and USA Network in the States, but probably most enjoy my involvement with the BBC in Britain. The whole operation is so slick and professional, and I've a huge appreciation for Sue Barker, who can turn out line after line on numerous subjects. She's known tennis since she was a girl, and never let it be forgotten that she won the French Open, which is a magnificent achievement if you compare it to the standard of Britain's top female players these days.

Sue's real accomplishment is being able to work on so many other sports. Her Olympic coverage has been excellent, and when you sit next to her in the studio you're aware of working with a consummate professional. I think I'm fine doing matches, but I struggle a little bit with interviews, and I'm interested to learn more from the best. I would probably be better talking to somebody about music because it's something that has become a passion.

Commentating and the Senior Tour keep me moving around the world, and though everyone on the road always complains, we all know we'd miss the life. I'm a rolling stone and I've been that way since I was fourteen, and it would be extremely hard to stop - but I'm not sure whether I'll again become a coach to any top flight players in the near future. My experiences with Philippoussis and Rusedski aren't really times I'd like to repeat, though I would gladly work with players as talented as Tim Henman.

I can't see it happening however, after offering my services when he split with David Felgate and not getting a reply. Tim is such a gifted player who hasn't yet got even close to realising his full potential. Sadly I think he is still a bit gun-shy of me, after the time I was misquoted as saying I thought he was too upper class and not hungry enough. I tried to explain to Tim's agent, Jane Felgate, when

I wrote to explain that I was hardly a boy who was brought up on the wrong side of the tracks with holes in my trousers. The article was all about British tennis and getting street kids to play, but everything got twisted around and taken out of context.

Living much of the time in London and practising regularly at the LTA's headquarters at Queen's, I obviously have set ideas on the problems of British tennis. Let's face it, they have had just two players of note in more than a decade, and one of them is Canadian. To my mind, the real problem is the standard of the coaching, which is dreadful, and the worst coaches are those who played and didn't quite make the grade; this is largely because they are perpetuating their bad habits, which were probably outdated practices in the first place, and teaching them to young players who are supposedly the best bets for the future.

The LTA have spent a huge amount of money to lure a Frenchman like Patrice Hagelauer through the Channel Tunnel. There's no argument he did a magnificent job in France and was largely responsible for their great strength in depth on both the male and female side. I understand there are fundamental problems in the British tennis attitude. But I question what has Hagelauer done in Britain so far?

A couple of years ago a British youngster called Lee Childs caught my eye. He's got a serve like a rocket, and as everyone knows, if a player is going to make it these days, the prime requisite is to have a weapon. Yet he was far from the finished article, and there were so many areas in which he needed top class guidance.

From what I could see, Childs seemed a nice lad and extremely willing to learn - and yet he is still with the same coaches. What is the result? His ranking has gone seriously backwards at a time when he should be making great strides in the other direction. I

So what comes next?

would have loved the opportunity to work with Childs; surely the input of somebody who'd actually won Wimbledon and been to the top, with an aggressive and attacking game, would have been invaluable to the youngster. The LTA knew perfectly well where I was, but did I get a telephone call? Exactly the same can be said about other British residents, such as Peter Fleming and Peter McNamara.

The LTA have sent one player to the Cash/Hopper Academy, and I hope that relationship can grow. Come what may, it's so clear that the LTA need to get their most promising youngsters away from home-grown coaches. I'd be lying if I said I wasn't disappointed never to have been asked to work with any British kids, despite living in London for sixteen years.

Peter Mac, who has now taken over the reigns with Philippoussis, feels much the same. He and I go way back to those Deepdene courts in Melbourne, and it's an undisputed fact that Aussies do make good coaches. Generally speaking, with a few notable exceptions like Laver, Hoad and Rosewall, we are not the most talented of players, but we are great competitors. Consider somebody like Darren Cahill, who guided Lleyton Hewitt all the way to the number one spot, and has now been snapped up by Andre Agassi.

I'm really not surprised that Killer has become such a respected coach. He's always been an extremely intelligent person, and as a player was very clever on the court. His coach was Bob 'Nails' Carmichael, and the reason for his nickname is self-evident. Nails was a hard taskmaster, and drilled that strength into his players. I always had trouble beating Killer because he knew my weaknesses and worked on them. I'm not sure how good Killer is on the technicalities, but he's not going to change Andre's game at the age of thirty-two; it's an interesting situation to watch, but Andre is such a tough competitor and so good mentally. The trick will obviously be to keep Andre motivated with so many other things happening in his life.

Perhaps I'm a dreamer, but becoming Australia's Davis Cup captain remains an ambition. Admittedly it's a no win situation because people only ever expect Australia to win, and defeat equates with crashing failure. In my case, I can't really see it happening with the current leadership of Tennis Australia because the president Geoff Pollard has always been very much a John Newcombe man. Perhaps some changes at the top will give me more of a chance, and I defy anyone to question my commitment to the Davis Cup cause over the years. Those two finals against Sweden at Kooyong remain in my handful of proudest memories. After all these years of antagonism, I'd dearly love to bury the hatchet with Tennis Australia and be respected for what I achieved in the game for my country. I honestly feel there's only a few stopping it, two of whom I've recently mentioned.

One secret ambition of mine is to see a bust of my head unveiled in the garden at Melbourne Park. Every year Tennis Australia induct a player into their Hall of Fame at a special dinner during the Australian Open, and this year I was deeply upset to find I was the only past or present player not to be invited to the function. I've even got my own tuxedo these days, and I'm quite prepared to put on a bow tie, so there would be no embarrassment. To my knowledge every other Australian who has won a singles title at Wimbledon, or even represented their country, is honoured in that garden. How much longer will my achievements be ignored?

I believe I can best serve tennis in Australia by raising future players at my academy, doing things my own way and breaking

So what comes next?

new ground. When all is said and done, I feel very lucky to have savoured the great moments of winning Wimbledon and two Davis Cup finals. Life is all about experiences, and in my case there's been the good, the bad and the very ugly. Perhaps this book is a way of venting some of my disappointments; there have been far too many things that have been locked up in my mind for too long. But life is all too brief to worry too much about the past, and I now believe it's so much more important to continue enjoying fantastic experiences with loved ones and friends. If some people don't want to come along for the ride then that's their decision, but fine by me.

And I suppose that takes me full circle to that sweltering July afternoon in 1987 when I scaled the Centre Court's architecture. It was something I'd planned and long dreamed of doing. I suppose it's what I'll always be remembered for, and if that is the case, I can happily live with it. My path up to that point was exactly straightforward, and it certainly hasn't been since. But how boring it would be if every Wimbledon champion was exactly the same.

When I watched Goran Ivanisevic tearfully tear off his sweat-soaked shirt and throw it to the crowd fourteen years on, I knew exactly what he was feeling and let me tell you, it's a wonderful emotion. When people talk about Wimbledon they so often quote the poem *If* by Rudyard Kipling, and that's hardly surprising because it's there overhead as you walk onto Centre Court. No offence meant Rudyard, mate, but personally I've never been a great fan, so I'll go with something a little more contemporary. The line of a song entitled All Star by the band Smash Mouth immediately came to my mind as a perfect description of Goran. After twelve months of reflection and travelling back through the various chapters of my life for this book, I've concluded it kind of fits me as well: Only shooting stars break the mould.